POUND WISE

LIST OF WORKS BY OSBERT SITWELL

From the portrait by James Fosburgh

OSBERT SITWELL

POUND WISE

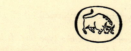

HUTCHINSON OF LONDON

HUTCHINSON & CO. (*Publishers*) LTD
178–202 Great Portland Street, London, W.1

London Melbourne Sydney
Auckland Bombay Toronto
Johannesburg New York

First published January 1963
Second impression March 1963

*This book has been set in Bembo type face. It has
been printed in Great Britain by The Anchor Press,
Ltd., in Tiptree, Essex, on Antique Wove paper.*

For

BETSEY WHITNEY

with affection

CONTENTS

INTRODUCTION

I had decided to call this book *Pound Wise* before the growing popularity of adding 'wise' to almost any noun in the English language had given it a horrid smartness. Nevertheless, it seemed better to me to retain the name, for it is not used in that sense.

Pound Wise, then, is representative of my work in prose—or at least of part of it, for novels and short stories are not included. The majority of the contents made their first appearance in print in the pages of weekly papers and magazines, some of which are now extinct. The main part was published in book form, in *Penny Foolish* and *Sing High! Sing Low!* 'A Letter to My Son', however, occupied an entire issue of *Horizon* and was afterwards printed by itself as a pamphlet. Many of these pieces are concerned with foreign travel—as, for example, in China—which has since then apparently changed out of all recognition—and in Guatemala. One thing though they have in common: they were nearly all written before the dissolution of the British Empire.

OSBERT SITWELL

I

WHAT IT FEELS LIKE
TO BE AN AUTHOR

Hunting the author, painter and musician is a traditional and popular sport. In this country poet-baiting at an early stage assumed the place of bull-baiting. The critics drove Keats to death, Shelley to Italy and Swinburne to Putney. . . . After visiting the old Protestant Cemetery in Rome, and seeing there Keats' tomb, bearing on it the inscription: 'Here lies one whose name was writ in water'—words written by the poet himself and placed there at his especial request by his friend Severn—after reading, in addition, his letters, it is, I apprehend, impossible to doubt that the critics *did* kill Keats; though the bare recording of this fact in any public journal still causes them to defend themselves, crying out that if he were so weak a creature as *that*, then there was no hope for him, and it does not matter. Thereby they shirk a statement of the real truth, which is that it was 'grand sport', because, for killers who love their work, to tear to pieces a poet like Keats, one of the most sensitive beings who can ever have lived, with genius, too, so

clearly indicated in his appearance that they could be quite
certain of the quality of their victim—for, says Severn, he had
the 'hazel eyes of a young gypsy maid in colour, set in the face
of a young god'—this, all this, must have constituted it an
infinitely more enjoyable sensation than, for example, to hunt
Tennyson and fail to kill him.

A poet dead has always been worth a dozen alive, both
literally and metaphorically. . . . This should have been particularly brought home to the public by the death of Sir William
Watson some years ago. The facts of his career as presented in the obituary columns must have caused a pleasant
glow to warm the heart of many a reader. . . . Every poet
becomes a 'Famous Poet!' on the posters announcing his
demise: but here was one who, to a name familiar enough for
easy lip-service, joined every attribute that such a being should
possess; he had lived and written in the reign of good Queen
Victoria (a great aid to any poet), had remained uncomfortably
poor during most of his life (as poets ought), was yet a knight
(it is not often, by some strange coincidence, that the knight
of today is a poor man) and, further, had been gifted—so the
obituarists united to declare—with that elusive quality 'the
authentic note'; of which I hope to have more to say one day
in an essay entirely devoted to it. Yet he wrote verse which the
man-in-the-street—who, together with the Archbishop of
Canterbury, is recognized today in this country to be sole
arbiter of art, as of politics and economics—could easily understand, if only he would read it. . . . And many, no doubt,
wondered, as they perused the columns before them, what was
really the life, the *private* life, of an author.

None: he has none: comes the answer. Whether poet,
novelist or essayist, a writer possesses, when his profession is
compared with other trades, one supreme advantage combined
with disadvantage—he can never stop working. Everything he

sees or does is, in a sense, work; as much as writing itself. Thus he can never be idle for a moment, never live for the sake of living, never take an absolute rest. When he says: 'Now I will stop work,' it is only in order to begin labouring in another medium. Moreover, being in this way both inside and outside his work, he is at the same time, or should be, abnormally sensitive and abnormally insensitive. In consequence he is able to watch himself in action at the dentist's or when annoyed by some noise at night, and to observe with amusement his own responses and ruses.

If, however, the author has *his* own way of looking at life, so have the members of the public *their* way of looking at him. They well know that every writer—and more especially every poet—is sent down from above as much for the counselling of all aspiring amateurs as for the entertainment of the crowd: and they consider that his sense of duty should oblige him to read carefully every manuscript forwarded to him, accompanied by the usual egotist's screed, and then annotate it and comment at length upon its merits.... All this the author must do without payment: indeed it is only fair, since writing in general consists of pure inspiration, poetry in particular being crooned, as it were, directly across the ether by the Great Invisible Crooner. No hours of labour, therefore, are needed for composition.

Ever has it been thus with poetry since, instead of being sung, it first began to be written down. Doubtless Chaucer, Shakespeare, Ben Jonson, Dryden—although manuscripts in those days were less easy to land on authors by post—found themselves similarly victimized. Pope, we know, felt himself obliged to spend countless hours in inventing excuses for not reading the imitative echoes of his own verse with which unknown persons continually favoured him. In consequence, he incurred much blame for the lies he told so profusely in order to avoid having to hurt the feelings of innumerable young people. And unless the world has changed, moreover, not only *young* people—for we seem, really, to be a nation of would-be poets rather than of successful shopkeepers. Old ladies and young ladies, cabinet ministers and porters, housemaids and aldermen and gamekeepers, hunting men, fishwives and interior decorators; all of them appear, at one time or another, to have essayed The Easy Art. . . . And war, which stirs the emotions and numbs the brain, only increases the number of aspiring poets and addled poems.

Nevertheless, these treasures which every post brings to an author of any celebrity constitute by no means his most serious infliction. His standing being that of an unpaid public servant, he is expected to bestow his time and the benefit of his advice upon anyone, whatever his need may be, who sees fit to claim them. And how diverse is the range of the necessity! It varies from giving instruction in the proper control of a hot-water bottle in the winter bed to an opinion upon psychic dancing or the principles of Schopenhauer. Chaperonage, too, apparently forms part of his job: for only a little while before the war, a lady of whom I had never heard, but who wanted to write a book which obliged her to contemplate spending some hours every day in the Reading Room of the British Museum, telephoned to command me to escort her there every morning, and to fetch her back home every evening; because, as she phrased it, 'The museum's such a grimy old place, it makes me feel quite nervous going in and out of it by myself'. And, on another occasion, a stout woman rang the front-door bell, and when I answered it, put her foot between the jamb and the door so as to prevent my shutting it, and demanded that I should take down in embroidery—one of the few arts of which I am altogether ignorant—the colours that she would sing to me—and, at this point, she burst into loud, unbidden song.

In growing numbers, too, there are the hordes of charity harpies begging books, a most unpleasant and persistent species. I refer particularly to the organizers of bazaars for eleemosynary causes, who never think twice before demanding from an author, almost with menaces, a signed copy of one or more of his works: though at the same time he is expected to pay his taxes and contribute in the ordinary way to deserving objects. And how frank and unabashed in tone is this great army of cadgers. 'Our idea is', runs a paragraph in a letter, headed 'Famous Authors Books Fund', which has just reached me from a hospital situated in a distant part of the country to that in which I live, 'to collect autographed books from famous authors, and auction them to book-lovers and well-to-do people.' (I like particularly, do you not, gentle reader, the distinction so wisely drawn between 'book-lovers' and 'well-to-do people'?) 'All of the money', it continues reassuringly, 'thus raised will be put to the Fund. The Appeals Committee will be tremendously grateful', the writer goes on, 'if you will autograph and give us a copy of one of your books, preferably the book which you consider to be your best, as that will add to the interest of the sale. . . .' So even the gift of a volume, and its signature by a 'famous author', is not enough; no, he must deliver judgment upon himself as well! . . . Yet the writer of this letter is in private life a nice, kind person, I should hazard, who would never dream of writing to a fishmonger, saying 'Our idea is to collect your best fish, ask you to sign them and then auction them to fish-lovers and well-to-do people.' He only writes in this way because he, together with the general public, shares the crooning conception of the author's work which I have adumbrated earlier.

Both of them consider that printed books fall upon the author like manna from heaven. Never does it begin to dawn on the acquaintance who says to you, with the insinuating whine that authors know so well: 'You never sent me your last book!' that he is demanding the equivalent of a postal order for 25s. Yet he would seldom dare to ask you for that amount outright. On the contrary, as his accompanying wheedling smile indicates, he regards his request as in some mysterious way a compliment to yourself. For every fool, however double-dyed in his folly, considers that his wishing to read a book must flatter its author. Or perhaps he bases his request on economic grounds of a different sort, understanding the real truth, now so often denied, that the only kind of money worth having is inherited, unearned money, and thus feeling that, if you earn the money by writing, you cannot mind giving it away, for you will certainly not have time in which to spend it.

Sometimes, of course, the organizers of bazaars are more generous and provide the books themselves: but even this can end badly. I remember, in this connection, a friend who asked me to sign some of my books which she had purchased and was giving to be auctioned for charity. Being vague by nature, she sent me round the *Forsyte Saga* instead, with a note saying: 'Would you mind signing these as you so kindly promised. . . .' I did not feel I could disappoint her, as apparently I had given my word, so I signed them and they were auctioned, but I never learned what prices the admirers of Mr Galsworthy gave for these unique items.

The most peculiar of all the special attitudes which members of the outside world manifest towards writers, though, is that reserved for them by servants. They take a kindly care of us, as if we were rather mad children, albeit they generally refuse to look upon authorship as a profession and regard themselves as entirely free to interrupt their masters whenever they feel inclined to do so. . . . I remember, for example, how when I asked a servant, now dead, whether my sister was busy,

[16]

because I wanted to show her a letter I had just received, he replied at once: 'Oh no, she's only writing!' And there can be little doubt that some deep instinct guides them very surely to burst in at *the* critical moment of inspiration, and generally to pursue the author with radios, gramophones, bumping, singing, stamping, smashing, dusting and other ingenious tortures.

Yet, I suppose, authors have only themselves to blame for conduct of the kind I have described. They are for the most part a kindly, talkative lot, interested in everything and everybody—even if the interest is, perhaps, a little professional, like that of Granny Wolf in *Red Riding Hood*. And often, after the pattern of all artists, they are passionately conceited and self-centred, which tends to render them slightly ridiculous. 'Let's have a little fun with them. Let's stick a pin or two into them and the bubbles they blow'; that is the general reaction to them. But if the author hits back, then his opponent, the Little Man—that degraded and hideous personification of a contemporary ideal—yells to his brother: 'Look! He's hitting someone smaller than himself!', forgetting, though the Press daily and flatteringly reminds him of the fact, that, however small, it is the Little Man who composes the big battalions: the packs, flocks and droves. Collectively, indeed, his methods resemble those of the herds of dwarf pigs which sweep through the forests of Central America, harrying and killing any living creature they meet that is bigger than themselves. They chase their victim for miles, and when they catch up with him gore him to death. If a man climbs a tree to elude them, they saw through the trunk with their tusks, and so get him just the same. Yet individually these little black porkers would harm no one, and are said to make charming pets, and can often be seen in the cities of their native region going shopping with their mistresses.

But I wander.... The reasons for the Little Man's attacks upon anyone over the normal size are, of course, easily to be

B [17]

comprehended. He is playing for safety, as well as enjoying the fun, and, further, there is the common desire to hit something bigger than yourself, to spit at the creative forces, to burn books, to debunk the great, to picnic in the ruins of a temple or palace—and, above all, the hitting is due to fright, downright funk. The Little Man suspects an author—often wrongly—of being 'clever'. This, by itself, would terrify him, but there is, in addition, his permanent, haunting nightmare of 'being put in a book'. A kind of humiliating form of individual preservation, he feels it to be, as though he were a foetus or freak preserved in spirits of wine in a bottle, for future ages to wonder and wince at. . . . And the duller-minded and more boring he is, the more he dreads this fate, which he regards as inevitable if he should meet a novelist, for the Little Man is unaware that his own fear of 'being put in a book' is surpassed only by the author's terror of the little beast getting himself there; an exploit which may involve a libel suit and impose upon the writer the payment of several thousands of pounds in damages.

The Little Man, therefore, relies upon persecution to rid himself of his terror, and constantly seeks—and finds—new methods. Of these, noise is the chief. The arrival of an author in a hotel, for example, inspires the most extraordinary phenomena. All the parents staying there will, swayed by some peculiar herd instinct, at once bestow upon their children the most raucous and ear-splitting toys, whistles, croakers, toy trumpets, crackers, miniature whizz-bangs, hooters, watchmen's rattles, plates to smash, fog-horns and dogs that have been taught to bark in an especially prolonged and attractive manner, and are encouraged to exercise this art by their dear little masters' perpetual teasing. And then, without adventitious help, the children themselves can cry and shout and sing —and do we not all love children's voices? . . . Down below, perhaps, a child of about fifteen, with fingers like a fox-terrier's paws, or sometimes, you may think, like an elephant's feet, is being given lessons on a piano by a professional torturer, who does not mind what suffering he inflicts on innocent listeners so long as he obtains his fees. This is the kind of pest who should be prosecuted and imprisoned. . . . The man in the next bedroom is learning to typewrite by day, and practises his snoring by night. (When you make a complaint about a snorer, he will always protest that he has 'never been known to snore before': and I think this is probably true; his unconscious mind has been tempted by the proximity of an author.) During the daytime, in every direction sound Salvation Army bands, the bands of the mutilated and every kind of professional howling and bawling by beggars, while the perpetual dripping of taps, tattooing of hot-water pipes—now cold—and an occasional burst of wireless news or music, gives variety to the nights.

Many other methods of annoying an author are known, however, to the *cognoscenti*. Invitations, for example, are extended to him, not by friends, but by those who contrive to remember his existence only at certain periods. Thus, every time a book appears, he is sure to receive an invitation from Lady Flinteye, or from soulful persons who claim to have known him in some other existence which they have rendered tragic for him, and who are determined, equally, to prevent him from enjoying this one. . . . Worst of all, there are the clubs run for artistic ladies; institutions which exist to enable their three hundred members to boast 'I met Mr So-and-So at dinner', and, more especially, to provide a meeting-place for all those who wish to insult at their ease any painter, author or musician whom they have been able to decoy thither to eat their rather indifferent food. Moreover, it meets the difficulty that etiquette precludes them from being rude in their own or in other people's houses: but in a *club*, specially organized for the purpose! What *could* be better! For the Little Woman favours sex equality and intends to be every bit as rude as the Little Man. . . . And how expert she has become! . . . I remember my initial experience of one of these meals. I was placed next to a gentle-looking, white-haired old lady with a soft manner and a slight but genial palsy. She turned to me at once, and said with a sweet, old-fashioned smile: 'Do you know, Mr Sitwell, I believe I've read nearly all your books'—a pause (during which I clamped across my face a mask of expectancy and pleasure appropriate to the coming compliment), then she added, *con brio*: 'and I don't like a single one of them!' . . . The insults are, indeed, often ingenious and sometimes amusing, even to those who are the object of them. On another occasion, I remember, I was introduced to a woman who was sitting next to me. . . . She at once burst into tears. My voice, I am sure, showed the interest and concern that I genuinely felt, as I enquired what was the matter. Giving a loud, yelp-like sob, she replied: 'For a long time I have looked forward intensely to meeting you, and now that I *have* met you, it is *such* a disappointment! . . .' It was impossible not to sympathize with a display of so much virtuosity and feeling.

Men, nevertheless, are no whit behind women in this direction. Thus, I recall an incident after a large dinner-party in Madeira a few years ago, when an individual, who was obviously a prey to a peculiarly intense inferiority complex— for he was stressing his individuality in the most painful manner by means of an eye-glass strung on a wide ribbon, and by a red-lined evening cloak, and every other possible, and impossible, attempt at originality of outward aspect—came up to me, solely in order to be rude. . . . By this time, for I had already been writing for many years, I knew that look in the eye, so when, by way of prologue—having already been carefully introduced to me once—he said: 'Your name is Sitwell, isn't it?', I replied loudly and clearly: '*No! Shakespeare!*'

However, he proceeded: 'Well, I know you are an author; and I want to tell you how much I despise all people who write books.'

'You ought to try to read one of them,' I suggested.

I should, perhaps, merely have replied: 'Little Man, You've had a Busy Day!' Because some instinct seems to prompt such people to be insolent to—it is true—all authors, but more particularly to that precise type of author who can most neatly or most severely answer them back. . . . Is it kind, one might enquire, to be rude to Pope or Dr Johnson or Sheridan or Shaw —or Sitwell? Is it *kind*; but, above all, is it *wise*?

2

OLD WORLDS FOR NEW

Now that all the talk is of new worlds (whisper to me, you who are with me waking and sleeping, where I have heard such talk before, was it during the Trojan Wars, the Punic or the Wars of the Roses?), now, I was saying, that all the talk is of new worlds, I feel that I myself am bound for the old, a Columbus in a hurry to reach home. I have caught a glimpse of a new heaven and earth fashioned by Woolworth's and the B.B.C. from the wreckage of tanks and the spidery carcases of aircraft, and I prefer that which grew out of the fallen porphyry pillars of the Forum and of temples that had been cast down.

It is, you will tell me, a matter of taste, or, perhaps, of morality. The Common Man finds Woolworth's convenient, and therefore It Fulfils a Function, therefore the things it sells are not only useful, sometimes, and cheap, but a thousand times more beautiful than the antiquated products and goods —for there are no arts in this world of which I speak, but only products and goods—of Egypt, Greece, Rome, Italy and France in former times.

To which I reply, with rodomontade, that for more than twenty years I have collected and made worlds, both old and new: some that existed, some that existed only as I saw them— and for me alone until I gave to my generation the key—and some that I created. Of the worlds existing in the past, I saw one in Cambodia, and handed it to you floating upon the wings of kingfishers, another—or part of it—in the swamps and mountains of Guatemala, in those vast churches, dark and cloudy with incense, the floors of which are sprinkled with rose petals and glitter with stars of candlelight: vast churches built for the Christian chairman of a board of ruthless, obsolete gods, naked heathens—but that world I reserve for another occasion. Then there were the worlds, more familiar, of Spain and Italy, or the particular ancient Mediterranean world which is so difficult to focus, and which you can enter, for instance, through the Lion Gate at Mycenae, a world built momentarily anew by the same sky, and the same stream rushing with surly strength through that gully which cuts off every other approach; a world of vast bronze helmets, gold masks and echoing tombs. . . . But one of the oldest worlds of which for an instant I caught sight was at a garden-party given by Prince Pu-Ru in April 1934. Let me, then, try to catch that moment, though first we must have maps and charts and Chinese pedigrees, and generally become prosaic.

Prince Pu-Ru, a cousin of the former Emperor Hsüang-Tung—Emperor of Manchukuo—was, at the time of which I speak, the only member of the former Imperial Family allowed to reside in the northern capital. This forbearance on the part of the Republican Government and the City Elders was due to the esteem in which he was held throughout the length and breadth—and, in this connection, the phrase cannot be regarded as a cliché—of the whole country, as being the chief modern exponent of the art of calligraphy, the basic art of China, and the leading draughtsman of his day. The smallest fragment of his writing would change hands at public auction for several hundreds of pounds. He and his wife, also a member of the Manchu Royal House, lived in a palace—or rather the portion of one, since their residence had originally formed a wing of the Imperial City, until the Emperor Ch'ien Lung had severed it from the main body, and presented it to one of his younger sons; from whom the present owner is descended. And you must realize that the word *palace* here always denotes, not a single building, standing by itself, but an organization of groups of tiled and painted pavilions in a series of gardens, and also that, because Peking is built of houses of one storey, except for the Forbidden City and the Gates, it covers an immense area. It contains huge thoroughfares—planned, it is said, by Kubla Khan—and innumerable small, thronged streets, and then, suddenly, you will come to some backwater; a broad *cul-de-sac*, it may be, where it seems as though no one ever passed. The houses are ripe with age in this empty sunshine. The grass grows between the cobbles, there are no stalls for food or tea, no children, in their broad, padded coats, stamping and tumbling in the dust, no piebald dogs, no old gentlemen carrying bird-cages in which their pets are waiting only to be uncovered before they start their song. There are no street sounds, no echo of gong or wooden clapper or bell or tuning-fork, no cries of the men who sell the innumerable delicacies of the season: spring chicken, ducks fattened in cellars, dumplings, smoked fish or the common water-chestnut or sunflower seeds. . . . It was out of such a broad and stagnant street, or *place*, as this that you entered the palace of Prince Pu-Ru.

The Prince was not a rich man—there are few rich men in China, except, it may be, for various atavistic missionaries and their children, or the sons of former statesmen of the Dowager Empress or the relatives of retired palace eunuchs, for graft and favour, not commerce, brought the great fortunes of the East. In consequence—and because the Prince was an artist—the place had remained unspoilt. The bright exterior painting, vermilion and green, of the halls was dry and flaking, and the ceilings and walls showed in places the ingenious, sombre lacquering of the snows of this year and yesteryear, which three times every winter roll a carpet of thick swansdown over the flashing golden tiles of the Forbidden City, and the herring-bone-ribbed grey tiles of the Tartar and Chinese cities. In the first room, in which we waited, I remember that two pots, containing diminutive fruit trees in flower, stood between the windows; those dwarf trees that were grown in Peking for house decoration, with the significant and distorted line of their small, crooked branches, and with blossom—cherry or peach—the precise counterpart of that which you see in a Chinese painting. Soon the Prince came in, and I was presented to him. He was a sturdy figure, in a dark-blue robe, with a face broader than the ordinary Chinese face, and thoughtful and kind in its cast. He talked to me for some time, through the friend who had brought me, and who now interpreted, albeit, indeed, the exquisite courtesy and dignity of his manner needed no translator. Before long the Princess joined her husband and helped him to show us—for my friend was a celebrated connoisseur—some of his treasures; small bronze vases of great antiquity, and a huge carved emerald which had belonged to that great collector, Ch'ien Lung. This stone had a rippling surface like that of water, green water, containing a lost unfathomable depth of light. Of the purest colour, it was the size of the Princess's foot—remarkably small, though the feet of Manchu ladies had never been bound. . . . All this time, from behind a pane of glass in the wall—the windows, of course, were of oiled paper—a very beautiful Chinese girl, her face painted in a florid, extremely stylized manner, and wearing an elaborately embroidered Chinese robe of blue silk, was watching us. But presently, when tea was brought, she came in to wait on the Princess. . . . At the end of the interview the Prince told us he was giving a garden-party the following week; and invited us to be present.

The importance, as it turned out, of this function was that it proved to be the first Manchu social event that had taken place since the Marshal Feng Yu-Hsiang's troops, doubtless at their leader's inspiration, had forced their way into the Forbidden City, and the young Emperor had been obliged to escape, some ten years before. And, when the afternoon arrived, it seemed as though, in itself, it might have been worth waiting for through a whole decade. Certainly, in England, it would so have seemed. But in the climate of northern China such a day at such a time is to be confidently expected. The seasons are unbelievably regular in the incidence of their weather. Each fall of snow in the winter, each gradation, almost, of temperature can be predicted. Thus, at the winter solstice, it is customary in Peking to make a 'Nine-Nines Chart of Lessening Cold', composed of nine patterns and eighty-one small circles, or else to paint a plum branch in outline, bearing on it nine blossoms with eighty-one petals, so that a circle or a petal can be struck off each day before the fulfilment of the spring. . . . But now the Feast of Excited Insects (on the morning of which day, it is said, the herons return to the moat of the Imperial Palace, leaving for the south again about five months later, on the evening of the Lantern Festival) was long over, spring had come, its Feast of Ching Ming, or Pure Brightness (when all good citizens wear circlets of willow, sweep the graves of their ancestors and burn coloured paper money on their behalf, so that they can purchase little luxuries beyond the tomb), had gone by. Each day seemed finer than the last, and the effervescence of spring was everywhere to be felt, in the fairs held within temple precincts, in the streets, in the broad roads or in the quiet lanes, by the lake of Pei-hai, by the moat, by day and by night.

The advance of the year was so rapid you could almost hear the branches of apple and quince and wistaria creaking with the life within them, almost see the sticky buds first appear, and then unfold and open into their spice-breathing cups and tongues and turrets. And, since the object of this party was to see the crab-apple trees in bloom, no afternoon could have been more fitted, more consecrated by Nature herself, to this purpose. It might have been fashioned solely for men to savour the scent and essence of such trees in flower, and the gay, sheepskin clouds, flecking the blue dome of the sky, were translucent as the clustered petals themselves.

We drove to the palace in our rickshaws, and were kept sitting therein for a minute or two in the deserted space outside, while—and this time I noticed them particularly since on the last occasion, too, I had seen them and had asked my friend who they might be—two bands of middle-aged men ran out from a lodge each side to open the stout wooden gates. They stood now, as we passed through, hanging on to the doors in order to have an excuse to scrutinize us minutely, staring at us with a curiosity of so intense a nature as to proclaim that it had not been properly satisfied for many years. The whole troupe consisted of about twenty persons, ten on each side, and they were dressed in long robes of vellum-coloured cloth. They were tall, a few of them inclined to fat, but one thing they all shared in common: their rather colourless faces, on which many lines were deeply incised, bore an oddly weazen look, like that of green and wrinkled apples. I had been sure, when first I set eyes on them, that somewhere, not long before, I had come across beings of this same order. . . . And then the memory had come back, of the tea and gossip—albeit incomprehensible to me—that I had enjoyed with the ancient inmates of the Ancestral Hall of the Exalted Brave, an almshouse for retired eunuchs in the Imperial service which I have described in a chapter of *Escape With Me!* But the youngest of those pensioners had been at least fifteen or twenty years older than these, the last recruited eunuchs of the Forbidden City, who now confronted us. Hither they had fled from impending massacre—although they had first made sure that their young royal master had also eluded it—on that terrible night in 1924; here, in this palace that seemed to stand forgotten in its large grounds, off the main ways of the city, they had found a sanctuary with Prince Pu-Ru's father. And, though now they could discover no means, as formerly, of making great fortunes, though now they were not living in the lavish grandeur in which for so long the people of China had been obliged to keep them, this curious and artificial sept perpetually recruited from the ranks, nevertheless they at present constituted its only living representatives in the whole of China; anomalous beings who were actually still pursuing their duties, which were the same as those of the eunuchs who had guarded the divine thrones, ever since they were set up, of Babylon and Ur, the Indies and China, Byzantium and Turkey.

The gardens seemed immense, as we got out of our rickshaws and began to walk. Inside the boundaries of their walls, crowned with yellow tiles, were groves of old cypresses, the frond-like arrangements of their leaves lying upon the air as though they were layers of blue-green smoke, there were eighteenth-century water-gardens, now dry but full of wild flowers, and there were the sunk gardens wherein flourished, with gnarled, rough trunks, the crooked and ancient fruit trees which constituted the chief pride of their owner. As we approached the pavilions, we noticed how many guests had already arrived. And although there was nothing political about this gathering in intention, the atmosphere was heavy and strange, laden with feeling for the old régime, for here, today, within this green domain, walking slowly as tortoises, hobbling, waddling, trudging, a few of them almost crawling, were all those who had come through from one world into another. Most of them, indeed, appeared to be very old. Some had been in hiding ever since the death of the Dowager Empress, some since the first revolution, some merely since the flight of the young Emperor; none, you would have pronounced with certainty, had ventured out for at least a decade.

Looking at them, it was at once possible to see that these Manchu nobles, in spite of their infirmity, and though very different from their ancestors, the simple warriors, with their outlandish ways and barbarous foods[1]—that belonged more to the tents of tribes wandering through the vast plains of Manchuria and Mongolia, and over the wild mountain ranges, than to the inhabitants of palaces—were yet incontestably the members of a ruling caste. Though they approximated now to the Chinese, in the same manner, let us say, that the English families settled in Ireland came to resemble the Irish—nevertheless, their faces were heavier, their noses more emphatic, they had all the air of those in whose blood existed the capacity and inclination to command. Old, old men, their beards thin, their benign but resolute faces wrinkled round the corners of

[1] These foods survived in perhaps a modified and more civilized form until lately. A Manchu civil servant, who wrote just before 1900, has left in a book he wrote (*Annual Customs and Festivals of Peking*, by Tun Lich'en, translated and annotated by Dr Derk Bodde. Henri Vetch, Peking, 1936), an account, for example, of a delicacy called Manchu Cakes, made of sugar and koumiss, this last being a fermented liquor made of mare's milk and a typical food of the nomads of northern Asia. These cakes, he tells us, 'are cooked during the night, when the weather has become extremely cold. Their pure whiteness is like frost, and when one has them in one's mouth, it is as if one were crunching on snow. They have a special flavour of the north. They are made into the shapes of plum flowers, or that of squares joined at the corners. . . .'

their eyes by the hot suns of the Chinese summers and by their bland smiling through several scores of years, they had, since the collapse of the Imperial power, remained in the discreet seclusion of their households and ancestral temples. Today they had come out, and their famous names and titles, now forgotten in the city outside, had been announced with a renewed flourish. Many of them supported their weight on sticks, many leant on the arms of younger relatives, and a few were so frail that they had to be aided, or even carried, by two men. But they had come out, and they all wore proudly the robes of maroon and mulberry and puce that belonged to their race, and—though this last was an indictable offence in modern China—some of them, or of those who supported them, boldly paraded pigtails.

The Princess was the only woman to be seen, and as she and the Prince went the round of the guests, obeisances were low. A certain feeling of sadness, it is true, permeated this almost ghostly congregation. The very welcome, even, which the eunuchs at the gate had accorded to each guest well known to them, the shrill cries of recognition and enthusiastic squeaks of greeting, contained, too, something of a nostalgic quality. In this enclosure, this oasis of the past, a lost world revived. The hoarse, ritual shouts of the Eight Banners as they greeted the Son of Heaven, moving through the courts of the palace as the sun moved—so it was held—through the sky, seemed to be audible again in the distance to sentient ears. These old men could recall so vividly the precise unique walk, a kind of conventional totter, as though upon stilts, decreed by the usages of antiquity for the Emperor of China, and the unique Imperial voice, inhuman—and so, godlike—loud and high, of which the very recollection was dead (though once I was fortunate enough to hear an imitation of it, given by a Russian who had been received in audience by the Dowager Empress—but he was rather drunk at the time, and nobody except myself would listen). Outside, each man was a stranger: outside, each man was a shadow belonging to the past. Now, it was only within the compass of these walls that there existed yet a sense of relative importance, that everyone could chart with exactitude the identity and position of each man present. Outside, there was nobody to whom to talk, nobody who remembered *anything*. . . . And, kindling in this new warmth, the guests, after greeting their host and hostess, passed on, beyond the pavilions, in the direction of the orchards.

Perhaps they could scarcely be termed orchards, because the trees, being grown for their blossom rather than their fruit, were irregularly disposed, and were fewer to the given area than is our custom. Bent, contorted with age as the old men who were now on their way to inspect them, they must have been planted some two centuries before. Each of them might have been shaped by the green fingers of a Chinese God of Growth, each was as exquisitely placed upon the green turf as any figure upon a scroll by the hand of a great artist. Perfect in their balance and grotesque posture, some inclined, at the precise angle best calculated to display their unexpected and singular grace, while one tree, even, lay on its side and blossomed on the ground.

Slowly, painfully, the old men hobbled along the crooked, paved paths that zigzagged to these trees. When they reached them, they were conducted up small flights of stone steps, so fashioned that, saving where the steps showed, they seemed natural rocks that had cropped up through the turf or had fallen from the sky. These flights, their tops level with the tops of the trees, are thus placed near apple and pear and peach and quince and cherry, so that the connoisseur can obtain a perfect view of the blossom. Even to a newcomer, inexpert in the flowery lore of the Chinese, from each different plane, the particular view of the tree for which the step had been constructed offered a revelation of a new world; of the same kind as when first you fly in an aircraft above the clouds, and look down upon their fleecy humps, white and golden—except that clouds disperse, are opaque, and do not favour an ordered development.

To the Chinese amateurs of the garden, however, these steps offer even more than to someone, like myself, who was fresh to them. In consequence, the old gentlemen persevered—for it was difficult for them to ascend such crags. Many of them took a long while over the process, and only gained the summits by the help, as it were, of guides. Next year, one felt, they would require ropes as well.

Once there, they would remain for a full hour, matching in their minds the complexion and fragrance of the blossom of previous years with that before them. Then, after the general examination of the crop, came the more intimate tallying of one branch, one flower, one bud, with another, and finally it was necessary again to consider the entire grouping and design. But the bees, inordinately busy and managing, behaving as though they were old women in a market, got in the way, and even the less industrious butterflies obscured the view with their gaudily decorated sails or dragged down a petal too heavily when suddenly they perched upon it. . . . Critical appreciation of this high order could not be hurried. After all, it was better fully to use now the powers of judgment with which the years had enriched them, and to apply their trained abilities in this direction, for, in the order of things, they could scarcely hope to see many more of these flowery harvests.

So, they stayed on. . . . But, alas, it was time for us to go. We said good-bye to our host and hostess, and turned away towards the gates, towards the new world of Salvation Army shelters and American Mother's Days, of corrugated iron and cocoa. But, as I looked back, I could distinguish in the distance the tops of the trees, so old, yet so intensely alive, producing these living hives of fragrance, living translucent clouds of snow and roses, dusted with powdered gold, and on the top of every flight of steps I could see, too, a decrepit dignitary of the extinct Empire, his robes of maroon or burnet causing the blue of the sky to vibrate more intensely. Each old man stood, outlined, motionless above the blossom, staring down at its frothy intricacies, waiting there with a certain solemnity, it seemed, and a proper sense of the occasion—for even tomorrow this perfection would be tarnished and it would be too late to form a considered opinion, even one day would have made all the difference; each old man waited, thus quietly under the immense blue dome, as though he were a watcher on a tower, or the guardian of an ancient shrine calling the faithful to worship.

3

DINING-ROOM PIECE

I WANT now to paint for you a still-life of things that are eaten in far-away lands, with, in the background, the likeness of those who evolved the dishes and, beyond them, a glimpse of the strange and imposing landscape which brought them forth. This picture aims to be a piece of the kind that was once so popular, hanging in every large English dining-room, but has now been set aside; by Snyders, or—as in the superlative examples of this *genre*—by that artist and Jordaens in conjunction. Differences, however, will at once be manifest, for instead of the peacock or the death-divining swan forming, as it were, the feathery explosive nucleus of my canvas, and lording it over the corpses of turkey, lobster and domestic fowl, here it will be that bird of fabulous beauty, the quetzal, who queens it over iguana and armadillo, and the background will resemble ruins depicted by Pannini rather than some Flemish hall. . . . But you shall judge.

The quetzal, indeed, plays a part at the beginning, for it is the national emblem of Guatemala, and was formerly, before the Spanish Conquest, the sacred bird of the indigenous clans. Clothed in green plumage of incredible brilliance and loveliness, and in appearance akin to a bird of paradise, it is so shy, so rare, as to be almost legendary except in the inmost prides of zoological gardens the world over. Nevertheless, even the coinage is named after it, a franc is—or was—a quetzal; and the strain of imagination touching practical affairs, which this nomenclature exemplifies, runs through the whole natural life, and begins to form a national style inspired by the original people of the country, albeit in many directions it is also intensely Spanish. Everywhere this Indian influence, Maya or Aztec, is to be felt; everywhere, beneath the disguises it has assumed, this national flavour obtrudes—and not least in the food.

It pervades everything—the things to be bought and sold, the houses, the clothes and, above all, is to be detected in the dark interiors of the gigantic churches, cloudy with incense, glittering with threads of gold where the flickering light catches the gilding; because all the illumination comes from the floor. For an hour or more each worshipper kneels on the stone pavers, strewn with rose petals, within a circle of candles that form, as it were, the footlights, and gesticulates, threatens and implores the Christian Deity for help, in one of the innumerable Maya dialects—and then leaves the church and returns to some dark nook in the mountains, there to renew the same pleas to the monstrous stone images that his tribe still worships in secret. Everywhere, as I have said, you will find the old gods evoking the old culture within the Christian forms; and it is surely more sensible to cultivate this sentiment to the full than to reject it—and yet, where deliberately it has been set aside, that, too, goes so far to the other extreme as to introduce an original atmosphere, and so I will mention here that many of the larger villages and towns in Guatemala have in their dusty

centres, or in no-man's-lands on the outskirts, set in a gesticulating swirl of cactuses, and with, behind them, the essentially
non-European outlines of their numerous volcanoes, a Doric
temple, erected in white plaster by dusky workmen. These
were decreed by the edict of a former President, in love with
Greek culture, and determined to forge a classical pedigree for
his country: the plaster is already falling, and the temples look
anaemic, mean, unhappy; poor white trash, in fact.

The provisions for every *ménage* in Guatemala have to be
bargained for at the market. It is impossible to obtain supplies
outside, because the peasants throughout the country so much
enjoy the occasion, which develops, for the man into a kind
of club for drinking, and for the woman into the equivalent—
though certainly more democratic—of Ascot and Longchamp.
If you meet these Indian peasants upon the road, and stop them
—they are running—and offer to buy some of the chickens,
ducks, pigs, vegetables, fruit and flowers, under which they are
weighed down, for treble the price they could, at the best, hope
to extort for them from tyros in the market-place, they will
assuredly refuse, otherwise they will miss the talk, the fun of a
function, discussion of scandal and the showing-off of clothes.
And upon *clothes* we must lay emphasis. Living for the rest on
fruit and a little dried armadillo, in semi-transparent establishments woven of wattle, with mud added to it for substance,
both men and women lavish their whole fortunes—and they
are not peons, are by no means so intensely poor as the natives
in other regions of Central and South America—upon dress.
These costumes vary entirely in cut and in colour with each
village, but in every case their origin is to be sought for in the
Spanish fashions of two or three centuries ago, though the
decorative motives which they embody are of Indian inspiration. They add a wonderful splendour and strangeness to the
landscape and a sense of fantasy to the towns.

It is for these reasons, then, that the broad tracks along the sides of the roads are perpetually crowded with Indians, always at the run, padding along on their silent naked feet at a particular quick running trot, for they never walk, and markets are frequent and universal. And thus it is that in the morning, when the forests and the plantations of coffee and sugar round the city of Antigua are still thick with dew, and when, as the sun rises, the world of insect life within these balmy wildernesses sets up with voice and castanetted wing so great a clamour, loud and brief as a shriek, a sound that can only be described as a rhapsody of triumph, these peasants in their dresses, diverse but always gay, can be seen converging from all sides upon the city, the women trotting too, some with long plaited pigtails of coarse black hair hanging down behind, and some with a baby fastened to their backs by a shawl, its nose level with the mother's shoulders.

I have chosen Antigua for the market, since though this is no finer than another, I know it the best. And though the scene lacks the Doric temple that graces so many of these towns, it has its own beauties and advantages of Nature and architecture. Formerly the capital of one whole quarter of the Indies, it was partly destroyed by a great earthquake in the 1760s, and its ground space is in consequence too vast for the present population, and therefore no wave of modern American construction has ensued. It remains today a partly ruined city of enormous, crumbling, seventeenth- and eighteenth-century churches, made of golden stone, or of adobe of the same rich tone, the intricate sculptural and arabesque decoration fitted in between the twisting pillars and round the pompous coats of arms upon the façades being the work of Indian craftsmen trained by the Jesuits. Some of the façades are so covered with deeply incised decoration that they look in the distance as though they were scrawled all over with handwriting. A few of the palaces—

notably those with the three arcaded storeys in the chief *plaza*—
exist only as to their fronts. The sky now shows through the
windows of their theatrical *décor*; but the majority, in this
resembling the houses of Andalusia—from which province,
surely, the conquistadores who first settled here must have set
forth—are of one storey, enclosing *patios*, and therefore sus-
tained less injury than the lofty and aspiring churches. All these
old palaces have fine iron grilles over their windows, and doors
of smooth cypress wood with ornate bosses and designs of iron
nails and studs, almost Byzantine in appearance. And several of
them, of which the finest example is perhaps the former
university and present museum, were designed by an eclectic
architect from Seville, who lived here during the forties and
fifties of the eighteenth century, and whose declared aim it was
to invent a manner which would represent the style wherein
the descendants of the Moorish builders in Andalusia *would have*
worked, had their ancestors never been turned out by the
Spaniards! And this ingenious adaptation of Saracenic, embodying rococo themes, which he deliberately evolved, is
singularly delightful and to be seen nowhere else, even in
Guatemala. The resemblance between, let us say, certain courts
of the Alhambra and that of the university here, with its gaily
fretted arcade and its lion-fountain, is unmistakable; though, in
addition, since all the workmen employed were peons, the
Indian influence is again to be felt.

In this town, then, the great market—for every day there is
a market of a kind—takes place twice a week. More even than
on Sunday, and though—in spite of the comparative size of the
city to its population—the life in it is always vivid, vital, it
imparts a tremendous air of festival to the days on which it
occurs. In the first light of the morning the peasants begin to
arrive, and you detect the well-known silent padding on the
pavement. Soon after, a military band is heard practising. It is

time to set out now, for, as elsewhere, the market here must be visited at an early hour. The streets are deserted, since everyone has already started, but on the way you notice the bakers' shops, for bread is not to be bought in the market, and the bread of Guatemala will be the most delicious and varied that you have ever eaten. At breakfast three or four kinds of roll at least would appear, in either private house or hotel. Otherwise, the shops are rather empty; empty vaults with cigarettes, rank cigars and postage stamps exposed for sale. But you must hurry.

The market is held in the gigantic *plazas* formed by the chapels, refectories and cloisters of a roofless monastery. . . . In flawless sunlight, the rays of which, though you feel them on your body under your thin clothes, are never *too* hot, this fantastic setting acts as background for a spectacle that never allows the visitor for a moment to forget his surroundings; the violence of it reminds him that, though not so far from the Equator, yet Antigua stands at a height of some five or six thousand feet above sea-level, upon the central plateau of Guatemala, and so the tropics have not sapped the energy of the people. Moreover, wherever you move here, you will see the feather-tufted cones of the two enormous volcanoes, their bulk being the colour of the bloom upon purple grapes, except when snow covers their tops; mountains which dominate the scene.

You see them, these monstrous twins, rising far over the tops of the towering, broken walls of adobe and stone that frame the market, over the sagging cornices festooned with tropical weeds and foliage, over the immense and disintegrating arches, laced with grotesque decorative motives, through the gaping windows. The best view of them, perhaps, is to be obtained from the one large roof which still exists, a green meadow supported upon arches. Mounted thus, and squatting upon the ground with their wares spread round them, in brilliant sunshine or under the flickering mauve-blue shadow of jacaranda trees that have seeded themselves within the precincts, or of square sails pitched above them, for their shade, on rough wooden supports, sit in long lines these beautiful little golden men and women, clad in dresses which create an amazingly rich effect; coarse homespun linens encrusted with embroidery that, being of fine design, coalesces into splashes of purple and mauve and rose and crimson, of blue and green and yellow and gold. The noise that rises in the air is hardly credible, the general chatter—for these people seem very gay, always chattering, except when they giggle silently, for they seldom laugh aloud—mingles with shouting, with the hammering of blacksmiths, with singing, and with the squealing of pigs, bleating of lambs and lowing of calves. In one room alone is there comparative silence, because the women in it—and you notice few here, except the cooks—are eating, resting and regarding one another, examining minutely each stitch of embroidery within range.

You might think this difficult, for at first, when you enter from the sun-drenched courts, it takes you a little time to see at all. Formerly a refectory, this room still possesses a roof and its windows are blocked up: no light enters save through the door from the cloister beyond; but the glowing charcoal fires of the cooks, who crouch above their stoves, stirring unknown concoctions, outline their figures and those of their customers, and flicker redly over the groups of mothers and restless, clawing children sitting on the ground. Eyes and teeth gleam from these sepia shadows, but everything else is gilded only in silhouette, seems to be smouldering, so that the forms take on most curious effects of light and shade, rich blooming darkness and sullen glow. Indeed, this interior, in the contrast it affords between the magnificence of its ruined setting and the unexpectedness of its inhabitants—the last people one would look for in such surroundings—can be compared in strangeness to those scenes of gypsies, fantastically garbed and feathered, feasting in the Gothic kitchens and dilapidated refectories of deserted monastic houses, which the eighteenth-century Genoese painter, Alessandro Magnasco, loved to depict.

But you must stop looking at the people and go to see what they sell and buy. First you will come to a cloister filled with flowers, placed within its lightly vaulted shade so as not to wither; huge mixed bouquets, arranged with skill which this race shows always in its use of colour, gigantic bunches of Harrisi lilies, of orchids, stacks of tuberoses, the scent of which lies on the air and wanders far, and many flowers of which I never found out the name, orange and flame-coloured and scarlet. But you must notice especially one flower, that here is bought either for decoration or to be eaten. This is the yucca; large spikes, clustering spires of cup-like blossom, creamy and green, ivory and white. The petals, cool, crisp and aromatic, of these flowers, sprinkled with their golden centres shredded over them, dressed with oil and vinegar and rubbed with garlic, form one of the usual dishes of this country. Texture and flavour are both excellent. The stalk is then cooked and eaten as a vegetable, but to me—though I seldom recognized what it was until I enquired—it seemed always rather tasteless and pithy, with a suggestion of soft wood and badly cooked root vegetables. . . . I cannot say whether these yuccas, though they look precisely the same, only larger and more florescent, are identical with those grown in English gardens, and I have not dared to find out empirically.

Passing on, you reach a court devoted to the sale of Guatemalan blankets, and, beyond it, another that displays embroidered shirts for men and shawls and scarves for women. In its turn, this leads into a colossal, sunny *plaza* where the native pottery is to be bought, mounds of earthenware pots and jars, their shape, the perfection of their irreproachable line, seeming more Greek than Spanish—a remark even more applicable to the neighbouring collections of flat dishes, made of an earthenware that is almost rose-coloured, which are used for cooking *tortillas*. Indeed, these large, flat, round plates resemble the discs of the *Discobolus*, so suave and stream-lined are they. From the next immense court, over which hangs a mantle of dust, issues that mingled lowing, bleating and squealing which you have already remarked.

Here, among the young pink porkers on string leads, who so resolutely make an inevitably ineffectual dash for freedom upon their short, apparently unjointed legs, here among the tufted calves attempting to escape—and indeed perhaps the cause of the general frantic behaviour of the animal world—sits a woman with a large round linen-basket full of the strangest cattle, the greatest living delicacy of the land: iguanas. These giant lizards, three or four feet long, are tied, like whitings upon an English breakfast-table, or the symbol of eternity, mouth to tail. Otherwise they would thresh out with their tails, which are spiked and can inflict formidable injuries. Their jaws, too, are bound together to prevent their snapping at and biting their prospective devourers, already bargaining over their bodies. Incidentally, the customers cannot poke them in the ribs, in the same manner in which they prod the calves and small pigs, to see if they are fat, because, even if an iguana possesses ribs—and at this point my knowledge of reptilian anatomy breaks down—the knobs and spikes of its armour would defeat prying fingers. Weight, alone, is the criterion.

A clean feeder, the creature lives in the tree-tops of the steaming jungles on sea-level, and subsists on the green leaves round it. The iguana-catcher is trained to net his prey, a difficult profession that needs a long schooling in these swamps and forests; or, again, it may be shot—sitting, I apprehend—and in these tropical regions 'a day's iguana shooting' is a popular sport, comparable to 'a day's partridge shooting' here. . . . Now it may be that the iguana is no pleasant object to look at. Its small eyes, pail-shaped snout and shark-jaws, lined with a saw's teeth of steel, are, I know, repellent to many. Even the reptile's best friends, indeed, will be obliged to admit that at first sight it presents a somewhat case-hardened exterior, and that its saurian countenance bears an unpleasing expression, both sarcastic and ferocious. But it is good, *very good*, to eat: and its cost does not amount to more than the equivalent of a shilling; two facts which must both tell in its favour. The ways of cooking it are many, but the best seemed to me to be roast saddle, cooked with herbs, and served in a circle of its own eggs with a rich brown sauce, flavoured with madeira or port. The saddle is white and tender as the best capon, and the eggs, too, are a suitable, and even delicious, concomitant, once you have grown accustomed to the idea of them.

If, then, iguana, *sauté* or roast, is the great indigenous delicacy of Guatemala, *tortillas* and *tamales* constitute the country's most ordinary dish. You can see them everywhere, in market, hotel and restaurant, in house and hut. The sight and smell of them is as common in town and village and jungle settlement as is the music of the *marimba*, the liquid-tongued national instrument of Guatemala, which sounds out in *plazas*, in crowded streets, in wattle-built villages and in clearings between the jacarandas and flamboyant trees. . . . But the word *tortilla* is deceptive. First you must clear your mind of its Spanish significance, for here is no flattened-out omelette, sprinkled with strips of tomato and pimento, but a bastard pancake, resembling the sole of a boot fashioned of oatmeal, or some substance like it, instead of leather—though certainly leathery enough. *Tamales*, on the other hand, are more interesting: small, flat, hot, square packets of savoury maize, of a brown colour. The varieties are endless, but they are always very hot and aromatic, always square or rectangular, and always cooked and served in a neat green casing of banana leaf, which the consumer himself has to unwrap (this, perhaps, psychologically, is one of the secrets of all tempting food: it must give its consumer trouble, not make things too easy for him; that is why a cold lobster should never be separated from the shell except by him who eats it). In addition, *tortillas* and *tamales* seem in every instance to be permeated by a subtle and curious flavour, difficult to identify, but akin to the smell of incense—perhaps due to something used in the fires upon which they have been cooked.

In these two dishes I have just described, and in a very fragrant and sustaining paste, made out of *frijoles*, or black beans, the Indians of this country find their chief nourishment. Unfortunately the native liquor, also made from maize, which accompanies them, is a vile and brutish spirit, immature and immediately intoxicating. Two small glasses would overwhelm any European, and among these simple people, though more inured to it, the results are often distressing.

In the market you can see, too, the dried halves of armadillo that I have mentioned earlier (they have ribs, you will notice), which present a painfully smoked and desiccated appearance, and other food of the sort. Piled up, in a corner near by, are brightly coloured, juicy and often rather tasteless tropical fruits, mangoes or custard-apples—these last of many different kinds, but all with their dark and scaly skin, which seems to indicate that, as a dessert, they belong to the same order of dinner as does the iguana for roast, and all possessing a cool, very sweet flavour of mingled banana, pineapple, eau-de-Cologne and turpentine. Custard-apples in mounds are rather beautiful, but not so effective as the hillocks of *serpoté*, many of them cut to display their yielding, flame-coloured flesh, and of grapefruit, tropical oranges with green rinds, and bergamots and limes, as refreshing and fragrant as they are decorative. . . . But you must turn away—it is time to leave the market now, being nearly eleven. Already the wings of the dust hang with a midday heaviness over the city. The peasants are furling their sails, putting their wares in boxes and packing up. Having eaten their meal in the refectory, others of them lie down in the most cool recesses of the cloisters, there wrapping themselves, head and body, in their home-woven blankets, preparatory to a siesta. It is time to go. Life in the market is dead—in the town outside, too, until dusk brings a revival, or until darkness brings the hour of pleasure. Tonight the *marimba* band gives a concert from under the arcade on the second floor of the Governor's Palace in the *plaza*. There are six of these long, wooden instruments, and two men play on each of them, by beating the keys with very flexible wooden gavels, thereby producing as liquid a music as that of carillons, or of falling waters or the tongues of fountains. Those peasants who have not far to go, and have not yet run home, sit on the stone benches of the garden, planted with strongly scented night flowers, or stroll about in the feathery shade thrown by arc-lamps spluttering above the fronds of the tall pepper trees which line the square and the diagonal paths that run through the garden. The concert lasts for two hours, tango after tango, rumba after rumba, and the audience sit, many of them, listening in silence, intently, as though they had never heard the instrument or tune before.

4

FORTUNE-TELLERS

During both day and night Peking—I write of this great capital before the Communists engulfed it—is profoundly quiet; peace reigns, in spite of the more minute sounds; sounds such as you will discover, perhaps, in no other large city in the world. In the day-time there reach you, of course, the shouts and cries of coolies running, their bodies like shining copper in the noonday sun, and, in addition, the more diminutive and insect-like notes which compose the symphony of Peking life; a composition orchestrated on the grand scale. Indeed, a thousand castanetted sounds, clangings and drummings and cicada-like crepitations, vibrate through the golden air and every now and then there will be wafted to your ears the gentle beating of a gong—not such a gong as summons all true Britons to their most hideous meals, but a sound that holds in it something tragic and not of this world, a mournful tintinnabulation. This signifies, to those who have become acquainted with the streets of Peking and with this kind of sound-hieroglyphic, that a blind fortune-teller is making his way through one of the numberless lanes, pausing every instant to lean on his long stick, the while he disengages his other arm and sounds the gong which he carries in his right hand. For in Peking those who cannot read the signs of the day before them, who can hardly tell dark from light, can plainly discern, it is believed, the course through the years.

The Chinese, indeed, are intensely superstitious, though they would hardly admit this, since they prefer to regard their practices as scientific; and, moreover, their superstition has often genuinely benefited science, for the fact that they possessed the earliest astronomical instruments in the world is actually only a by-product of their ancient reliance on superstition. Marco Polo, most accurate of historical observers, tells us that in his time there were in the city of Kanbalu (or Peking, as it was subsequently called) 'amongst Christians, Saracens and Cathaians, about five thousand astrologers and soothsayers. ...' (When I was there, there were almost as many—only instead of 'astrologers' we must read 'fortune-tellers'.) The Emperor, we are told, provided for them, so that they could spend their time in the constant exercise of their art.

Marco Polo also informs us that they had their astrolabes, upon which appeared the signs of the zodiac, the hours and their various aspects for the year. The different schools of astrologers examined their respective tables every year, in order to discover the course of the planets in relation to one another. From this they could forecast the weather and natural phenomena for each month of the ensuing year. 'For instance,' he says, 'they predict that there shall be thunder and storms in a certain month, and earthquakes; in another, strokes of lightning and violent rains; in another, diseases, mortality, wars, discords, conspiracies.' The predictions were recorded upon 'certain small squares' and sold to the public, and those astrologers with the largest number of correct forecasts to their credit were, very reasonably, ranked the highest in their art.

The early astronomical apparatuses used by the Chinese have many of them survived to this day. You can still see the shapes of some of these beautiful instruments outlined against the sky above the Eastern Wall. Two of them, originally designed for Kubla Khan, were taken to Berlin after the Boxer Rebellion in 1901. Referring to these, Bertrand Russell, in *The Problem of China*, says: 'I understand they have been restored [to China] in accordance with one of the provisions of the Treaty of Versailles. If so, this was probably the most important benefit which that Treaty secured to the world.'

Though these bronze machines for reading the heavens are no longer used, no Chinese would have started on any project or undertaken any course of action without acting on auguries, and many different methods of fortune-telling are, of course, in existence; such, for instance, as the temples of the Three Hundred and Sixty-Five Worthies; each of these represents a day in the year, so that you can tell what your fortune will be from the appearance of the worthy under whom you were born. . . . I remember being much impressed by the fact that my Chinese chauffeur, on enquiring from the custodian the identity of his tutelary guardian, was shown a great golden face so identical with his own that, unless he had moved, it would have been difficult to tell one from the other.

At every fair, too, there are those who divine by pouring sand on to the ground before them, and others who tell fortunes by an arrangement of beans or nuts. The blind, again, tell from the feel of the hand. But the oldest of all these methods, so its exponents claim, is that of telling the fortune from the lines of the face. And this art is not one to be lightly undertaken, since ten years of intensive study are needed for it. Those who practise this style of prophecy are men of professional repute, called in for every wedding of wealthy people. The fees seem high. Though life in China is inexpensive, to have your fortune told by this method costs at least a pound, while if called in, following on a marriage, to foretell the birth of children, the charges of the soothsayer mount still higher. Women being still despised, if he forecasts the birth of a daughter the charges will be reduced; but a prophecy of this nature is so unpopular with any but the most freaky parents that he would scarcely venture to make it.

You can imagine the scene. It is a hot day, and so you are sitting in the courtyard. The painting of cornices and doors and windows—the cornices in bright blues and greens, the doors and windows in the shade of red lacquer—glow in the spring sun, the light of which attains a particular brilliancy in this country. The doors stand open on to the quiet street beyond, guarded by a devil-screen which protects you from visitors both earthly and aerial. The bushes, maple or lilac, send a flicker of shadow over the intent face of the diviner and record their shapes on the paper windows, which gleam with a slight translucence. The man regards you with a pitiless stare; no line in your face escapes him. He begins at the forehead and reads down. A Chinese servant helps him by translating his forecast, but this is not so easy, for a simple fact may be of considerable portent. When, for instance, I was informed that in ten years' time I should grow a moustache—and this, indeed, was to be one of the central events of my career—I did not at first realize the political importance which is attached to such an embellishment in China. Only a person of power would dare to indulge in those few drooping and sparse hairs. . . .

The idiom of the language, too, is often picturesque. The fortune-teller prophesied the birth of several male children of my impending marriage. Though they would eventually attain success in life, there were difficulties ahead; when, he prophesied, I told them to go to the east, they would go to the west.

5

THE SUMMER PALACE, 1935

I N 1860 the allied armies destroyed Yuan-Ming-Yuan, the
most romantic and beautiful oriental palace in the world.
This was the work of Lord Elgin, whose father some years
before had removed from the Parthenon the marbles which
now bear his name attached to them. His son was now bent
upon other artistic achievements: and indeed, at the end of his
visit, hardly one stone was left upon another. And yet to this
very day, as you wander through the desolate courts, a faint
perfume of the former palace still lingers in the disposition of
the gold-lacquered fields and hills, and in the artful windings of
the stream. For the rest, there remain one or two smashed
bridges and a plumed arch or two bearing the remnants of
Jesuit rustication; but while you pass, the little children in their
padded winter coats, which resemble eiderdowns, are hammering at them for their amusement with huge bits of stone or
logs of wood, far too heavy, you would have said, for their
years.

After the destruction of the palace it was three decades before the Empress Dowager faced the question of a new summer retreat; but eventually even the garden courts of the Forbidden City, even the pavilions of Coal Hill, that artificial mountain raised in the middle of Peking, failed to compensate her for the delights of country life, and, carefully choosing the situation, she decided to build the new Summer Palace on a hill between the Jade Fountain and the ruins of Yuan-Ming-Yuan. At the back of it there still existed, almost complete, an abandoned Summer Palace of the Ming emperors: and this, no doubt, influenced her, both in her choice and in her designing of it. It is the fashion among many people to deride the Empress Dowager's creation, because of the late period of its building, but, in fact, the palace and demesne are as national in style as anything of an earlier period, and while a certain vulgarity is to be observed in the detail, I can at the same time confidently assert that nowhere else in the world at that period would it have been possible to evoke so beautiful a home. As for the grounds—lakes and peony-terraces, as well as streams and bridges—they are lovely beyond criticism, quite as beautiful as anything made five hundred or a thousand years before.

Of course, the Summer Palace cost an exorbitant sum of money, and money at that time was not easy to get, for China was already in course of being exploited by the foreigner. The Empress Dowager, resourceful as ever, decided to create a great fleet to meet the threat of the Japanese navy. Having announced this, and having obtained a grant of the necessary money, she then quickly appropriated it for the building of her palace, and provided no ships at all. The Chinese incline, in patriotic moments, to bewail this fact, but the truth is that, even had their fleet been built, they would certainly have lost it, just as did Kubla Khan, against the Japanese. . . . (One day, perhaps, the Chinese armies, but never a Chinese navy, may prevail against the Japanese.) It is well for them to avoid naval battles, especially against islanders. And even had they won, even had a few rusty cruisers and battleships survived, these would offer little of interest or beauty now, while the Summer Palace, which since the fall of the dynasty has always been open to the public, lies within easy distance of Peking and provides a pleasant day's picnicking for those of the population who can afford it.

The particular beauties, as I have said, of the Summer Palace are its waters and its bridges. The camel-back bridge is one of the most beautiful in the world, and every now and then it seems as though the Empress Dowager had been inspired by the famous Royal Park of Pei-hai—once the pleasure-ground of Kubla Khan, and later adapted by one of the Ching emperors to the pleasures of eighteenth-century life. It seems, indeed, a development of the same themes of lotus pool and marble balustrade. Herself a great gardener, the chief pleasure of the Empress Dowager, as an old lady, was to wander among the flowering shrubs.

But the Chinese conception of flowers, which she shared, is a very different one from the European. The great national flowers of China are the peony and the chrysanthemum. Of the chrysanthemum I cannot speak, for I have never seen it bloom except in Europe; but certainly the peonies, balancing gaily upon their special terraces, beneath an awning to protect them from the fierce sun of the Chinese summer, attain to a hitherto undreamed-of perfection; especially the tree-peonies. In colour they range through every shade from lotus-pink to so deep a purple that it is known as black. The buds have been cut off here and there, and a great art has inspired the whole of the growing of the tree, while the terraces enable the onlooker to view it from a thousand different angles; for that, indeed, is part of the Chinese theory of gardening. Thus a blossoming tree must always be viewed from above, as well as from beneath and at the side, and for this purpose are constructed those miniature mountains of rock which at times, when the trees are not in flower, seem so meaningless. But who that has seen it can ever forget the flowering of a cherry tree, when viewed from this particular unusual altitude? For it reveals a vista of winged life at which, before, one could only guess from the deep murmur inhabiting it. From above, as the blossoms lie displayed in the sun, you can watch the going and coming, the endless journeying of the bees and the fluttering of the swallow-tail butterflies.

The cultivation of wistaria, too, has attained in China a degree of excellence unknown here, and the blossom is treated in various and original ways. Sometimes an old vine is hung through a lattice, so that each drooping head is framed in a square; sometimes a stout tree has its serpentine branches supported by painted props of wood which look as though they were fashioned of coral, or, again, it is encouraged to writhe over a shallow pool so that it may be mirrored the better. And in these pleasances are found to perfection the natural stones which, in a Chinese garden, so often take the place of statues. Indeed, for a well-shaped, honeycombed piece of natural limestone rock a Chinese connoisseur is willing to pay the most extravagant price.

But it was the peonies, I think, that were the cause of my seeing the grounds of the Summer Palace at their best: for the Mayor of Peiping—as Peking is now called—is a very important person politically as well as socially, and has his residence therein. Suddenly he decided to give a party. One day a large and beautiful envelope was handed to me, with a huge card inside, on which lay sprinkled a delicate inscription in Chinese. I induced my Chinese teacher to translate it, and his translation runs as follows:

[53]

Everything in the old capital is a fairy place with nice plants and flowers. The old Palace was a place for amusement in the spring-time, and whoever went there was glad to be alive. It is that season now. The air and clouds are very nice, cold weather has already left, the trees are in leaf and the birds sing. Everything causes the spring to smile. The whole demesne of the Yi-Ho-Yuan, the Summer Palace, was an old Palace for amusement. It has many good and famous things still remaining. Surrounded by hills, it is surprising how high the temples and buildings seem. The fragrance of flowers clings to our clothes and a nice lake ripples before our eyes.

So now I intend to have a party on the 6th May. Both foreign and Chinese high-class officials will come. When you arrive you will have the same pleasures as those who came in an earlier day. Furthermore, there are good trees everywhere, so that it is not necessary to roll the screens for shade. You will find kitchens in every place, and it will not be necessary for you to bring your wine with you. I am having this party as was done in olden times. It is just the same as the good party given in the Sung dynasty. I hope every friend will bring his family. You had better bring your handkerchief for sitting on the rocks when you wish. I can provide you with a jar of wine, and we can sing after dinner as we think of the past and contemplate the future. On that day you will give and get happiness, and we shall take a picture for a memory which you might like to see afterwards.

I beg your pardon for writing such a short letter, but I shall be much pleased if you will give me your company.

MAYOR YUAN LIANG OF PEIPING

And the Mayor lived up to his word. Although afflicted with severe toothache (which was said to be the reason for his wearing a bright-blue tie with his frock-coat—evidently it made the pain more bearable), he was to be seen everywhere, instructing people to take photographs of the company. Many great marshals and generals had come here for the occasion, and at every point you could obtain tea and wine, as well as many varieties of cake. Boats floated on the lake, boats with awnings, painted boats and plain boats; the yellow China roses and the peonies were in full bloom, and down the long-roofed, open corridors, decked in gay colours, walked the Chinese ladies, with their small feet and elegant robes, observing the flowers and watching the dragon-eyed goldfish performing their veil-dances in standing bowls of water.

6

MUNICIPAL RHAPSODY:

AN IDYLL (1920–1940)

THE seaside year is now nearing its zenith. The waves are quieting down beneath the soft summer rains, and the ragged old men no longer poke about for drowned treasure among the seaweed deposited by the storms: while the rival teams of schoolgirls, who during the winter months used to play hockey upon the sands, have laid aside their clubs and made way for the platforms of pierrots and other entertainers licensed by municipal authority; now, led by mistresses dressed in sensible tweeds, the crocodiles walk in prim procession along the more distant, untrodden golden sands which every day the sea unrolls for them afresh.

Today is a great day, the opening of the Municipal Carnival. Entertainment is no longer unorganized, and every joke and happy outburst of laughter has been long and carefully prepared. Through the mists, the incipient sea-fogs of the early morning, which shroud so far the floral violence, municipal gardeners, carrying upon their arms brass labels, as though they were the loquacious but indistinguishable porters who carry luggage off French boats, can be seen dimly, balanced on ladders propped against the concrete pergolas of the Italian Gardens, here tintacking down the errant branch of an ice-pink Dorothy Perkins, and there shaking the dew off more ponderous, pendent and scentless blossoms. (A chrysanthemum has here been invented which is larger than all others, and blooms—if such a word can be used of such a flower—in shaggy, camphorated perfection throughout the entire summer.) Protected by movable screens of canvas and by overhanging rocks, a few sub-tropical plants, yuccas and palm trees wilt in sad advertisement of the climate, and dew—more owing to the intense cold of the past night than to the mildness of the morning—has laid a mirror-like sheen upon excessively trim lawns. Soon, however, the sun appears—at first a poor, lost, red balloon floating uncharted in this grey vacancy. At once the gardeners climb down their ladders, place them in tool-sheds disguised as Swiss chalets and Norwegian houses, and wheel out their little green-painted motor-mowers, which stripe the grass with patterns in a lighter green, the while their humming imparts, in spite of the facts declared by the thermo-meter, an indescribable atmosphere of summer. Up and down, up and down, they clip these lawns, above the sands; the morn-ing tidiness of which, alas, even they will never rival.

The holiday-makers by now begin to saunter ox-eyed along the promenade, determined to obtain their money's-worth of staring. A dull sense of expectancy pervades them: they seem to be on the look-out. And, indeed, today is a great day, the first of Carnival Week. For months past the coun-cillors and aldermen have sat in conclave in the carved-oak chairs within the red-velvet Council Chamber, discussing plans for this occasion. Even last year, in preparation for it, a large, cream-coloured square of Regency houses had been thrown down, and the wind-cut trees, in the garden fronting it, pulled up, so as to make way for a municipal battledore-and-shuttlecock court, combined with the latest 'Lido' and soda-fountain. Only a few days ago this had been declared open by a jubilant Lady Mayoress. . . . But today is even more important: today takes place the Battle of Flowers, modelled upon the delicious, southern gaieties of the Riviera. Alas, since this year, except in the gardens belonging to the Corporation, the flowers are very backward, the solemn, red-faced crowds have been forced to rely—instead of throwing carnations and opulent roses—upon a plentiful supply of confetti, streamers and Jubilee medals made of chocolate.

First of all there rolls by (a sigh of interest passes through the crowd) an enormous papier-mâché car entitled *Progress*, in which are borne aloft a mammoth bomb, a monster radio, a gramophone and the advertisements—for by this means the Corporation saves the pockets of the ratepayers—of number-less patent medicines. The maladies to which the conditions of their lives expose the members of a democracy are here freely emphasized: there is no attempt at censorship. Behind the chariot of Progress, so beautifully painted and gilded for the occasion, comes a car, drawn by stage horses, containing clownish yokels in yellow wigs, smocks and top-hats, and armed with pitchforks. Now arrive towering Carnival figures, like the exaggerated ghosts of ventriloquists' dummies. A red-faced woman suddenly hurls a paper rose at the Lady Mayoress, and all the children blow noses, dance and clap their hands. Next marches past the band of the local Yeomanry or Terri-torials employed for the occasion, and braying lustily along. The defectives, removed in the summer from their winter playground, the sands, and usually immured in houses at this season, have been brought out to watch the gaieties. It seemed a shame that their shortcomings should deprive them of such a simple, yet delightful, pleasure. Poor things, they have suffered enough, and their guardians whisper and confide to one another innumerable secrets; but the scene appears to excite their charges, to work them up to curious and unexpected frenzies, and their attendants are forced to murmur soothingly to them. One shakes from head to foot without ceasing; another barks like a dog; a third grimaces at the spectators. . . . Perhaps it was a pity, after all, to bring them.

Now the whole procession wends its way down to the sands; wherefrom, for the moment, the platform and the pierrots in their glittering white clothes have been removed, and crowds, still greater, collect to watch the fun. The civilian municipal band takes over from the military, and, caged-in on one side, as though they were rare animals, from the wind's attack, the members of the orchestra indulge their curious, nostalgic fancies; sometimes Dvořák, singing of the negroes shuffling through the orange-hung darkness of the South, and sometimes Tchaikovsky, celebrating the hot-house delights of Tsarist Russia, the gypsies, the waltzes and the lights that gladdened its polar nights. . . . And now, the sun comes out, reveals itself for all the crowd to see, and the happiness of the councillors, the Fathers of their People, is at last complete.

7

THE LADY WITH THE
PINK FEATHER

WILL the Lady with the Pink Feather, I wonder, if these words catch her eye, think the worse of me? I hope not. . . . It was thus. . . . I had been asked to lecture in, let us say, Devonshire, to an institute connected with an amateur association: and my lecture had been announced some weeks previously. Several letters reached me. First of all I received a letter from the President, recalling the fact that we were cousins (though she had never previously seemed to make much of this relationship) and hoping therefore that she could rely on me to *stand no nonsense* from the Vice-President, should I meet her. She was of opinion that I should not like her: a disagreeable, interfering old woman, who needed to be put in her place. I was not to mention this letter, of course, but should I find myself called upon to deliver a few severe rebukes to the lady in question, I was to be aware that I should have, behind me, the tacit support of the President. . . . But the letter which really interested me was exceedingly long, and one which I was obliged to read over many times, before I could fully obtain its gist. A diffuse letter, half frank, half secretive: it began by being concerned with nothing in particular, and only gradually the truth leaked out, only gradually its purpose suggested itself. Boiled down, the appeal was this. The writer, who bore the rare but not unsonorous name of Albinia, was a married woman and a member of the Association. She and her husband, she wrote, were great admirers of mine and of my brother and sister; took so great an interest in us and in our work that, led on by their enthusiasm, it might be that they had in some way or other, for instance by the use of Christian names when referring to us, and by relating instances of their acquaintanceship with us, produced the impression on other members of the Association that they knew us . . . well, rather better than our acquaintance actually warranted. Besides, she had only just remembered that, as a matter of fact, absurd as it might seem, we had *never* met. . . . However, the moment of trial had come, she and her husband could not bear to miss my lecture—and, indeed, if they did miss it, what would their friends think of them? Yet, if I showed no sign of this friend-ship which they had claimed, *where* would they be then? . . . Really, she felt she *did* almost know me. Did I feel the same? . . . She would be standing by the platform, and would be wearing a pink feather in her hat. . . . Surely I would not pass her by?

As I say, the purport of this long letter, the request in it, gradually emerged. Would I, for the sake of saving two human beings from agony, claim them, though I did not know—and, in fact, had never seen—them, as my friends? The request, in itself, I thought, was a compliment, for it indicated a belief, born of reading my books, that I *might* do so; that I was a person to whom it was possible to make this very unconven-tional and, indeed, extraordinary appeal. . . . At the same time,

I decided that the letter would have been more to my taste if it had been shorter, written in the style of a confession.

However, I decided to do the thing handsomely. The day came, I passed up the hall towards the platform, by which little knots of people were standing. I approached them, to greet the President. . . . A little way off stood a nervous but rather good-looking woman, wearing in her hat a pink feather. . . . As though suddenly seeing her, I threw my arms open, exclaimed in a stentorian voice of surprise: 'Albin-ia! You here!' and printed a hearty kiss upon her cheek. . . . I noticed a flush of pleasure as she returned my greeting, and that is all I know of her.

8

ON GHOSTS

O NLY by night do I believe in ghosts: and then more especially in a house that lies buried in the depth of the country and in which there is no electric light. That there are *manifestations*, on the other hand, I am persuaded by day as well as by night, and if these appearances are what they seem, or if they simply produce the impression of being ghosts, will to me, for one, ever be immaterial. Whether they prove merely to be lifeless impressions, stamped upon the surrounding air in a photographic way through the strong yet surviving emotions of the persons who inhabited this room or this house some centuries ago: whether they take shape through a trick of the atmosphere or encounter us through some fault in the flowing of the time-stream—so that perhaps we give the ghost as great a fright as he gives us (that is to say, that he returns to the people of his age, declaring: 'I have seen a peculiar being walking along the passage, dressed in baggy sort of knee-breeches made of cloth, and the most fantastically ugly coat') or whether they indeed be *revenants*, can make no difference to the fear with which these apparitions will always be regarded, and which no explanation, scientific or otherwise, can allay.

A great many ghosts, I take it, are the result of boredom. Just as small boys, when enduring the *ennui* of a private school, invent mysteries for themselves, and hear footsteps—or should one write the more interesting 'footfalls'?—on the gravel at night, so a few people, imprisoned in the sad magnificence of a decaying country-house, may be forced to invent for themselves nocturnal apparitions. The whole of the Romantic movement (with which the modern popularity of ghosts is very nearly connected) was, I think, the result of the growing boredom then beginning to afflict the most sensitive minds of the time. Perhaps, even, the apparition which was seen by Charles I (said to be Laud, but in reality Stafford, for partisans of the King changed the identity of the visitor, fearing that it might be harmful to his cause if he had seen the ghost of one whom he had so much injured) was the fruit of the long *ennui* which his imprisonment had engendered.

Superstition is so deeply rooted in human races, even the most civilized, that I do not know how it will be eradicated. No amount of reading of Sir James Frazer's *The Golden Bough* will ever quite liberate our minds. It will take many thousands of years before we can face the next world—or the lack of one —in any form without a shudder. Even now the inhabitants of great cities are only just freed from their fear of wild animals; to emancipate them from these more intangible terrors is altogether a more difficult affair.

Dr Johnson, foe to all exaggeration except that of natural appearance, held the opinion that no anecdote, however wittily related, was amusing unless in strict accordance with fact. 'Is it true?' was the rather astringent test which he applied to every story told him. Now, however, when most fiction is slightly falsified truth, and each biography is a neatly verisimilous work of fiction, the application of this standard would seem more than ever necessary. Certainly it has always seemed to me that the telling of a ghost story is never justified except by the good faith of the narrator: and, alas, most true ghost stories are not only pointless—which does not matter, for, in the absence of motive and clue, may, indeed, consist the whole effect of such a tale—but crude and unexciting.

I know several people who have seen ghosts, and many who have been through curious, if slight, experiences. I myself have, as I suppose, talked with a ghost, or, at any rate, with someone who was not there—though I should say talked *to*, rather than *with*. During the 1914–18 War, at a moment when I was very over-tired, my company had to take over some front-line trenches. We arrived just before dusk. There was a rule, as most readers of then military age will remember, that the men should 'stand to', with rifles on the parapet, at the moment of dusk, for it was one of the most common times of attack. I came out of my dug-out, which I had just entered, and saw a man, in the corner of the bay opposite, with his rifle on the ground, leaning against the wall of the trench. I spoke to him saying: 'How many times have I told you to get your rifle on the parapet?' and continued in the same strain, when suddenly I realized that no one was there—only a rifle leaning against the wall. . . . This experience was not in any way terrifying, but, all the same, however explicable through fatigue, it did bring with it subsequently an uneasy feeling that you could not trust your own senses, just as the man who has survived an earthquake distrusts for a time the solidity of the earth.

9

THE GHOST IN THE GREEN MASK

THE story of Dr Goodfellow's visitation is of interest; for the occurrence, however slight, and of however familiar a type, has unusual features, one of which is the reliability and intelligence of the person to whom it happened, and another the curious insistence—seemingly quite beyond the necessities of the case—with which the apparition sought to attract the doctor's attention.

One evening I was sitting at dinner alone with Dr Goodfellow. Upstairs a relation, of whom I happened to be extremely fond, was lying ill; and this serious illness had, during the last two or three months, formed the foundation for a friendship between the doctor and myself.

Knowing, as I did, this invalid, it was impossible not to admire the combination of tact and wisdom, the tempering of firmness with intuition, which the doctor had displayed. He lacked, too, the professional optimism of the English practitioner. He was about forty years of age, and a giant in stature; altogether he seemed a rather remarkable person.

The talk turned on the progress made recently in mental healing and the understanding of nervous disorders, and finally I enquired whether, among the many incidents of a medical career, there had ever occurred to him any event of which no ordinary explanation could be furnished.

Dr Goodfellow at first denied any belief in the phenomena of thought-transference or apparitions. Indeed, so strong was his conviction that it seemed completely to have banished from his memory for the moment the singular event which might have caused him to abandon it.

He was silent for some seconds, and I could see in his eyes a memory trying to rise, like a fish, to the still surface of his consciousness. At last it reached him, and rather unwillingly he admitted that, once, something unusual had happened to him.

As a student, at the age of seventeen, Dr Goodfellow had worked in the smallpox hospital at Glasgow. It was at the time of that alarming outbreak which coincided with the Boer War.

To lessen the risks of catching or spreading this virulently infectious disease, it was the rule for workers among these cases to wear a special uniform, consisting of loose white coat and trousers and a green mask, with a beak-like nose, attached to a close-fitting cap. However necessary it may have been, this livery must have added a grotesque touch of further horror to the scene, dehumanizing the doctors and workers as they glided in and out of the carefully shaded rooms, making them seem, in the delirium of the poor disfigured victims, rather the personification of the disease—as though the deadly microbes responsible for it had for the moment been allowed to assume quasi-human form in order to plague and torture the wretched sufferers—than what they were, courageous and sympathetic volunteers for its combat.

[67]

Working with Goodfellow was a student named Fairfax, whose most intimate friend he became. But such friendships of adolescence are apt to be volatile, and, when Goodfellow left his comrade behind in Glasgow, in order to study medicine in Paris, his letters to Fairfax, his letters from Fairfax, became more and more infrequent, and finally, after a year, stopped altogether.

Goodfellow's new life, coming at the very moment when his vitality was at its greatest, and the transforming of the scene which framed it, filled him with the intoxication of existence which comes—if at all—but once in a lifetime, and completely obliterated for him the thought of anything but the actual moment. Fairfax was forgotten, absolutely forgotten.

The young Englishman was working in the medical college which was under the charge of the famous Monsieur Blois. For a year a room was found for him in the establishment, and then he was allowed to move out into a lodging of his own.

He was singularly fortunate in the one he now rented, for it was a delightful room, the panelling of which was painted a soft, clear grey, and, what was more important, it had three wide windows looking out on to a garden.

It was the sort of room that exercises an influence, both invigorating and calming, on the mind of its occupant, however unconscious he may be by nature of his environment.

The door faced one of the end windows, and between them was a very charming mantelpiece. The bed stood with its head against the other wall opposite the chimney, but there was a considerable space on each side of it.

The only drawback that Goodfellow found to his new lodging was the absence of electric light. But this deprivation was in the day-time fully compensated by the light which poured in.

Here the young man lived for some years; during this

period he never heard from Fairfax, nor could the latter have been aware of his present address.

One night, during his fourth summer in Paris, Goodfellow came in about eleven o'clock. The windows stood wide open, and from the garden below drifted the warm air of May, scented by the pale, Persian shapes of the lilacs as they were fanned by their gentle slaves, the winds.

The room was drenched in moonlight, so pearly bright that it was as though daylight were being filtered through deep, clear waters.

A sense of rest and contentment seized on him, and, puffing out the candle, he swiftly fell asleep. Out of this peaceful but heavy slumber he was wakened suddenly, and with a feeling of disturbance. What had happened? . . . The clock struck two, and he looked round.

In an armchair by the window, facing him, and very distinct in the milky light, was a motionless figure in gleaming white clothes, and with a green beaked mask; an unearthly Punchinello, it seemed. Even apart from this sad, fantastic uniform, the build and poise of the visitor proclaimed it as his forgotten friend Fairfax.

Goodfellow knew that he had locked the door before going to bed. Fairfax was certainly ignorant of his address, and in any case would hardly call on him, in the middle of the night, clad in the garb of the Glasgow smallpox hospital.

The figure remained there motionless. His friend called him by name, asked him what he wanted; but he sat on there under the moonlight without moving.

Fear overcame Goodfellow; he could not find the matches, and the figure sat on. He feared that it was a hallucination, that he might be going mad. He buried his head in the blankets, and turned over towards the wall. It was some minutes before he dared open his eyes.

When he did so, the figure was opposite him once more, had moved to take up its position on a chair by the wall near him. There the masked creature sat, again rigid and immovable. Goodfellow fainted: but when he came round his visitor was no longer with him.

The next morning he made sure that his door was still locked.

But the concierge complained, when he came downstairs, that a funny, stiff figure in fancy-dress had knocked him up in the middle of the night and asked for the young Englishman upstairs: so that the apparition was able, evidently, in the illogical way of ghosts, to enter certain rooms without human aid.

Goodfellow was so perturbed by the whole occurrence that he contrived to sit next to Dr Blois at luncheon—for the head of the college often lunched with the students—and confided in him.

The old Frenchman enquired laughingly what he had eaten for dinner, when, just at that moment, a telegram was brought informing Goodfellow that Fairfax had died the previous night, shortly before two o'clock.

Under the will of the dead man he was appointed executor. Could he return to England as soon as possible?

Fairfax had died of pneumonia, following on influenza, and had left behind him a wife and child of whose existence the new executor had been ignorant. But why had he adopted that strange, ominous uniform for his appearance; why had he not spoken?

Dr Goodfellow had never had an experience of this kind before, and has never had one since.

10

THE BEST YEARS OF LIFE

We can watch how the years built themselves up; how they began, out of darkness, with small visual impressions that even today are borne back unexpectedly on a tide of summer scent; the smell of hay, for example, or of some particular flower; the smell of box hedges or of seaweed drying on the rocks in the wind, or, it may be, of some pungent food.

But these sensations, agreeable though they were, are not coherent enough to justify us in describing infancy as 'the best years of life'. . . . Afterward there came, for me at any rate, a year or two of unpleasant grappling with the primary problems of Latin and arithmetic; an epoch infested also with a certain magic derived from the study of atlases and books of history: for then insinuated themselves into the consciousness all those queer names—names which seemed to stand for so much, but in reality conveyed so little; Ethelred the Unready, Canute, William Rufus, Richard Cœur-de-Lion and many other such high-sounding syllables. . . . Yet all these things we accumulated, in reality constituted—so one was given to understand—only a preparation for 'the best years of life'.

At last dawned the awful morning which, convention led one to believe, formed the threshold of them. School to me had always been an intimidating prospect, and I shall never forget the sensation of gratitude that I experienced towards the only person who, in advance, told me the truth about it. He was an acquaintance of my parents, considered rather a worthless, feckless and extravagant being, but, guided by some instinct of genuine kindness, he interviewed me before I went to school, gave me a sovereign, and said, at the same time: 'My boy, most people will probably tell you that the next few years will be the best years of your life; but don't you believe a word of it. They will be perfectly horrible and a dreadful waste of time. You must never expect to know a moment's happiness until you grow up.'

This information was, at any rate, encouraging and of use, for had I really, when at school, believed that it *was* the best that existence could offer, the blackness of despair which engulfed me would have been even darker. Several years of life at a private school followed: and then I moved to Eton, with its beauty, ineptitude and snobbishness; and from there proceeded to an army tutor's. These last months were, rather unexpectedly for one of my temperament, enjoyable.

After that came a year of agony during which I was attached to a cavalry regiment; a life fit only for horses and dogs—which were, indeed, considered by the officers (and very rightly) as being by far the most important members of their community. I escaped, eventually, to join my own regiment, and in it spent a year or two of great happiness. But the 1914–18 War broke out, and quickly put an end to that.

[72]

I am prepared to think that the long, the—as they seemed—
endless years which were wasted in a horrible, deplorable and,
as all now see, pointless struggle, *might* perhaps have been the
best of my life; but since I was a soldier, and not a politician or
an army contractor, they were certainly the worst and most
harrowing. Not only all that and more, but they were, in
addition, the most boring. The war ended; but even so great
a relief could not rid me at once of the great burden of unhappiness it had engendered.

Nevertheless, the year after the war—I was twenty-six—
proved one of the most agreeable of my life, for then one was
able once more to travel freely abroad, to recover all the joys
of European civilization, which had been in abeyance during
the whole war period. I visited Venice and Rome and the cities
of Spain. Even the Riviera, with its vacuous, rose-pink, middle-
class tidiness seemed a paradise. Moreover, during the years
that followed, I was, for the first time, able to work at a job
congenial to me—writing. And this added a certain quiet
pleasure—broken only by the fits of temper engendered by
criticism—to my life.

Yet, invincibly sanguine, one cannot help but hope that the
best years of life yet lie hidden in the future. . . . An old friend
of mine once confided to me that he had never known happiness until he reached seventy. I can quite understand his point
of view; no need to be afraid, at that age, of *giving too much
trouble*. A man of three score years and ten can advise and
interfere where he wishes, without the least dread of retalia-
tion: he is too old to be worried, but not too old to worry other
people. If, by that time, a successful author, he will have become automatically a 'Grand Old Man'. Everyone will laugh
at anything serious the 'G.O.M.' says (since there is his reputation for wit to be considered), and will be serious when he
says anything funny (because deference must be paid to

sagacity as much as to wit). Moreover, a 'Grand Old Man' can speak without being answered back. He can talk when he wants to, and be quiet when he wants to: and his silence will be considered no less pregnant than his utterances. . . . Would not these be the best years of life?

II

ON PRIVATE SCHOOLS

Those who come of Anglo-Saxon breed are people of strange and savage customs, especially where the young of their race are concerned. The more wealthy, the more fortunate, bring up their children until they reach the age of nine or ten in circumstances, if not of luxury, at least of happy plenty. Every little ailment is attended to immediately, and they go short of nothing they want. Their diet is carefully studied, they are taught the rudiments of many obsolete crafts such as riding and old-fashioned politeness; while they learn, too, the names of cinema stars, wild flowers, butterflies and of the various brands of milk chocolate. . . . And then, suddenly, just as they have reached an age when their intelligence and sensitiveness, which have after this fashion been encouraged, can respond to the stimuli of their surroundings, they are whisked off to places of dreary internment, called private—though now more widely known as prep—schools, where the most extraordinary tribal values and standards prevail: and though these, as it were, labour camps are varied according to their years, they remain in one or another of them (unless they have the good fortune to be expelled with ignominy) until such time as their characters have been formed in the same hard, dense and unpleasant mould as that of those who teach them.

The arguments bandied about in favour of English schools as a form of upbringing seem to me very faulty. The chief one in current use is to name some man, notoriously a half-wit, and say: 'Look at *him*, now! He was never at school.' But then, since schools in this country are the established rule, the fact that he never entered such a place of learning merely indicates that he was always mentally wanting. . . . Otherwise he would have been sent to one, willy-nilly; for, if they belong to the comfortable classes, the parents of any child who is not sent to school remain, among other parents, until death, under the intolerable, atrocious stigma of being 'unusual'.

And yet what strange, Spartan modes are these, to apply to boys of whom their parents hope that they will, when they grow up, one day rule their country, governing it, fighting for it, thinking for it! I believe that the children of working-class homes, though (as we hear so frequently stated) 'denied the opportunities which money affords', are better, more kindly and more sensibly brought up than the children of those possessed of money to spare. . . . Notwithstanding, directly a poor man has made a sufficient fortune to enable him to do so, he sends his children to 'a good school': so strongly anchored in our blood is the instinct for this sort of education.

What, then, does 'a good school' signify; what qualities indicate it as such? . . . Difficult to define, these special marks of differentiation are, perhaps, easier to describe from personal experience. At the moment, however, I will deal only with those places in which are confined the very young, leaving the 'public schools', as they are called, for a later scrutiny.

Thus myself, for example, was placed at a particular private school, which in those days had become fashionable, because—as frequently before I went there, I heard my elders remark to one another with an air of contentment—the headmaster was 'the best dribbler in England'. Innocent in those far-away times of the meaning of Association Football terms, this phrase used greatly, and often, to puzzle me. What could be the purpose, the significance of this so desirable and yet, as it seemed, mystic accomplishment; one, moreover, which so ill accorded, as far as my experience went, with their code of nursery behaviour? Nor, when I came to think of it, had I ever noticed that my parents chose as their friends those endowed with any special aptitude for dribbling.

But what a life ensued for me when at last safely placed under the tutelage, spiritual as well as mundane, of this grand, though well-meaning, dribbler! What vistas I see again of fog and rain and wet grey flannel (I can still smell it), of plungings through ink in the morning, and through mud in the afternoon, of pens and benches and indiarubber, of food which, though intended to be healthy and plentiful, was in reality of an ancient-British, Stonehenge variety, and finally, of occasional nostalgic lectures, mostly about the Holy Land, accompanied by lantern slides and delivered by various aged clergymen, each with a different kind of impediment in his speech; that is to say, that one would indulge in an ordinary stutter, another betray an inability to pronounce the letter 's', substituting for it the letter 'f' (so that he conferred, as I see now, upon our everyday speech the feeling of those old books in which the long 's' occurs), another would whistle at unconjecturable intervals, thereby imparting an extra, if unusual, interest to his discourses, another would have no roof to his

[77]

mouth, while again another would, from time to time, lose his voice altogether and mouth at the assembled school after the manner of a rebellious goldfish.

Then, too, I recall those hideous, appalling school concerts, where in an atmosphere of unscented soap and scented brilliantine, blossomed that clean, sportsmanlike sense of fun which, together with a rare aptitude for Alpine accidents, is the badge of English schoolmasters all the world over. . . . A series of hymns to the wheezy following of a harmonium also presents itself in my memory: until, at long last, the term ended in a frenzy of ritual. Thus a certain day was appointed, forty-eight hours before the school broke up—called 'pay-day'—on which every boy could pay off old scores without fear of rebuke, 'bashing' and being 'bashed' to one's heart's content. These were hours of black eyes, missing teeth, bloody noses and whirling fists. . . . During the last week, too, of holding their usual class during the afternoon, the masters would, as a further treat, read aloud a few chapters from some incomparably boring novel by Sir Walter Scott: and there would be more chapel and prayers than ever, and a certain amount of speech-making, to be followed by an 'end-of-term-supper', greatly appreciated by the young. Now, at last, the school cook could manifest in a thousand ways her hellish ingenuity: tipsy-cakes, crazy concoctions of cream, turned inside out by a thunder-storm, almonds, synthetic jam—containing wooden splinters intended to summon up in the uninitiated the idea of rasp-berries or strawberries—and custard, vied with quaking jellies that radiated the most terrifying green and red fires, volcanic and sulphurous, and little cakes, composed equally, it seemed, of coco-nut-matting and cold cream.

These may seem frivolous objections to a school: but what did we learn? To support the Navy League, and to shirk the necessity of lessons by means of shining at games. . . . We learnt, too, that in our free country stupidity was no disgrace. (This lesson was subsequently emphasized by a public-school education.) Indeed, I know of nothing more saddening than to visit a young relative at such a school: for the child that one knew as a delightful, original being, full of affection, has been converted into a horrid, stupid, hard-hearted little boy, his head full of shibboleths and cricket averages. That which most concerns him is whether his trousers are turned up at the ends, like those of other boys, and whether, after all, Jenkins will play for the school.

12

ON PUBLIC SCHOOLS

Public schools are to private schools as lunatic asylums to mental homes; larger and less comfortable. The public school, it is true, allows more individual liberty than the private school, and it must be admitted that up till the time of the war no special effort was made in these institutions towards education. This, where an intelligent boy was concerned, constituted an advantage. It did not waste his time, it did not oblige him to fill his head with useless tags of Latin and arithmetic, but instead afforded him the necessary leisure in which to read and to think.

Since the beginning of the nineteenth century the public school has injured incalculably the English governing classes. It has weakened them, and sapped their strength. The remark, attributed to Wellington, that Waterloo was won upon the playing-fields of Eton, in the end became more responsible for the loss of the Boer War and the length of the Great War than any other hypothetical epigram of any other great man. It will be noticed, to the contrary, that when a particular streak of political acumen is visible through the generations of any family, the members of that family were never sent to a public school.

The popularity of the English public school arose with the industrial revolution and the necessity, which the middle classes then began to feel, of becoming gentlemen. In result, the public schools developed merely into so many large-scale factories of that boring and emasculate commodity, the English Gentleman. To be an E.G. it was necesssry to possess a fixed income and a certain *savoir faire*, to hunt and to have very little education; and it was towards this goal that the public schools aimed. But alas, the middle classes were not successful in their ambition; because, by sending their sons in over-whelming numbers to the public schools, they fashioned them —though it must be admitted, without meaning to—in their own mould. Games were now substituted for blood sports. And, much as blood sports are to be condemned, at least a certain primitive force and purpose inspires them.

Dr Arnold, as Lytton Strachey pointed out in *Eminent Victorians*, was one of those most responsible for the nineteenth-century development of the English public school. It was in his day that the boys, no longer allowed to roam about, observing birds and flowers and butterflies, were first obliged, instead, to concentrate their ambition and energy upon the pursuit of a football, cricket ball or some other spherical object. Even now, compulsory games are still in force, so that at this moment, all over England, poor little boys are being compelled to spend their time in this unutterably boring manner. . . . Let me offer them one word of help and advice. . . . If they must play in a compulsorily organized game, then let it be football; which can only last for a short time, during which it is possible, with a little trouble and with the aid of the specially armoured boots

F

that etiquette decrees for such an occasion, to inflict considerable damage on those who deserve it. A cricket match, on the
other hand, can endure for three days and fill the soul with an
almost intolerable sense of *ennui*.

Here I should like to recall an incident. Some years ago the
Provost of Eton, Dr James, sent a circular round to all old
Etonians, inviting them to subscribe sums of money in order
to buy more land for playing-fields. This letter was addressed
to myself among others, and in reply I offered to send a cheque
if the Provost would ensure that these playing-fields should not
be used for the odious habit of compulsory games, which had
ruined the minds of so many of the most intelligent of my
contemporaries. . . . Alas, on this point, he would offer no
guarantee.

I seldom visit Eton now, so bored was I during my time
there. Indeed, the most agreeable hours I spent in that place
were during the recurrent few days of each winter term in
which the town was flooded. This imparted a certain remote-
ness and watery, Dutch interest of detail to the landscape and
pleasantly varied the normal course of the day's work. Moreover, there was then, given good luck, a chance of catching a
severe cold through getting wet, and the comfortable prospect,
in consequence, of being able to spend a day or two quietly in
bed, reading, without being forced to see either masters or
comrades. Anything, indeed, like a thunderstorm, that lifted
life a little out of its ordinary rut, made it more bearable, and
even a school concert, full of boys singing:

> At Flores in the Azores
> Sir Richard Grenville lay,

was less intolerable than the more normal hours of *ennui*.

And then the masters! Public schools are so obsolete that
they yet rest upon an old monastic basis; the majority of them,

[82]

even to this very day, still favour clergymen as headmasters—an absolute anachronism. It is difficult, of course, to be a schoolmaster—we all admit that: but a clergyman is the last man in the world to be allowed to deal with growing boys; for, whenever a clergyman becomes a schoolmaster, he always tends to become either severe and cranky or playful and self-advertising.

As I have said, I seldom visit Eton now. Too many pitiful ghosts haunt its lanes and quadrangles, and the mere sight of a master slouching in his cap and gown down one of its narrow alleys fills me with misery. But the other day I spent an hour or two there, and wandered round the cloisters, observing the alterations that had taken place. The chief change seemed to be the enormous number of memorials erected to my contemporaries: for I belong to that unhappy generation which came of age during the years in which the 1914–18 War broke out, and most of my friends and enemies at Eton are now either maimed or have long been dead.

It had always seemed to me that schoolmasters particularly love memorials: stained-glass windows and Gothic lettering, carved-ivy borders and brass eagles; and in this direction wars no doubt added an interest to their lives. Just think of the wall tablets and the windows that have been unveiled! Think of all the singing in the school chapels, of the choir practices, and of the many charming little ceremonies which have celebrated the fulfilment of that education which I saw in progress round me. Throughout my school years I felt that, if this education were intended to turn out a type, and if that type were going to rule the country, some great disaster must be on its way for us. So strong was this impression that, while still at Eton, I asked my father, who had also been 'educated' there, whether the boys had been as stupid in his time as they were in mine? He assured me that they had been, and this comforted me. But I think he was wrong.

Well, the disaster came; and the public schools are still devoted to the same ideals, and thus will be ready for the next disaster which they are helping to bring about. The community which they turn out is now, therefore, to be regarded, not so much as one of English gentlemen, as of English dead. They constitute, in fact, no longer factories of gentlemen but, instead, so many corpse factories.

Their methods are antiquated to such a degree that it is almost impossible to remedy them. From the class-conscious point of view of those who dread government by the workers, the most desirable thing in the world would be democratization of the public schools. If miners and millhands could only be educated at Eton, there would never be any strikes, or if there were, these would be unsuccessful; would mean no more than an Eton and Harrow match. Always teach people of whom you are afraid 'to play the game'; in other words to be hoodwinked throughout life, and to be contented with conditions with which they have no right to allow themselves to be contented.

13

GAMES (1)

AS A MENACE TO THE COUNTRY

MY FEAR and detestation of games is founded in the first place, I think, in love of my country; chiefly, then, on patriotic grounds I abhor them. . . . When England was making her way from a small island to the principal power, first of Europe, and then of the world, no organized games existed in this fair land. Almost the first mention of them in our history is the unchallenged fact that Drake nearly missed destroying the Armada through untimely indulgence in a game of bowls.

At school—and, when discussing games, one must, alas, inevitably hark back to those places of incarceration and torment—the authorities arm themselves with the excuse that the playing of them prepares a boy for leadership in the life which is to follow. . . . But, that being so, where, I ask myself, are now my—or your—great contemporaries in the worlds of cricket and football? . . . The answer is, of course, 'Still playing them!' (though that an adult would, of his own accord,

engage in such orgies of futile infantilism is hardly credible!) . . .
As to qualities of leadership: was a particular devotion to golf
or cricket ever recorded—to take a few great English names at
random—of Raleigh, Marlborough, Henry V, Peterborough,
the Black Prince, Pitt, Fox or Nelson; any more than of such
negligible highbrows as Shakespeare, Milton, Pope, Keats or
Blake? . . . To look further afield, neither Alexander the Great,
nor Caesar nor Napoleon, seem to have had much time
for this sort of thing; yet each one of them, you might
have thought, displayed a certain capacity for inspiring his
men.

Of course, we are compelled to admit that our governors
in the Houses of Parliament have, for several decades or so,
played golf: but then consider to what a pass they continually
lead us! Does anyone nowadays think favourably of politicians
as such; has not their very name become a byword for plati-
tude, banal blatant blather and incompetence? . . . Indeed, it
may be claimed that golf nearly lost us the first war: many of
the statesmen who allowed us to blunder into it were golf-
addicts.

One of the foremost methods of propaganda by which our
opponents kept up their flagging spirits during the 1914–18
War, and prevented their people from giving in, was the
statement that, if the English won, they intended everywhere
to introduce compulsory games; nevertheless, since we were
nominally victorious, the nominally vanquished, looking round
after the battle for the cause of their failure and our success,
decided 'It must be due to games! They say so themselves,' and
proceeded to inflict on their own countries this barbarous
English habit.

Sometimes I wonder. . . . Abroad we are still held to be the
most subtle diplomatists in the whole world; we have now
taught other nations 'to play the game'. Is this a piece of

deliberate, diabolic guile: for the practice of games, by inculcating a blind, 'My country-right-or-wrong' team-spirit, teaches a nation to be warlike without being certain to win and, when actually engaged in the struggle, to fight as though playing a game; with the Almighty looking on as an omnipotent umpire, ever there, ready to declare a 'foul', should one occur? . . . Have we, then, of a purpose set their feet on the wrong track? And, as I hear of our continual defeats at the hands of France, Germany, America, Italy and Greece, a thrill of patriotic emotions runs through me and, murmuring: 'There Is Yet Hope,' I wonder if, after all, this particular objection of mine to games—as a menace to the country—may not be mistaken? Perhaps we shall be more evenly pitted, one against another, in future. . . . We have taught young foreigners, too, how to waste *their* time and undermine *their* health.

When all these arguments have been stated, it remains indisputable that England was built up with the brain rather than the foot (although it is this member which every schoolboy from the age of eight to eighteen is now taught to regard as all-important) and that, in the world as it was, the national mania for games did, I apprehend, help considerably to lengthen the duration of the war. The 'team-spirit', of which in those ugly and ever-deplorable days we heard so much, undoubtedly prolonged it and, as well, aided the final exhaustion: for the end of the shambles resembled the result of a tug-of-war wherein one side suddenly lets go. The Allies sprawled on the ground: and there, indeed, they continue.

Further, while the game-playing spirit endures, so long can there be no peace in Europe: because it inspires us always to support the weaker side; which policy, however noble in intention or as a gesture, is dreadfully, horribly unwise. Directly a nation begins to be prosperous and powerful, we, for our part, begin immediately, almost automatically, to dislike and disparage it. But, in future, would it not be better to try to form an alliance with the strongest—rather than the weakest—group of powers? . . . Alas, we shall never even attempt such a thing: for it will be time to 'have a go at the other fellow', time to enter for the challenge-cup again!

14

GAMES (2)

AS A PERNICIOUS INFLUENCE ON THE INDIVIDUAL

FAR, then, from preparing a boy for leadership in adult life, all that the school obsession for games really accomplishes is to afford a pleasant existence to him who likes playing them. To others, however, compulsory-games come as a disaster, as well as a bore. (I hyphenate the words, since for them—as for modern warfare—a new designation should be invented, both having long outgrown their names.) When once they become compulsory, they cease to be games, and, with that, all their virtue—for what it was worth—dies. Indeed, upon the individual, they exercise as pernicious an effect as upon a country. For example: how brutally ugly they are to look at, with the single possible exception of lawn-tennis, a harmless, silly, rather pretty dissipation! Consider cricket: it does not even possess the dramatic, exciting side to it—and certainly not the splendour of pageantry—that go far towards excusing the bull-fight in Spain. It is thus infinitely more degrading to the spectator.

And here, perhaps, we may touch on another problem; the influence of games on those who watch them. At school, of course, small boys are often compulsory spectators of games, as well as compulsory players. They cannot help it. It may be, even, that they find it less boring, if much colder, than to join in the sport themselves. . . . As for the adult—if you can call him such—spectator of games, though it necessarily damages his esthetic sense, I do not in other respects take a very serious view of his failing. It must be very dull for him, poor man; but, at any rate, it must be *healthier* for him than if he were to *play* himself. Moreover, through this process of substitution, he may in time get rid of the craving. Further, the sight of a crowd on the way to a football ground should, in certain directions, help to reassure us. Some there are who have pronounced England decadent, have alleged that enjoyment is now the order of the day here: but let us remember, for their refutation, the thousands who will sit in the rain for hours in order to watch a football match. Surely *that* is a sign, a symptom, of the toughness and vitality of the race? . . . Let us recollect, too, that, though foreigners might misconstrue the complaint that some of its addicts have registered of recent years (that cricket was but dull fun), reasoning that this indicated an enfeebling of the national fibre, yet the only suggestion —put forward by the same people who complained—for the brightening and speeding up of the game, was a proposal to lengthen the natural span of a Test Match from three to four or five days!

But to return to our sheep (and what sheep they are!) the influence of games upon those who play them is quite a different matter. After all, cricket, golf and football, whether to watch or to play, remain merely so many devices for wasting what is, so far as we know, the only span allotted to mankind in a world full of wonders: for, though it may be argued that they often occupy but a very small portion of twenty-four hours, they are yet so tiring that the rest of the day must likewise be spent in stupor. Thus, for instance, whenever you hear someone remark: 'After a day's hard work, I go to the theatre to be amused, not to be made to think!', that person thereby announces himself, you may be sure, a game-fiend. Such fatigue results from over-exercise, from using the wrong muscles in the wrong way, at the wrong age, but never from brain work. A healthy man can derive more pleasure from the use of his brain than from the use of his feet.

What, then, you ask, gentle reader, is the cause of the 'game-habit', hardly less injurious in the end than that of opium or hashish; how do men, reasonable in other respects, acquire it? . . . Usually its origin is to be traced back to schools: but, in after-life, it springs, as a rule, more immediately from over-indulgence in food. People choose to think that over-eating can be remedied by over-exercise. It is a vicious circle. Over-exercise makes them over-hungry. Once you take to it, violent exercise becomes a necessity throughout your life. You cannot do without it. The game-addict, unless specifically equipped for his career by Nature, must, in order to 'keep fit', play—or should we write 'take'?—more and more games. (Here, in parenthesis, note the coincidence that the word *take* is, through some process, perhaps, of unconscious identification, used of both exercise and drugs.) As with soporifics, the need for games increases with the years that pass. But, since the constitution of a man can only withstand this sort of life so long as he is young, directly he grows too old, too exhausted by exercise to indulge in it any longer, he dies. (It is, of course, common knowledge that athletes are apt to die young, their systems outworn, their hearts and nerves run down, the power of resistance at an end.) . . . Yet actually two brisk walks of from twenty minutes to half an hour each, or a swim of fifteen minutes a day, are quite sufficient to keep a man healthy in body. But there also exists the mind. '*Eat less and think more*' should be the slogan of all who have leisure.

Some game-fiends, exceptionally strong to begin with, do contrive, by one method or another, occasionally to prolong their existence into middle age: and nothing is more sad, more despicable, to the really healthy man, than to see these poor tortured creatures running all over the place in sweaters, racing over the muddy ground, and toiling over golf courses, in a constant, ineffectual effort to regain the health which all these exertions, all this morbid attempt to escape from the reality of life, have destroyed. If you ask them what they are doing, they pant out, peevishly enough, that they are 'trying to keep fit'. . . . But what for? What, indeed, can be the purpose of trying 'to keep fit', when all their time is absorbed in doing so? Against what hour of trial are these wretched victims of delusion preparing; for deathbed or Day of Judgment?

Yet games have their uses. There is, after all, a good side to them. The game of golf, for example, can be played alone—a great advantage. Further, a golf course, a cricket ground, a football pitch, each acts as a temporary internment camp for all those who practise, or are interested in, the particular vice to which it is devoted. Thus the man free of these habits and healthy in mind and body, can look at his watch on a summer day and say to himself: 'It's safe now: all the worst cricketers' ('worst' being used in the sense of most addicted) 'are at Lord's or at the Oval; all the worst golfers are isolated on their "blasted heaths". I can now walk abroad without fear of being bored by a single one of them.' . . . Lastly, as I have stated, such games soon intern their habituals even more securely—this time in their coffins. For Nature very sensibly concludes that if a man will, of his own choice, thus waste his time and energy, this world cannot hold much interest for him. And so, cutting down his life's span by a decade or two, she, with combined wisdom and kindness, removed him from it. R.I.P.!

15

ON BROADENING THE MIND

'Travel,' you hear people say, 'broadens the mind'—as if that were a recommendation!—and, in consequence, it is often suggested to many young men of the more leisured classes as a fitting close to their education. Another instance of our illogicality: for the aim of education, I take it, is to enable the child to grow up into a man well equipped to grapple successfully with life, and so be happy in it. Yet surely one would presume on looking round, that, to attain this end, the absolute essential was to have not only a narrow, but a resolutely shut, mind? And why, for example, seek to broaden a mind, when several hundreds, or even thousands, of pounds have already been spent upon a continuous and very expert course of narrowing it—by means of the private-school and public-school systems?

Travelling does, indeed, open your eyes, the eyes of even the most unobservant, a little to the future; which, if happiness is your aim, is inexpedient. It is not, for example, encouraging, nor does it tend to promote the *bourgeois* belief in human progress on which contentment largely depends, to journey through China and find the Chinese people, with their strange instinct for the future, everywhere repairing the walls, long disused, of their towns and villages, and putting up new ones where necessary, in preparation for another thousand years or so of chaos. . . . And, again, to observe the different rites of different religions, which yet all present so close a parallel to those of your own Church, might arouse disturbing thoughts. You should never, if you value happiness, allow yourself to question your beliefs. Indeed, if you lack them, you should go out and find them, for, just as the Chinese are rebuilding and patching their walls for their bodily security, so many people today return to narrow and outworn creeds for the protection and comfort of their minds. . . . Close your mind and shut your eyes, and you may be happy, and not only happy but great; for most really great men, that is to say, men of action as opposed to men of thought, have been narrow-minded and lacked vision. What man not blinded by a single purpose would have dared, like Clive, to conquer India (and has *broad-*mindedness enabled us to keep it?). . . . Alexander the Great, as a boy, is said to have tamed his horse Bucephalus by riding it towards the sun, so that it became dazzled, blinded to all else, and in like manner he allowed the thought of conquest in later years to narrow his own great mind, so that he could perceive nothing but its blaze.

In politics, then, never entertain a doubt, nor in religion: if you are an esthetic conservative, condemn out of hand all modern poetry and painting, but without reading or seeing it; or if a radical, despise all ancient things, forbidding yourself to recognize the worth of Raphael or Titian, El Greco or Gainsborough. The pleasure you will obtain from scouting them is quite equal to any you might derive from a more broad-minded appreciation of their beauties. Assign to your personal or inherited belongings a special artistic or historical interest, and to your home, even if it be one out of a row of two hundred similar houses, a particular air of handsomeness and comfort; think your carpets softer, and your children better at sport, than your neighbours'. And, above all, acclaim, without knowing any other, your own land as the most beautiful and most just, the least selfish and most intelligent, full of the best-dressed men and women, the most profound cricketers, the most subtle golfers and the best tadpole-fishers of any country in the world. . . . That way lies peace and contentment.

In all truth, a man whose mind is said by his fellows to lack breadth is from the first in a strong position where life is concerned, well adapted for its struggles, and certain of happiness, even if congenitally unfitted for conversation. And nothing can be done about it; the narrow mind narrows further with the years, inevitably; in the same way that the broad mind broadens. . . . Thus, to strike a personal note, my whole life has been spent in an endeavour to narrow rather than broaden my outlook, and to debase rather than improve my mind: but it has proved a hopeless struggle. I was afforded every advantage in that direction; I was sent to good schools and taught cricket and Latin: and yet it never made me into either a good cricketer or an adequate classical scholar; in only one direction did I show promise, by preferring my own native language to that of other countries, a preference founded, no doubt, on laziness, but a necessary ingredient of the narrow mind. . . . Finally, in, as I suppose, despair, those responsible for my welfare decided that a cavalry regiment would prove the best finishing-school for me, and accordingly I was for eight months attached to one of those now obsolete institutions: but did this, even, make for my happiness by destroying my intellectual and esthetic interests? Alas, not in the least! I could still see not one, but a thousand sides to every question, and, in consequence, still found myself inclined to waver mournfully in my opinions.

As for that cavalry regiment, it was, indeed, an extraordinary, and even useful, experience, enabling me at an early age, and without travelling to distant and unhealthy parts of Africa, to make myself acquainted with the customs and comprehend the mentality of the members of any primitive tribe. No life shared with savages of the Congo or with the web-footed natives of New Guinea could have been more strange; none could have seemed so far removed from the life proceeding round it. In all other aspects, indeed, it constituted the antithesis of travelling, for everything was a restriction. The objects, a stranger would have pronounced, to which these barbaric clans were dedicated must be horse and dog (even the crocodile, formerly venerated by the Egyptians, was a more sensible and seemly object of respect). Of all animals the horse influences the average Englishman to the greatest extent; the magical creature seems able to conquer his whole interest, his whole life, and to prevent him from thinking about anything else. A special language, even, of hoofs and hocks and fetlocks and a thousand other such terms, has to be used in his worship; a language as complicated, to express a process of thought, subtle as any needed for the comprehension of the more involved problems of higher mathematics. Moreover, the devotee must dress in special clothes, and bestow every hour upon his god: that way, too, lies happiness.

Such experiences, even if they do not successfully straiten the mind, do, in a sense, help a little to prepare their victims for life. However much of horror and *ennui* the world may hold; whatever, for example, your experiences of first-class modern warfare, they will probably, nevertheless, come as a relief after days spent at school. Many a youth, leaving school

G [97]

to join the Army during the war, found life in the trenches less of a strain upon the nerves than had been everyday school existence, infinitely preferable to it in every way. In that sense Waterloo was perhaps really won upon the playing-fields of Eton. . . . So let us narrow our minds and take heart for the future.

16

IN PRAISE OF INDOLENCE

THERE was a time when laziness, now proclaimed as a virtue, was condemned as a vice. 'Satan,' they used to tell us, 'finds some mischief still for idle hands to do.' . . . But many people now realize, only too well, that, in order for this proverb to contain truth, the word 'idle' should be rendered 'restless' or 'busy': because over-intense activity is often a form of nervous disease, a kind of mental St Vitus's Dance. The idle man is usually a good-natured one; at worst, harmless; whereas the men who do the harm, the Napoleons and Lenins and Hitlers and rabid newspaper-peers, are obliged by their natures to be for ever frantically striving. . . . Poor creatures, they cannot rest until they are worn out. Pleasure has little meaning for them, and they are the victims of continual indigestion; mental, not less than physical. Avoid, I should counsel you for your own good, the man who has no use for sleep and says so: it is the sign of one who wishes to be a superman, and who will, if you give him time, undoubtedly tell you that he glories in battle and he considers that Effort is the Aim of All Life. Beware, too, of the sort of old people who subsequently, in their obituary notices, are said to have 'remained active until the end'.

Effort is of no avail in itself; nor should it be necessarily awarded admiration. It requires, often, as much effort to lose a battle as to win it; because the stupid commander, aware of his inferiority, has to be even busier than the clever one, and tends to fussiness in detail. Cleverness no more consists in an infinite capacity for taking pains than does genius; they both consist, rather, in an infinite capacity for inducing others to take the pains for them; and the right ones, at that! The generals and statesmen, on both sides, who were responsible for such endless disaster and loss of life during the 1914–18 War were, on the whole, a painstaking and unimaginative body, always busy, and indeed inclined to parade the fact. The Devil himself is evidently a busy lost soul, endlessly coming and going about his work. . . . The lazy man has seldom forged or murdered. All the grand embezzlers and treasure-rootlers during my lifetime were all intensely *busy* men. (Activity, indeed, was a constant advertisement for them.) Further, both religious communities and germs begin to persecute only when they are active.

Effort for Effort's Sake, then, as a doctrine is outworn; he who follows it might as well devote his life to dumb-bell exercises for all the good he does. And, in fact, almost the only effort which it is worth making continually—and that more for the sake of self-respect than because of any positive utility— is the effort to combat human stupidity. It can be done, though, quietly; very quietly. . . . A word in time—like 'Why?'—saves nine; so that, when people begin offering you such sentiments as 'You see, *I* believe in . . .'—whatever it may be, Christian Science, a Big Army or the Survival of the Fittest—always

interject 'Why?': for a belief which has so urgently and swiftly
to be introduced into conversation is sure to be mystical rather
than reasoned, the result of faith rather than of thinking. And
faith should serve as the basis of a religion, but never of an
opinion.

Consider the Epochs of Effort. The Victorian Era was the
most consciously devoted to this curious ideal; the chief effort
being, in reality, to sell something. The singular fact emerges
that Charles Darwin, albeit a great man of whom most of the
Victorians intensely disapproved, nevertheless through the
medium of his theory of 'The Survival of the Fittest', did much,
however unconsciously, to give them support. He imparted to
their often iniquitous proclivities an ethical foundation; because, for each rival merchant knocked into the workhouse, for
each business man assassinated, for every native murdered or
enslaved in order that his land might be appropriated, the
persons responsible for these results could, when occasionally
their consciences stung them, always comfort themselves with
the reflection: 'It can't be helped. . . . Survival of the Fittest,
and all that. . . .' The theory was applied to everything in the
universe; the very laws of the universe itself were interpreted
in terms of Effort and Will. And it is only of recent years that
more probable but very opposite explanations have won
acceptance from science; such, for example, as the one which
tells us that the earth, in the course which it pursues round the
sun, and the moon, in the course which it pursues round the
earth, are not following any dictates of Effort, but are, instead,
merely following the Line of *Least* Resistance! . . . And who
knows but that many of those who prate of Effort and of
Doing are not, in fact, following the same course? It is more
difficult for many of them to think than to act; while to think
straight would be more difficult still. It is easier to demand
than to think out the results of the policies you are demanding.

I should not, therefore, perhaps so much advocate laziness, as strive to uphold the cause of mental activity against physical, and of honest mental activity against dishonest. . . . Yet there is much to be said on behalf of sloth. Nearly every great invention has been the result of natural indolence in the inventor, and in its turn has helped on the cause. Some child, working in a factory in Victorian times, found it tedious to turn a wheel: by the clever adjustment of a piece of string to another wheel he found it would continue to work of its own accord. This was a 'labour-saving' invention: in other words, it pandered to laziness and was the result of it. But, also, it saved the proprietor expense, and so we were spared all the talk, to which we should otherwise have been treated, of the beauty of labour and of the joy of work. This has always been the course of true invention.

As for the benefits of physical activity, the idea of 'regular physical exercise' is another fruit of the conception that to keep busy is necessarily an admirable thing in itself. And exercise, excessive physical exercise, kills more people in a year in England today than do many diseases of which men stand in dread. It is, perhaps, itself a disease of the spirit. . . . Alas, if only those addicted to it would sit down for half an hour with the same solemnity they apply to golf, and devote this time instead to thinking, results might be achieved that would astonish the world! As it is, they prefer to dissipate their energy in perspiration.

Where myself is concerned, even, I have never yet been able to attain to the pitch of sloth which is my object. Seven years spent in the Army made me, against my better judgment, to some extent an exercise-addict; so that, my system craving it, I must always obtain an hour or two of sharp walking a day. I have tried to reduce it, but have failed. . . . On the other hand, the waste of time thus incurred reduces my capacity for work, and so, in a sense, constitutes laziness of a kind.

[102]

17

THE WHITE MAN'S BURDEN

CERTAIN people exist whom the experienced can at once recognize under the classification of the White Man's Burden; and, indeed, the cleverer among them acknowledge such identity of their own accord. These happy beings, by no means confined to any one class, are those on whose behalf others willingly work themselves to the bone; who can, without danger to themselves, become implicated and entangled in a thousand troubles, and yet, whatever the cost in labour or money, will always be rescued, though this salvage work will entail an absolute lack of exertion on their own part. They ever float on the surface, in bright, never-ending sunlight, wearing perpetual and quite natural smiles. They go anywhere they want to go, do anything they want to do, and yet no evil consequence will ever befall them. Providence reserves the pains which, according to every moral rule, their behaviour should incur, for other people. They are debited, reader, to your account and mine.

The White Man's Burden, as I have written, is not confined to any one class; we have all seen the labourer whose bicycle is wheeled along for him by his comrades, the shopkeeper whose business is carried on by domestic slaves; but certainly he is most to be sought, most at ease, most active, in an artistic environment. Eager to attend parties, he can sit up all night without feeling in the least debilitated next morning. He never works, for his work is a pleasure to him, and the harvest of his agreeable labour he disposes of with a born facility. Publishers scramble to accept his books, directors of galleries rush after his pictures. He can paint or write music as easily as he eats and drinks—not that this in itself indicates that he necessarily paints or writes well; in instance of which the reader will remember the story of the discerning lady who, expatiating upon the work of a novelist remarked finally: 'Dear Mr Dash . . . he writes as easily as he breathes . . . but then some people don't *like* being breathed upon.'

But it must not be thought that the W.M.B. is in any way a parasite; far from it. He labours, but with more ease and with more pleasure than the average man. No: that which distinguishes him from his fellows is the fact that everybody—even those who do not like him—are always willing to labour, indeed slave, for him without comment. Further, the W.M.B., by nature clever and intuitional, seems as a rule to be conscious of his birthright, and is therefore inclined to be difficult and a bully. When, however, for a moment he forgets his genius, he becomes the gayest, most amusing of companions.

Many of us have a streak of the W.M.B. in our composition. I myself was always conscious at school, and, of later years, in a military hospital, that my comrades would look after me without much effort on my part. Yet I could never attain to the full stature of a W.M.B. I have to be pleasant, and to work a little, to gain my effects; and, alas, I am always forced to rescue myself from the troubles into which I fall.

Of course, those who do not understand the nature of these rare beings remain to a certain degree unappreciative of them; and this accounts, I apprehend, for the unflattering portraits which we find of them in literature. The finest example of a White Man's Burden to be depicted in a novel is, I think, Mr Skimpole, of *Bleak House*, with his peaches and champagne, his charm and his wit (his wit seems to me undeniable), but Dickens has misunderstood him and, by an underlining of his faults and an underrating of his very real distinction, has in this case spoilt the balance of character. Mr Skimpole, it is plain, realized to the full his destiny; and this was apparent to Dickens. He knew that he would ever drift on the tide of life, enjoying himself, supported, as a great ballerina is supported, by a crowd of satellites, by a mob of struggling, eager, drowning friends and relatives. *Somebody* would always come to his rescue. Meanwhile, as we see, he pursued his delightful, his effortless, way, a child of pleasure.

'This is our friend's consulting room (or would be, if he ever prescribed), his sanctum, his studio,' said my guardian to us.

'Yes,' said Mr Skimpole turning his bright face about, 'this is the bird's cage. This is where the bird lives and sings. They pluck his feathers now and then, and clip his wings; but he sings, he sings!'

'These are very fine,' said my guardian. 'A present?'

'No,' he answered. 'No! Some amiable gardener sells them. His man wanted to know, when he brought them last evening, whether he should wait for the money. "Really, my friend," I said, "I think not—if your time is of value to you." I suppose it was, for he went away.'

Not even the French or Russian revolutions, had they occurred in his time, would have been able to spoil his manner of life or dispossess him of his birthright. The Communists would have laboured on his behalf as willingly as his rich friends.

Another characteristic of a W.M.B. is his inevitability: impossible to avoid him. For example, on one occasion I was on a visit to Paris, where I had not stayed for many months. At any rate, I felt as I journeyed there, I have escaped seeing Smithers (as we will call him); for I was angry with him for the trouble to which he had put me, and I knew that he had been left behind in London. That evening, however, I visited a *boîte*, and there he was, in the doorway, waiting to receive me. I explained to my companions that I could not face it. . . . We left, deciding to visit another *boîte* instead. But there he stood again, waiting for us, expectant and unsurprised, though we had gone there directly in a fast car and he could not have been aware of whither we were going.

Many other curious points require elucidation. Thus, though the W.M.B. often accomplishes much good work—and if not good work, at any rate, much work—he seems to the outward eye to have all eternity at his disposal. Never in a hurry, always able to drop in and see his friends or, in his turn, to receive them, his books appear as though they were mushrooms, grown in a night.

And not only does Providence itself take care of the W.M.B.; there exists invariably, attached to him by some invisible thread, a special kind of human being. Just as the crocodile is inevitably accompanied by the crocodile-bird, so the W.M.B. bears always with him, at his beck and call, a type of individual whom we may christen the 'retriever'. Retrievers, of course, exist also on their own, and are sometimes to be found elsewhere than in the wake of the W.M.B. Divided into several groups, they nevertheless fall roughly into two main classes: firstly, those who collect all your former acquaintances

—people who have bored you twenty years ago, and of whom with great difficulty you have rid yourself—and then, without warning you, fling them at you in a lump, asking you to tea to meet them or, at any rate, organizing an encounter of some kind, without explaining who is going to be there; secondly those retrievers who burrow you out in order once again to expose you not merely to your own bores, but to your own liabilities—such as the W.M.B.

For instance, you will say to your W.M.B. that you are away, offering several excuses. At once the retriever will come round, will worry you until you forget your excuse, will force you into saying yes, you will come to tea, suspecting no link between them. You will go, and there you will again meet your fate. . . . The best retrievers of the collecting sort are those who live in country houses. In these vast depositories they can secrete any number of former acquaintances of yours, people whom you have forgotten long ago and with difficulty, and then, without a warning word, bring them over and unload them on you in your own home.

18

RULES FOR BEING RUDE

BEING rude, I suppose, is an art, like any other, governed by strict rules and subject to a code. It requires, for its full development, either native genius or, at any rate, an inherent talent. . . . A lady to whom George Moore had read a story, once remarked: 'What enormous talent you have, G.M.', and received the reply: 'No, I started with a very little talent, but I have cultivated it every day.' . . . In the same way, there are those among us who, born with however small a talent for being rude, have cultivated it to a truly remarkable extent.

Let it be clear from the beginning that by a *natural talent* for being rude, I do not intend to signify natural rudeness. A man naturally rude is indeed temperamentally, but very effectually, barred from ever gaining any results from his insolence. He is merely rude—'a rude sort of chap'—whereas to exercise the art of being rude, to extract from it the utmost flavour, you must be, by nature, kind and generous, and have, in addition, acquired beautifully polished manners, so that your rudeness

tells to the full. Thus it will be seen that the pleasures of rudeness are essentially those of an old and civilized society; which
explains why the eighteenth century was the grand epoch, the
golden age, of rudeness as of so much else. It is of no use to be
rude in the backwoods: there, among so many too liberally
gifted by Nature in the same direction, you would be merely
another backwoodsman. Further, avoid at all costs being rude
without intention; do not ever allow yourself to become a
rudeness-gusher, with a perpetual supply of that commodity,
on which the world can depend.

Consider the technique of your art, by no means an easy
one. It is difficult, even, to find a subject upon whom to
practise. First of all, let us establish that those—if any—to
whom it is permissible to be rude, must be of your own age,
sex and standing: never be rude to those older or younger or
poorer than yourself. You must, in addition, carefully select
your setting, your background. Just as if you were a great
pianist, or a great violinist, you must have an audience to
inspire you to the full use of your powers: yet you must never
be rude in your own house (a great pity, for it would enable you
to grapple with your foes with much more facility); nor must
you be rude to them in their own homes (a still more grievous
injunction, because meditate for yourself upon how enjoyable
would be a daring Jameson Raid or verbal hold-up of your
enemies in their own beastly homes); nor, again, must you be
rude to them in the houses of common friends, of neutral
powers, as it were.... I have even heard an old gentleman once
lamentatively protest: 'I'm surprised, that's all: rude to me in
my own motor-car!' ... Thus it becomes plain that the path of
true rudeness never did run smooth, is beset with difficulties
and trammelled with the reddest of red tape.

What pitch, then, what scenery, should you choose for
your brief battle (it must be brief, too, very brief, to be

[109]

effective)? How can you entice your quarry, all unsuspecting, into the street, and there assassinate him with a word: for being an enemy he would, unless bent on the same errand, scarcely wish to find himself in your company? You must, I apprehend, make a careful study of his ways, in order to meet him as though by accident, all unwary, walking along the pavement or entering a place of amusement. A railway carriage, again, offers a splendid *décor* and no opportunity for your quarry to escape.

On the other hand, if you are thoroughly acquainted with the canons of your art, with the commandments that govern its exercise and the old-fashioned limitation which tradition has placed upon it, your knowledge affords you several pleasures and advantages which ignorance would forfeit. Thus you can meet a person—as he thinks, by chance—in the street, and be very rude to him without his having any cause for complaint (it is all the more startling for your victim), or you can be extremely cordial and polite in the house of a common friend one night, insult him the following evening in a restaurant and then go out of your way to be amiable once more the day after. . . . This adds perplexity to insult. . . . And, though you follow the old rules that framed the impromptu nimble wit of Lord Chesterfield and the stentorian and calculated insults of Dr Johnson, yet modernize your technique, making it adaptable and elastic, with plenty of give and as much take. . . . But do not dash at it: remember you must play your opponent for weeks, as though he were a trout in some liquid stream. Disarm him with interest and amiability and the charm of your companionship, lull him into a fictitious security; then choose your opportunity, and do not spare his feelings. . . . Better still is it, if you can, to induce *him* to afford you the exercise of your art: persuade him, though he remains unaware of the process, to write to you asking for some favour, and then crush him.

As for the manner of being rude, never allow yourself at the moment to show any emotion, least of all anger. Dislike should breed contempt, but never rage: for such anger, after the fashion of love, has a flame to it, and offers heat, so that your opponent can avail himself of it and forge himself armour, and even, it may be, a sword. Conscious that he has made you angry, his replies now come to him all the more easily. . . . No. True rudeness should be cold, and at the same time perfect in form, exquisitely delivered, so that, going away discomfited, your enemy will ponder: 'Can I have heard aright? Did he really say it, really *mean* it?' will tell people of the occurrence, in order to have their opinion on it; will even, in his folly, deliberately ask their advice. . . . For many days he will turn it over in his mind, and in this way the wound you have given him will fester, scar him for life.

Moreover, should your opponent, too, be gifted, never grudge him the effect he desires. If he is rude, adequately rude, in return, show your pleasure and appreciation: but do not retort more than once. . . . Never allow rudeness to degenerate into a wordy duel, into a vulgar quarrel. . . . No, if you can, pick a moment when he is surrounded by friends—his friends— and then, into the momentary silence which the strength of your personality should be sufficient to enforce, interject a poisoned sentence. . . . Above all, eschew humour, that anti- dote to wit.

19

THE EDWARDIANS;
THE RICH MAN'S FEAST

A LITTLE while ago we used constantly to read in the papers such paragraphs as this: 'It is now the fashion to decry everything Victorian, and to speak of the great Victorians themselves with contempt.' . . . Before now, I have been myself accused of this heinous misdemeanour.

Yet I doubt very much whether these accusations were ever justified. Certainly to decry the Victorian Age was never the *fashion*; for—apart from Victorian morality, which has undoubtedly been discarded and which only, in fact, began to ravage the country after the Crimean War, when the failure of our arms and the first revelation to the world of the ineptitude of our generals led to a most virulent and bigoted revivalism— this epoch has always remained for the majority of English people the Golden Age. It was an age which they find it easy to understand; an age of plain-speaking and comfortable living, of easy interference with the affairs of foreign nations, of fogs, and of a convinced and sanguine patriotism. Its poets could be comprehended—only too easily—while its musicians chiefly wrote anthems, or tunes which, at any rate, resembled hymns already popular and familiar. The world was ordained, under English guidance—or rather, synonymously, under the guidance of the English Comfortable Classes—to advance from triumph to triumph; through steam to petrol, and from the electric telegram, as it was at first called, to telephone and phonograph. It was a wonderful, happy, if rather self-complacent age, in which there could be no suspicion of unexpected future developments; no seeds of decay existed. Even the ruthless satire of those humorous twins, Gilbert and Sullivan, could reveal no hidden sore. . . . As for the great men of the later Victorian period, as for those whom this generation is now arraigned for reviling, no words, it is true, were bad enough for them at the time: Darwin, impious atheist; Swinburne and Rossetti, mad *poseurs*; Whistler, horrid little American bounder; but the really good and great, the territorial magnates and millionaires, the top-hatted poets and the respectable painters, such as Leighton, were universally revered and personally adored.

These, then, were some of the features which helped to compose an age to which numberless people still remain faithful; so many, indeed, that one is driven to the conclusion that Victorianism must be a national rather than an epochal trait; a quality innate, if sometimes latent, in the British people. Today, with the pillars of the Victorian world lying shattered and smashed all round it, Britain rather touchingly yet clings like a child to Queen Victoria's voluminous and billowing skirts; refuses to emerge at all from behind them. . . . Who can doubt that the future will witness fresh outbursts of Victorianism from this country; any more than that, when Julius Caesar first landed among our naked, if exotically dyed, ancestors, even then some form of Victorianism, whether more primitive or not than in its subsequent full flowering, brooded dully over the country? Certainly Victorianism, as he shows us in the *Dunciad*, ruled in the early days of Alexander Pope.

Thus, if occasionally people have of latter years mocked the Great Age, this was but a pretence; only so that, by speaking and thinking of it, they could live in it over again. . . . But at last, I believe, the centre of interest has a little shifted: for the Edwardians can by now be seen in full perspective, and their rotund and splendid figures seem, more than those of their more severe predecessors, to engage the attention of the young.

What, indeed, are we to make of those gay ten years, that strange culmination to the long Victorian Era, or of the beings who presided over this essentially Rich Man's Feast? How are we to judge them, or that fat, placid, kindly yet exciting period, when the only voices that broke the harmony were the rough Scottish tones of Keir Hardie, denouncing the wealthy, the gallant accents of Lord Roberts, alone prophesying war, and the enraged and, it then seemed, slightly hysterical tones of suffragettes, as they chained themselves to the railings of Downing Street or slashed old masters in the National Gallery? What a delicious, halcyon period it was!

The attraction of these years derives in part from the fact that the King was a character, always able to make himself popular, and one who preferred to surround himself deliberately with certain people, rather than simply to accept or inherit those whom he found there; that he liked, in fact, to be amused. Thus for the first time since the death of his great-uncle, King George IV—and, as for that, for only the second time since the death of King Charles II—it became fashionable to be, at any rate a little, intelligent, and the possession of wit, and even of some eccentricity, was considered preferable to mere dullness, however worthy. Much outward splendour was joined to these happy circumstances, for the King understood the value of pageantry, and the shell and form of life, the big parties and entertainments, continued in the same mould as in previous reigns. The traditional English life still prevailed: so that, in effect, the members of the ruling classes remained true to traditions, in which—if they were intelligent (and then they sometimes were)—they could no longer believe.

Thus, though it deemed itself imbued with a new liberty, it was a tremendously conventional age; for, no longer believing in anything, the penalties for any breach of the code yet remained the same. The Victorian religious edifice had collapsed under its own weight, but the Edwardians continued to worship in it as though it still stood. Divorce remained unforgivable; though no stigma attached to the conduct that had caused it, unless divorce followed. Outward life was everything, and material prosperity was marvellously maintained and increased, until it seemed as if the substantial, vulgar dreams of the Victorians were, after all, to be realized.

Alas! that decade in which all men grew richer and all women prettier passed very rapidly. . . . And what did it leave behind it? Must we judge it by its works, of which the 1914–18 World War was the chief; by its Sargent portraits of hard-faced women in soft, filmy hats; by its lack of poetry and contempt for it; by the *Merry Widow*, that unique expression— as had been Gilbert and Sullivan of the late Victorians and Offenbach of the Second Empire—of the humour, romance and ideals of its period; by the bold, towering, cosmopolitan figures of Boldini, advancing, with ropes of pearls, out of their canvases; by the gold boxes and kickshaws of Fabergé and the sudden popularity of papers such as the *Sketch* and *Tatler*; or can we rely upon our own memories of it, as a period of intense sweetness and activity, when even the newspapers seemed more

concerned for the invention of new sweet-peas and the revival
of cookery than in the fomenting of wars, when everyone
appeared gay, and when people, even those who were not kind
by nature, were mostly good-humoured; when, in fact, hatred
had not as yet inherited the world?

20

ON PROGRESS

THE material heaven of the Edwardian reign, and of the first few years of King George's, seems very remote from the present time. In those happy days every faith, even the faith of the Socialists, was justified, for it looked as though, if wealth were to be redistributed, there would soon be enough money to go round. . . . As for the upper and middle classes, they lived in circumstances of profusion, and there was provided for them a constant flow of pageantry and amusement, which in no way was allowed to be spoilt by the frantic bustle which grew to be the mode in the later years. The great feudal families still maintained to a certain degree their influence, though even then it was weakening; but to possess many connections in the world of politics and fashion was an advantage, rather than a disadvantage, to more serious work. In the evenings the houses of the squares of London opened their doors; light poured out from the balconies, and with it came the music of the waltz; for jazz only began, with such tunes as

'Everybody's Doing It' and 'Alexander's Rag-time Band', in 1910 or 1911. The world anticipated no future but a continued steady progress, although one of the questions most frequently put to a dancing partner was 'Can you reverse?'

There can, I think, be no doubt that civilization itself is proving triumphantly that it *can* reverse. For example, in 1914 Germany exploded back into the times of Odin and Thor—that horrible German world where the heroes drank blood out of skulls and wore skins instead of clothes (and never did a race exist more unsuited by nature for the display of its bodies!). Many people in Hitler's Germany, too, it is said, actually advocated a return to the cult of Thor and Odin; but such an apostasy could make no difference, for whatever god or gods the Germans worship will always remain the identical barbarous gods under a different name. In any case, the old, kindly German of the time of Bach and of Mozart is dead, and the Wagner lovers have reaped their reward in the revival of a boisterous and fictitious past.

But while the appearance of the world in the years before 1914 of which we are writing was that of a great comity of nations advancing, more or less at a level rate, year by year, the impression today is of a hundred or so insane states—all, not advancing but diverging in different directions; backward, forward or sideways; but these alleys are no *culs-de-sac*, for at the end of nearly every one of them stands plainly destruction. The rate of their progress towards this goal is variable, but the pace has so much increased recently as to have become visible: it is as if microbes had grown so large that they had become perceptible, or as though one were watching a comet with its golden tail falling from the sky. But the eyes of the observers are blank with apathy, and human beings appear to reserve their terror for mice rather than men. Any idea concerned with the modern world of literature or art terrifies the average man, and also angers him; but, singularly enough, ideas in general do not frighten him—or, at any rate, do not frighten those who do not understand them. . . . A mouse, though, is something smaller and more tangible. And yet it seems strange that so many people should be more frightened by those soft and furtive rodents than by the enormous menace of events; a menace that surrounds them on every side.

Everybody, for instance, appears to be delighted to see a battleship launched. The prow is wreathed in flowers, champagne bottles are showered on it, flags decorate every building in the vicinity and old men make interminable speeches. The armament firms and the corporations provide lunches. The very people who stand on chairs in order to avoid a mouse when it runs into the room are precisely those who cheer most wildly when they see a battleship glide smoothly into the water; only launched that it may one day destroy their fellow-men. It is true, of course, that, comparatively, battleships can achieve but little harm; for they are obsolete—as obsolete as the sailing-ship—but this hardly affects the principle.

And the more frightened the human race becomes of the things it makes, the more it calls for the things of which it should be frightened; the more terrified we grow of the possible destruction that can be wrought by airplanes, the more stridently we demand more airplanes to destroy our neighbours. You can see many women who would run at the mere sight of a mouse, regarding with complacency some tank or cannon, erected in a public place as a memorial. Hardly ever, in any country in Europe, will you find an inscription under such a monument of a kind to discourage war. It is, therefore, a source of some pride to me that I am responsible for one of them. The parish council of my native village invited me some years ago to lend a small portion of land upon which to erect a cannon, presented to them by the War Office. I replied that this instrument of war was a very ugly thing, that my views on war approximated to those held by the Quakers, and that I could see no point, therefore, in lending them any land for such a purpose. They replied that my views were coincident with their own, and was I still adamant? To which I answered that I would lend the piece of land if I were allowed to write the inscription under the cannon, and penned the following paragraph, which to this day stands under the gun.

THIS GUN HAS BEEN ERECTED HERE TO REMIND THE PEOPLE OF ECKINGTON OF THE FOLLY AND WASTE OF WAR RESPONSIBLE FOR THE DEATHS OF SO MANY OF THE BEST OF THEM, AND IN THE HOPE THAT ITS UGLINESS AS AN OBJECT WILL FRIGHTEN THE CHILDREN SO THAT THEY GROW UP WITH A NATURAL HATRED OF WAR AND THE BRUTAL MACHINERY THAT ACCOMPANIES IT.

But such inscriptions are part of a dream that has vanished. Every nation seems determined to fight, if not in the immediate present, at any rate as soon as they have the armaments with which to do so. Our position is the old one of: 'To prevent the powder magazines from blowing up we must have the biggest one.' The higher branches of the human race at the moment have obviously dedicated themselves to suicide, and who is to stop them?

21

ON ADVICE:

ITS GIVING AND RECEIVING

Some countries, I think, are specially designed to tender advice and warnings; others, to profit by them. . . . Germany, for example, is a natural receiver of advice; and, indeed, since the autumn of 1918 until January 1933, was exposed to an absolute orgy of it. Never a day went by without her being treated to a warning on the part of France, and a few helpful, if self-righteous, words by ourselves. And much of this advice, leading in a thousand contrary directions, she took. Now, however, we are cognizant that, though we continue to offer, she will not accept our counsel. Because Nationalism demands that advice, like all else, shall be of domestic origin: and in that clamour, perhaps, we may find one of the secrets of Hitler's popularity; for he himself was disposed to be generous with this commodity.

Germany loves advice! To realize the truth of this assertion it is only necessary to wander round any German town, observing, pasted up everywhere, the amount of private notices

containing exhortations, cautions and injunctions. . . . More
than that, she loves to take advice, to obey—'to love, honour
and obey'. 'She', I write of the Fatherland; for the Germans,
despite their protestations, the beards, pipes and talk of Attila,
are an intensely feminine race; much more feminine than the
more delicate and charming French. (There are female elephants no less than female gazelles.) The French indubitably
possess masculine minds, with a love of independent thought.
Only because the Germans are a warlike—or, in other words,
quarrelsome—race, is it supposed that they are male-minded;
yet women, it is said, indulge in quarrels, even ferocious ones,
just as often as men.

The Germans, then, like to quarrel, but they also like to
carry out orders. And by a correlation of these two assumptions
eighteenth-century England, which employed German mercenary troops, discovered a perfect solution of the German
problem. After this fashion, the most warlike of the race were
killed off at regular intervals and, as we, at any rate, thought,
fighting on behalf of right. . . . And here, in parenthesis, I
would like to enquire with all seriousness, whether it would not
be possible, given the present circumstances, to find a similar
solution of European difficulties today? Why cannot an international body be given the power to employ a mercenary
German army to enforce—or, in the present journalistic cant
of the day, to implement—its decisions? So could the warlike
German tribes, perhaps, be induced, with an added feeling of
self-respect, to fight on behalf of civilization, instead of against
it. . . . Alas! in these degenerate days it is supposed to be wrong
to allow anyone but yourself to be killed in a quarrel picked
against you; a totally modern development of honour, and one
which must end sooner or later, if you have to deal with
sufficiently quarrelsome people, in the loss of your cause.

However, I must not wander too far. Germany, I was

maintaining, likes to receive advice. But it serves as a signal of general danger when she inclines to show herself to the world as an example; to become a mentor, to guide the feet of others and to show them the way. Then it is time to seek safety, because, historically and almost invariably, the results are as disastrous to the world as to the Fatherland. Thus in 1914 Germany was anxious to take the lead, eager to give, rather than learn, a lesson. She advised Austria, admonished Serbia, cautioned Russia and warned ourselves; the upshot of all this being that the whole of Europe became involved in war.

We English as a race excel in the offering of advice; and because of our talent in this direction, indeed, have been dubbed the Governess of Europe. The sad truth, however, is that though our advice is, politically, nearly always right and sound and wise, we seldom profit by it ourselves, and when we offer it to friendly nations this altruistic national trait appears to anger them more than any of our less commendable characteristics. Only consider, in example of it, our note to America in 1932 concerning the Anglo-American debt. The French, in their plain way, merely refused to pay, and were quite willing to incur the onus, if any, which attached to their default. But we, once more, were as free with our advice as with our money. We paid in full yet again, and at the same time indited a note; a little masterpiece, in the preparation of which, it seemed, an army of clandestine governesses might have been at work for years, day and night, at the Foreign Office. It was infused with an excruciating air of 'it-hurts-me-more-than-it-hurts-you', though actually its message in this instance was 'it-hurts-you-more-than-it-hurts-me'. His Majesty's Government, you will remember, was in one sense eager to pay; in another, reluctant. But this last sentiment was not as you might, after your vulgar fashion, have thought, founded on the desire not to part with the goods, but, instead, on the conviction of our rulers that the transference of so large a sum would injure the payee even more than the payer. They were, in fact, anxious to *safeguard American* interests. Financial dislocation and widespread disturbance would ensue, it was pointed out, in that great continent. . . . (And how right we were! . . . But then, if we had not made the payment, we could not have proffered such sound, if uncalled-for, advice to a foreign power: and much more gladly would we abandon any hope of obtaining a reduction of the unjust sums to which we were bound, than forgo our prerogative of proffering unwanted counsel.)

In this case, however, it might have been presumed that we had met our match; because America, having, as is widely recognized, a monopoly of public spirit and public virtue, will come forward to offer advice with—or to—any country in the world. (Europe's troubles are her own fault, because she remains heedless of the American example.) And so it was that, conscious as the Americans were of their own unselfish generosity and scrupulousness, the arrival of the English note, inspired by similar sentiments, became responsible for more consternation in Washington, and aroused more antagonism there, than would have been caused by any abrupt refusal on our part to pay.

And, just as some nations are born to receive, and others to give, advice, so it is, I apprehend, with persons. . . . More blessed to give than to receive. And alas, for myself, I am a born recipient. Never can I be alone for an instant without some kind person endeavouring, gratis, to improve my mind or manners; while, on the other hand, I notice that if ever I venture to *offer* advice, nobody takes it! But then, who thinks ever of acting on advice unless he is made to pay for it? Advice, they say, is cheap; but what of the hundreds and thousands of

[124]

pounds earned by lawyers and doctors? Is that cheap? Yet it is the *only* advice which is ever acted upon. So, when next called upon for your views on a personal problem, refuse to give them, if you value your own opinion, except for a heavy fee. It is kinder to him who seeks your aid.

22

ON THE HORROR OF SOLITUDE

ALAS, the day of the hermit is over! No longer are caves and ruins inhabited by sages and ascetics with flowing white beards and wild, fierce eyes. Yet the necessity for loneliness, for the possibility of meditation in solitude and amid inspiring and romantic scenes, makes itself felt, day by day, more than ever before. The very bungalows that clutter and litter the countryside are, in fact, a sign of it: since the inhabitants of each one of these ugly and crowded excrescences originally moved here in order to 'get away'; get away, that is, from neighbours and noise and everyday life. They are thus in rebellion against the intense gregariousness of the modern world; in which people are forced, not only to eat, drink and think together, but also to eat, drink and think the same things in the same way. Indeed, today the grave, that 'fine and private place', is almost the only one left to man.

For the herd instinct is in possession of the world. To such an extent, indeed, that solitude has to many become akin to terror. 'But I shall be *alone!*' one hears people exclaim in accents of despair: an attitude very opposite to that of the late Monsieur Pachmann, the exquisite if occasionally eccentric player of Chopin, who, when his hostess, having to leave him for a little, excused herself, saying: 'Dear Master, I do hope you do not mind being alone?', replied proudly: 'Madam, I am never alone: I am with Pachmann!' . . . And very good company, I imagine, he must have found himself. . . . But then the artist, though usually he feels more need for solitude, is generally a much more entertaining companion than the soldier, statesman or business man. To most people, however, this point of view is absurd, even incredible. Their conception of sociability is so strong that they are annoyed, even, if they see someone they know dining alone at a restaurant, condemn him straightway as 'mad': as though—apart from the fact that nobody in his senses would dine alone, or in company, at any public place of eating unless driven there by necessity or laziness—to dine alone were a form of lunacy. Yet, though personally I prefer eating in company, there is no doubt that the way in which to appreciate good food is to eat it by yourself, undistracted by conversation. . . . Again, of all the vices, the worst one is to be a 'secret drinker': and the accent is on the word *secret*. Than this, only to be a secret thinker is worse in the calendar of social crime.

'What can he do with himself, all alone like that?' So you hear people speak. But how difficult it is to be alone; an expensive business, too. You have to travel far, to Canada or Siberia. No longer is it possible to find solitude, as Wordsworth found it, among the Lakes. The Lake District is now but a car-park, a bin for orange peel; and Scotland, too, unless you are in a position to buy a deer forest, offers no shelter from the herd. . . . Once or twice in my life I have found places where solitude seemed peculiarly pleasant; but it was never long before others found it too, and invaded it, filling it with whistling sounds of appreciation. Worst of all, there are the kind people, the well-meaning, who *feel sorry* for you *because* you are alone, and make it their business to come and talk to you and to break up your thoughts. . . . You would think, for example, that in a sense it would be easy to be alone in a large boat, if you knew none of the other passengers. Not a bit of it; they will take pity on you, sure enough! 'We thought you looked so sad, sitting all by yourself like that!'

Alas, those are precisely the people who should themselves be alone, be made to be alone; be subjected, even, to periods of solitary confinement in agreeable surroundings, but without any possibility of recourse to wireless or gramophone, or conversation of even the most casual kind. For want of time in which to think, they have become thus idle-mouthed and slatternly minded. Even an hour of forced meditation would help them to reconstruct a little their thoughts and put their minds in order.

The most singular feature of this modern gregariousness, this avoidance by people of their own thoughts, is, however, that it has done nothing to help those who suffer from that terrible affliction, loneliness. Indeed, the fear of loneliness—the exact reverse of the longing for solitude—is more general now than in any former epoch, and one with which we must always sympathize, never mind to what extent the loneliness may have been earned in times past.

For often it has been. . . . Think, for example, of the old ladies, with that fear in their hearts, who for one reason or another congregate in those busy hives of idleness, 'private residential hotels'. (And why 'private', since privacy is that which their inmates hold most in abomination?) Often they have been driven there by their own hardness in times past, by their selfishness and their lack of consideration for their friends.

And now, by a genial stroke of Fate, several of them are collected here, under one roof, to worry and irritate—and, by means of that worrying and irritation, in the end to comfort—one another. It is better for them to form a herd after this fashion, better than to pine alone—and with them to be alone *is* to pine—in remote suburbs and refined watering-places. Moreover, for others it possesses the advantage of collecting them together in, as it were, a concentration-camp, until such time as Death shall seize them in its final and most lonely embrace.

Nevertheless, that from which they suffered was not genuine loneliness: the feeling of physical propinquity was what they desired. Real loneliness, on the other hand, is a disease of the spirit, and one of which the most sensitive and the most kindly seem, as a rule, to be the worst victims. Those liable to its onslaughts are no more immune from them in a crowd than on a mountain-top. Especially will it attack them if they are forced to attempt communication of ideas with uncongenial people. Thus a short visit to a crowded country-house may be a dreadful penance to them; far more severe than a month alone on a desert island.

To the lonely, as to the lover of solitude, books and travel form the best companions, lessening the sense of nervous tension from which they suffer. Communal amusements, such as cinemas, are best avoided; though in the enthusiasm of a great crowd, at a football match or a bull-fight, it is possible both to lose loneliness and to achieve solitude. . . . And the stupid, when they suffer from loneliness, find it removed by a war, with its accompaniment of 'mateyness': though I fancy that in the next, which we are all so busily preparing for ourselves, most of us will attain our final solitude, whether we have been seeking it or no. Humanity's next Great Beano may also be its last.

23

ON THE DECAY OF PRIVACY

THE two most important and expensive things in modern life are privacy and leisure, and though of the latter much is said and written, little or nothing is done to help us achieve more privacy.

Now leisure may lead to much evil, to acute unhappiness, illness or boredom; but privacy has no such drawbacks or dangers.

Every day, however, we are deprived of more of it. Model towns, for example, are built by wealthy and benevolent corporations for their workers.

What is the result? The worker has henceforth no seclusion, and is forced to live, as well as work, with his fellows. Or else he is obliged to inhabit one, perhaps, of a row of jerry-built houses or villas, in which every sound from every house is audible, so that, practically, he can be said to be living in the street. Thus the Englishman's home is no longer his castle, but either his fellow-workers' communal kitchen or else just part of his neighbours' street.

The world at large lives for the most part in public, eating in restaurants, travelling by Tube or omnibus, visiting cinemas or theatres.

This makes it all the more necessary to possess privacy in your home. But only the rich can afford it, for to secure this most elusive thing you must have plenty of servants to guard you against intrusion and a few rooms at the back of the house which, like Bluebeard's secret chamber, no person but yourself is allowed to enter.

Then there are the hotels wherein we stay; a hotel is a bitter enemy to privacy. Not only is one at the mercy of every stray and idle bore who happens to be staying there, but to keep oneself to oneself, hitherto regarded as a virtue, has now become a social crime. Indeed, it is not very long ago since, in a hotel abroad, I crept away from a room where there was going to be a dance, for I was tired after a hard day's work and wished to avoid the very bad and noisy band which was already striking up; but as I left the room an American visitor approached and said angrily: 'Have you no social ambition, may I ask, sir, that you leave this ballroom?'

And on another occasion an interfering old Scotswoman enquired why I did not give up writing books and take instead to politics?

And whither can we escape nowadays? It used, for instance, to be possible to find peace and privacy by walking down any country road in England.

Not so now; because the road, broad as the Grand Canal of Venice, is overlooked for its whole length on each side by long rows of incredibly hideous houses, while fleets of motor-coaches and motor-cars hoot and roar down it all day long.

There were the parks in London. Therein it was easy in former years to sit under a tree in summer and read a book:

but now we find ourselves in dear, benevolent Mr Lansbury's paradise, among dancing-halls, jazz-bands, carillons, round-abouts, swings, brass bands and paddle-pools; things which, of course, may be of benefit to the community in other ways but constitute a fresh inroad on the little privacy left us.

Then chief of the enemies to privacy stands modern science. It has armed every friend and foe with the most formidable means of shattering it in our own houses. Telegrams, wireless, motor-cars, telephones, are all ready to help the invader, not to succour the beleaguered. Formerly if a man wished to disturb a friend, he was put to the trouble of walking or driving to his house and doing it himself. Now, on the other hand, not only is the radius of his operations extended, in that he can motor eighty to a hundred miles if he wants to break in on someone, but, better still, he can do it by mechanical means at any distance—'just ring up'. To talk to someone in his own house, which is what the telephone amounts to, is an undoubted intrusion; is just as much to deprive a man of his privacy as it would be to shout at him through his window as he sits and reads. But the bore and the privacy-killer are now all-puissant, can disturb the peace of almost any family in Europe, or even America, at very little trouble, though considerable expense, to themselves.

Till recently the telephone-operator was our guardian; and how often we should have thanked, instead of upbraiding, her for giving some friend a wrong number! But we never thought of it, and only now, when modern science threatens everywhere to institute the automatic dial-system, do we realize our loss.

Apart from special instruments for killing peace, there are the ordinary noises of the street, which have immensely increased of recent years in number, variety and volume. The traffic, street bands, barrel-organs, church bells, radios and gramophones in neighbouring houses—all have made privacy more remote and difficult of achievement

For the clarinet at the street corner is as much of an interloper as a voice on the telephone, and, as we have pointed out, a voice on the telephone is as much of an interloper as a stranger in the house. And never a Sunday evening goes by but a part of the Salvation Army dances its noisy, albeit noble, way into the seclusion of our most private rooms.

What remedy is there? Only to increase as much as we can the privacy in our own home, by insisting on every member of a family being perfectly independent. No one must be allowed to be worried by importunate questions such as: 'Who is your letter from?' or 'Where are you going?' And the habit of such questions is fortunately easy to break; for they arise as a rule not from curiosity, not from any desire to know the answer, but simply from custom. The sole other remedy is to become rich.

24

ON SEX

IN MODERN conversation the word *sex* has to a great extent replaced the older, and somewhat more conventional, word *love*; a mistake, for such a label carries with it an infinite burden of science and pseudo-science. Thus if *Romeo and Juliet* had been written today, it would, no doubt, be described as 'a straight and stirring story of sex-appeal' rather than as a love story. Sex psychology is the term applied to love psychology and while, no doubt, it is in the general interest that the study of love should be scientific, yet, in another mood, it seems a little to resemble an attempt to harness two butterflies to a waggon.

I suppose no one will deny that certain persons display a genius in sexual matters, just as they might in poetry or painting, cooking or generalship (the vehicle of genius is one that it is impossible to criticize)? And this quality of sex-genius enters, I believe, into that other curious quality, glamour: which can never be quite described or analysed. Certainly it play its part in stage glamour. For instance, the peculiar sway which the late Gaby Deslys exercised over every kind of audience can be accounted for only by this kind of genius. Neither her legs, nor her clothes, nor her voice, nor any combination of these, were altogether responsible for the fact that when she appeared on the stage it became impossible for members of the audience to look, listen or pay attention to anyone else.

As for the alleged 'modern preoccupation with sex', Hollywood has accustomed us to placarded displays of sex-appeal; but if in reality the modern world were preoccupied with sex, we should hear very much less about it. Sex chatter covers a void. Indeed, only a very moral world can give birth to scandal. If the world of today were really completely amoral —as, for example, was the world of the Greeks—there would be no scandals and very little gossip, for no aberration would cause any surprise. Thus divorce, again, can exist to shock us only in a state of society where monogamy is the recognized institution. In a country like America, where divorce is every year becoming more and more common, soon only the long and happily married couple will surprise—and therefore ultimately shock—the community.

The frequency of divorce in America has produced two effects. Firstly, if morals have suffered because monogamy has suffered, at the same time scandals have very largely ceased to be scandals. Secondly, the fact that two persons may in every respect become tired of each other during the course of a few years has been recognized, and is now so well established in the minds of the people that it has lost its old power to arouse morbid curiosity and fester like a wound. After all, there are fashions in morality as in everything else. Forty years ago a Turkish pasha married to less than four wives would have shocked the Turkish nation, in just the same way, and just as much, as the man with two wives shocks us.

There are countries where the leisured, surplus female

population of England appals the inhabitants by its want of sexual experience; just as genuinely as the event of its seizure and subsequent disposal to a harem would shock us. The European standard of morality, then, may be just as much due to the fact that the average European is essentially monogamous by nature as to any inherent moral superiority. But this does not alter the fact that we have a code of behaviour natural to our civilization, and which it is thus useless to criticize.

From time to time it is stated that the old are shocked by the frankness of the young; but they are not half as much shocked by it as the young are shocked by their habit of muddling. The old muddled *themselves* into domestic unhappiness, just as they muddled *us* into the Great War. They resolutely refused to think things out, and by their insistence on their own code of morality often showed great cruelty.

For example, among them there still exists the extraordinary idea that parents who get on together very badly, and spend all their lives quarrelling and making their small children miserable, must not divorce, must not separate, 'for the sake of the children'. If, in these cases, the children were consulted, I think there would be very little doubt as to their decision. Further, though it may shock the old to think so, it is just possible that their children would prefer to have round them parents who were growing old happily, if polygamously. And, finally, at their age, they should stop being shocked. It is a privilege of youth.

Meanwhile, to prophesy: this age of frankness will wither before another age of discretion. 'Sex-appeal' will lose its sway over the hearts of the young and will take on a hundred romantic variations of name. It will become the fashion to disguise the sentiments just as, perhaps, once more to disguise the male countenance with whiskers. Indeed, it looks as if whisker and crinoline were the outward and visible sign of a wish to disguise the inner thoughts.

25

OUT OF SEASON

Lㅤondon is too large and straggling a conglomeration of
houses to be really much influenced by seasonal changes.
Yet even the most casual observer knows that London *has* a
season—almost as much as any watering-place or seaside town.
By no means, however, am I thinking of the summer months,
which for a few members of the richer classes still constitute
The Season: a recurrent phenomenon ever officially heralded
by the opening of the Royal Academy, an event sufficiently
depressing, one would have thought, to drive every esthetically minded person out of the town; nor of the tail months of
the year, now christened the Little Season by the Fashion-
plate Press; but, instead, of the month of August, when, indeed,
if only for a few weeks, London completely alters its aspect.

To begin with, the residential streets of Mayfair and St
James's are deserted (though how curious that so many people
should leave these regions, just when they become pleasantly
empty, in order to transport themselves at considerable cost to
summer resorts, just when those places become most noisy and

crowded), while on the other hand the rest of London suddenly turns either provincial or foreign. Super-provincial and super-foreign, perhaps I should write, for in Bloomsbury the squares echo to the massed intonations of Bristol, Sheffield, Leeds and Glasgow rather than to the usual cultured cooing which in more ordinary times caresses the ear, and its thousand temperance hotels are a-clatter all day with tea-cups: while, in the Strand and Piccadilly, every European accent can be heard, and this, and the eager curiosity of the strangers, impart an unwonted vivacity to these neighbourhoods.

But what of the places which, for their very livelihood, depend on a brief season; places which, from the point of view of fashion, are created afresh, as it were, every first of May or first of August, only three months later to sink back into primeval nothingness? . . . These we must examine after the last lingering guest has taken his departure and when blinds have been pulled down in shops, hotels and houses. Even now, however, behind one or two of these blank windows, may shrink and cringe a belated, timid figure, aware that, according to all the laws of his world, he should have left. Since, however, he has nowhere to go to, no friends and no funds, he is forced, sad ghost, into this miserable, shy defiance, though at night he may be able to sneak out and crawl round the crescents unobserved, an uneasy spirit revisiting the places of his former mundane delight.

Certainly such towns, dedicated to one season, present in their off-duty moments the certainty of affording surprises. . . . I remember, for example, spending a day in Mentone early in September, in the years before the summer-season vogue had spread so far down the coast. . . . It was the most beautiful day imaginable, with a few fleecy white clouds trailing above the horizon, but the aspect of the promenade seemed most singular. The carefully kept winter lawns were brown as slabs of chocolate, no flowers were visible except one or two geraniums in the last stages of exhaustion and the palms spun their tufts all dusty into blue air. The numberless hotels which face the sea were shuttered, their windows having a kind of roll-top-desk shutter let down over them, for the sake of security. . . . But, most striking symptom of all, under the *porte-cochère* of one hotel, in the street behind the promenade, stood an abandoned motor-car, looking twenty times its age; as if this were not Mentone, but Pompeii, and itself a recently excavated object of interest. What wild tale of adventure, one could not but wonder, what tragedy of missed trains and lamenting friends, lay behind this abomination of desolation? And how utterly broken, beyond mortal repair, must it have been for the members of so thrifty a race thus to abandon it!

Nothing, I think, is so melancholy as a ruined machine: yet human relics approach it in being pathetic. I had deemed myself the only foreigner in the town: though even then a few doubts had assailed me, for Mentone is something of a terminus; people drift there, can get no further without crossing the border (which requires initiative) and at the same time cannot return home. It has, moreover, ever been a favourite resort with the English—and, indeed, apart from San Remo, remains the best place in which to study English hats of the seventies, eighties and even earlier; hats comparable, in their involved design, to those which a decade or two earlier had so much astonished Théophile Gautier on his arrival in Gibraltar, after six months spent in a then hatless Spain. . . . I was turning over in my mind just what sort of ghost might haunt these streets, when all at once it materialized: the sad, but, at the same time, not altogether undefiant apparition of a middle-aged English lady, obviously economizing out of season, at a place which, alas, she could not afford to leave, but in which there was now no one for her to talk with—none of those lovely, impersonal, abstract, pro-British hotel-conversations. . . . As for her dress, she had attempted to come to some compromise with the climate, for she was shod in *espadrilles* and, after the manner of the natives, went stockingless, but wore one of those flowered chiffon dresses which have now practically become the English national costume, and was crowned by what I judged to be her second-best winter hat; a real confection of cherries, blue-satin and pink-satin ribbons, white currants and artificial roses, but one which was plainly not too well withstanding the onslaughts of the summer. Her face, which had been vigorously painted, and her hair, which must surely have been touched by Midas on more than one occasion, both emphasized the impression of poverty which emanated from her. . . . I watched her. She hurried across the street to have yet another glance at the English (Cotswold) Church, standing so stonily behind a low ivy-clad wall. . . . There was no fresh news. The same little white notice, pasted on one of the supports of the lych-gate, still announced in faded ink that the Rev. Douglas Surplice would return as Chaplain on December the twelfth. . . . There would be special Nativity services. . . . Yes, but across what a desert of wasted Sundays in Trinity! . . . She then recrossed the road to look into the window of the best cake-shop in the town . . . brioches . . . jams . . . panatone . . . crystallized fruit . . . those delicious biscuits, all with their prices attached to them on flags. I saw, though I did not at once interpret it, a sad connoisseurship gleaming from her eye; but then I understood, for, instead of entering, she hurriedly crossed the street again and dematerialized into a cheap, dull tea-shop round the corner. Alas! both body and soul were destined that day, and perhaps on many others, to remain unsatisfied. . . .

I turned towards the promenade. The car still stood under its *porte-cochère*, but I had already forgotten about it. Machines, decidedly, are less interesting, however curious their history.

26

ON A COMMON COLD

Common, indeed!
  A cold may be common: but it should not for that reason be despised. Many common things partake of the nature of a miracle; and a cold is protean, amazing in its diversity. What an inventive germ must lurk behind its malevolent manœuvres, behind these sneezings and coughings and red noses, these pains in the teeth and in the roots of the hair, these sore eyes and achings in the limbs, this difficult breathing, these voices, husky and grating, or speaking out of hearing somewhere, as it seems, in another dimension, from mouths that open and shut to no accompanying sound.

Common, indeed! Why, a common cold alters the very existence of him who suffers from it; not only, I mean, his mode of life but also the appearance and feeling of it, so that passing events, the very view from the window, are now seen by eyes that have not looked upon such things before. Pathos, together with a slightly hysterical humour, suddenly invade every accustomed act of our everyday existence. The very pleasures of life are transmuted as at the touch of a witch's finger: cigarettes become at the best tasteless, at the worst a torture of burning brown paper, emitting suffocating fumes; food holds no interest for us, and our animal appetites, if we are wise, become entirely centred on hot-water bottles and hot punch. . . . Oh! the joy of those cloves and that lemon infusing the steaming glass, and of the steam itself, which, so pungent and fragrant is it, can, even now, just faintly titillate the sense of smell. Boredom, again, holds no terror for him who now wishes only to lie down, or, better still, rest in bed, bookless and untalkative.

But most of all does the *common cold* alter the spirit, the very nature of the person it attacks. Those who have many friends are no longer eager to see them; while, on the other hand, the friendless, and even the unfriendly, at once become genial. If in dead of winter your telephone bell rings to ask whether Mr Snooks, whom you have never liked and have hardly ever met, and who, you are aware, harbours for yourself a feeling of very acute, though, as you are inclined to think unjustifiable hostility, may come to see you by appointment, suspect the common cold! I even remember an old and distant cousin of mine, who in all her life never troubled herself at all about my existence, calling on me as she was driving down to Ascot Races. Why had she thought of me? I wondered; no race-meeting could remind anyone of *me*, for never have I attended such a function. For a moment, until I saw that black-velvet nose, I was at a loss; but then I at once realized that this extraordinary feature really constituted but one more manifestation of microbic malevolence.

Other persons, again, usually of a lonely temperament, become of a sudden gregarious and pleasure-loving, afflicted with the desire to visit theatres, lectures and concert-halls, where for a brief hour or two they may splutter and sneeze to their heart's content. But these people you can distinguish at a first glance, by a certain look of self-importance, an air, too, of subtle triumph, which marks them off from the healthy of their tribe. Even those who, when well, present a forlorn and meagre appearance are invested with a certain strange radiance.

In addition, it must be borne in mind that persons undoubtedly exist to whom a cold is an obvious, positive pleasure. One or two of them occur in every community, however small, and in a household they are apt to form a reservoir of germs, which though dormant may at any moment enter upon hostile activities. Such persons you should compel to be inoculated, not because of any particular belief in the virtue of this operation, but because the pain of it serves as a powerful deterrent, and acts as a valuable moral lesson; they will be more careful another time, will think twice before attempting to launch a new series of germs. After this manner inoculation, however inefficacious in itself, forms a useful weapon in the armoury of hygiene today.

Of trades, those most addicted to colds as a habit are hairdressers and waiters, to both of whom their work affords various and splendid opportunities of spreading infection. Clergymen, I must say, run them pretty close—so that most country churches are, as it were, to be considered as refrigerators, in which germs can be preserved fresh and healthy during the week, until next Sunday the time comes for them to renew their attack. And next after them, in the strange and awful order of precedence dictated by bacillic virulence, follow the lady-novelists. Oh, those pitifully blurred consonants that fall from eminent mouths at the P.E.N. Club meetings! But, above all, if you wish to avoid catching a cold, never enter an English chemist's shop: for these shrines are

centres of pilgrimage to the infectious, and he who is gifted
with vision can see, when he stares into its windows, whole
cohorts of germs dancing round the huge bottles filled with
coloured water, and pressing their blue and eager noses against
the glass panes in their hurry to be out and at him. Doctors,
again, carry the infection into your own house; and, before
summoning a general practitioner to the aid of any member of
your household, it is well to read the passage in Marcel Proust,
wherein a doctor is described in the act of opening his black
bag, which property the author compares to the bag of Aeolus,
for as he opens it he releases all the battalions of bacilli, which
are to be seen whirling out of it, rejoicing to escape from their
captivity.

A common cold! Why, even the history of this germ is
interesting enough to rescue it from the possibility of any
appropriateness in the application of such a term. Indeed, it
boasts a descent of incomparable length. Long, long ago a
horrible and sudden plague afflicted mankind, then in an early
stage of development, decimating the race, leaving only here
a man, and there a woman, who was able to resist its ravages.
So numerous were the corpses of even the chieftains, that the
survivors could not dig barrows quick enough to bury them;
but from the survivors, whose children, again, were attacked,
though somewhat less savagely, by the children of these same
germs, are we descended; and from the germs, too, are
descended those which today are causing me—and perhaps
you—such hideous discomfort. A long and evenly balanced
battle through the ages, at the end of each era the weapons of
the opponents have varied. In the Elizabethan Age, poetry
itself entered into this wintry warfare; for 'Roosemary', we
read, 'is good for palses and for cowghs and good agaynst
colde and for the fallynge syckenes. Rooses be a cordyall and
doeth comforte the herte and the brayne.' Later, no doubt,

the patient was bled, as for every other disease; and now, in this age of steel, stacks of dead germs are pumped into our arm to feed, so the theory goes, an invisible but beneficent host which inhabits our body. All these remedies, I suspect, are possessed of an equal value.

And the cold, too, has played a noble part in world events; fighting, as you might have presumed, for ever on the side of England, its favourite habitat; since our climate is the best, most loyal and most abiding ally which this affliction possesses. Thus the Emperor Napoleon typifies, I suppose, the arch-enemy of England: he was defeated finally and for ever at Waterloo, by a common cold. Not the Duke of Wellington was his conqueror, neither Blücher—but this despised and altogether underrated bacillus. The Kaiser, a biographer tells us, on being informed by his doctor that he was suffering from a 'little cold', replied: 'It is a great cold. Nothing about me is little.' Herr Hitler was another very notorious sufferer. His cold at the time of the proposed visit of the English Secretary for Foreign Affairs was a much more historic one than the Kaiser's. Further, he suffered from hoarseness. . . . Caesar's troops must have sneezed their souls out. And, in addition, the common cold has often helped on English arms by knocking out one of our own generals at a critical moment, rendering him unable to speak the fatal word of command, which would have ended in the massacre of our poor troops. . . . *Common*, indeed, with such a history!

27

ON WORDS AND
THEIR MEANING

THE French are in many respects the most thrifty and prudent people in Europe. Something of Chinese wisdom and providence seems to attend their management of both private and public affairs. They are *so* sensible; they can, on the one hand, run their trains punctually, without the necessity of having a frowning and menacing dictator to preside over them, as in some Latin countries; nor, on the other hand, do their Governments find it necessary to torture or banish all those of whom they disapprove. Their judgment in public affairs is, at the same time, determined and defined; they act with courage and swiftness. Thus when Mr W. R. Hearst, a visiting American newspaper-baron, offends them, they ask him to leave the country: a thing we should never dare perform in England. Again, when they can afford to pay America no longer, owing to the increase in the price of gold, they do not argue for months, or, it may be, years, before making a decision; nor do they indulge, even, in the luxury of governesslike, it-hurts-me-more-than-it-hurts-you notes; they simply refuse to pay. What is more, the result of their actions in no way injures them; on the contrary, they gain still further the respect of the more barbarous nations and individuals with whom they are forced to deal.

And one aspect of—or perhaps one reason for—their refined civilization is the manner in which they use their language, with its eloquent, if thin, vocabulary. Certainly it is incapable of the richness to which ours is heir. Nevertheless, the French mean, to a much greater extent than we do, what they say. If they speak of a great poet or painter, they *mean* a great poet or painter: not a mediocre versifier or a sugary, incompetent portraitist, as these terms so commonly denote in England.

Similarly if, for instance, we take French journalism, we shall find many neat and amusing examples of the precise and scrupulous selection of words which they affect; and of their thrift, too, in this respect. For they assign to each word its exact value; a word is allowed to parade itself, neither at more, nor less, than its proper worth; and this leads to a heightening of meaning and an intensification of personality.

Thus, recently the *Matin* reported three police-court cases. In the first of these a young Armenian had shot and wounded his sister. Giving an account of this affair, in reality one of little consequence, the journal announced that 'the police asked themselves the reason for this gesture'.

In the second a workman threw vitriol at four persons, but fortunately missed his targets. This constituted an incident of greater importance; no longer did the police 'ask *themselves*' a question; nor was this ill-intentioned act allowed to masquerade as a gesture. No! this time they asked—presumably of the world in general—what was 'the reason of this *demonstration*'.

Finally, third instance, a man was discovered in a state of

[147]

alcoholic exaltation in the Place de la Nation. On this occasion the Parisian police, courteous as ever, 'invited him to calm himself'. Alas for Bacchic wisdom! The invitation—never, alas, destined to be repeated, which they had, after their fashion, so politely extended—was refused by him. Their next invitation to the errant one proved to be that he should accompany them to the police-station.

I fear that in English newspaper-reports of such police-court incidents we should find but few examples of this scrupulous explanation and description. Probably each would have been described as a 'police-court drama'.

Foremost amongst the dangers to which cheap literature and sensational journalism expose us is this threat to our rich, full-blooded language. True to our national character, we allow them every day to throw away, to squander without thought of the morrow, the inherited riches of our speech; riches accumulated during centuries of poetic exploration.

Sometimes, under these unfortunate influences, words are drained of their vitality, become pale and anaemic; sometimes on the contrary, inflated and unnatural. Such words as 'wonderful' and 'magic' no longer bear any significance at all, while often the meaning becomes stunted, dwarfed and crippled; as in the word 'tragedy'. In the past this term was applied to the work of the Greek dramatists, or to such stories as those of *Othello* and *Macbeth*; but now it is used indiscriminately of any death as the result of a common orgy (in itself a devitalized word), of any over-indulgence in narcotics, or of any squalid murder in which neither victim nor murderer has any hint of greatness; in which neither could ever be hunted by the Furies. The difference, again, is the difference between Mycene and a third-rate—or, as for that, first-rate—night-club; between the bee-loud tomb of Agamemnon and the grave of a rich manufacturer in Aberdeen or Sheffield.

Then there is the word 'romance'; originally applied to the deeds of chivalry and of the high love that inspired them; later used to describe *Romeo and Juliet* and the story of Perdita. What strings of poetic memory formerly vibrated at the very mention of this word, now used to designate any trivial coincidence—the marriage, let us say, of two people who met for the first time through a collision of their standardized motor-cars—or the meanest and most sordid of vulgar divorce-court episodes!

Countless other words are equally abused. The word 'beauty' stands now, at the best, for prettiness—and often for ugliness itself. The word 'literature', again, is applied to the accumulated rubbish sold on railway bookstalls. The result of this is not only the debauching of our language, but the debasement of our values in life, so that people in general have no longer any knowledge where they stand. A man is described as a 'great' writer, while somebody else is a 'great' golfer or 'great' spillikin player. Such are the values of the newspaper words of today. And, of course, nearly every actor and actress is a 'great' actor and 'great' actress.

To prescribe the exact remedy for this state of affairs is difficult. I suppose a constant reading of the classics would enlighten anyone as to the comparative merits of various writers. As for the stage, perhaps the best course is to read Shakespeare, and then if you are fortunate enough to find a play of his running at one of our West End theatres, to see it acted. Nobody, I think, can accuse the work of Shakespeare of being better off, than on, the stage. The reason that we prefer to read his lines is, then, because they are so often badly acted and spoken. On the other hand, to see a performance at the Old Vic or Sadler's Wells is always a pleasure; for there we find no pretence; there, at least, words still have their meaning.

28

ON THE BELITTLEMENT
OF THE GREAT

THOUGH the majority of fashions scarcely outlives the span of a year or two at the most, yet at least one still prevails, and continues to give signs of growth, which started many years ago: the vogue for belittling the dead—that is to say, the dead who, either through their own abilities or by virtue of heredity, occupied great positions of trust, respect and responsibility in their lifetimes. Dig up their faults, show up their weaknesses, rootle about in the dust of ages for those things they hoped forgotten; at the best, let them appear to us, in our plus-fours, the funny old pieces of upholstery that they were, with their wigs and velvets! This seems to be the attitude of the writer of today towards the past. . . . And, in a sense, it is easy to understand, being the result in part of that very justifiable disrepute which the still living generals and statesmen have earned for themselves by their repeated and signal failures. Since the laws of libel compel the author to suppress the truth about the failures and oddities of the living, instead he exaggerates or invents those of the celebrated dead.

The methods of posthumous belittlement are numerous and diverse. One of the most successful, however, is the adoption of a spurious familiarity, by which the writer puts himself, and every reader, on Christian-names terms with the subject of his book. It is a kind of *tutoyer*-ing through the centuries, the style of the gossip-writer applied to history. Just in the same way as in the Villa of the Knights of Malta, outside Rome, the architect has arranged for visitors peeping through the key-hole of the front door to obtain a magnificent yet intimate view of the dome of St Peter's, so these modern historian-bio-graphers only require the reader to look through the keyholes with which they provide him, to obtain an intimate view of the love affairs of King Henry VIII, the writhings of King Louis XIV in the grip of that singular indigestion to which he was victim all his adult life, or the *accouchement* of Queen Victoria. King Henry, it goes without saying, is always referred to as 'Hal', the Roi Soleil as 'Lulu', the Queen as 'Vicky'. Indeed, this type of writer deserves the classic rebuke which I once heard delivered by a worldly old lady to a young man inclined to this same sort of misleading reference: 'Mr Merely, how different we are in our outlook, I notice you always address the Duchess of St Dodo as "Duchess", but refer to her in her absence as "Muriel"; whereas I always call her "Muriel" to her face, but, when she is not there, refer to her in front of other people as "the Duchess of St Dodo".'

In this particularly intimate writing, as in so many other directions, America originally gave us the lead; but only too readily have we followed it. Almost the worst instance is the book of an American author, an incredibly bad book which purported to be a life of that genius, the first Duke of Marl-borough, and in which that great soldier and statesman was referred to throughout as 'Jack', as though he were a boon companion whom the author had met every night in a speak-easy. Indeed, the Duke of Marlborough seems to be a favourite for such treatment (which doubtless was one reason for Sir Winston Churchill's decision to write a life of his ancestor and show that interest could be maintained by the inherent won-der of the life and vigour of the writing, without any such artificial aids), for pages can be taken up entirely with his sup-posedly treacherous character. And even if some of the alleged facts were true, what do they amount to, and who cares? It has been charged against him sometimes, for example, that he accepted money from King Louis XIV, receiving it as a bribe to allow himself to be defeated, and then, instead, defeated the French king. . . . And what action, let me ask, could be more patriotic: a double defeat inflicted on a rival and hostile power in the realms of both finance and battle? much more patriotic than rout in battle alone. Only the ghost of King Louis XIV ('Old Loo') has the right to complain.

To return, though, to belittling by means of names, it is one thing for Ben Jonson to refer to 'Will Shakespeare' and quite another for a modern author to do so (for some reason 'Ben', though familiar, is a necessary distinction). And what of 'Kit' Marlowe? Then, again, there are those who love to refer to Chaucer as 'old Dan', under the delusion that 'Dan' was his Christian name, instead of being a misreading of 'Dom', which probably indicated his position as a great man at Court. Indeed, this method is so popular, in the writing of both biography and romance, that even the title of a book must hint at it. . . . Thus we are given, as a robust belittlement of Queen Elizabeth I, the title 'The Tudor Wench', although, on the contrary, other knowing writers have recently insisted that the poor Queen was in reality, all the time, a man dressed up as a woman.

Biography is, admittedly, a difficult medium, and one which many, too many, persons—some with misused ability, and some without any qualification at all—attempt. When writing a life, the author must remember continually that it is the subject of his book, not its author, which will make that book interesting. Biography, except autobiography, should never be selected as a means of self-revelation and interpretation; for no sensible reader wants personal or modish views of a great man.

One sin in which all the modern writers of biographies, even the more competent, indulge, is that of oblique reference. This was initiated—together, indeed, with the rest of modern biography—by Lytton Strachey. In his essay upon Gordon in *Eminent Victorians* that delightful author suddenly switches off on to Rimbaud's journal, the effect being one of surprise justified; for though some persons hint that the document is a forgery, the quotation which follows does, at least, contain reference to the General. But in the end, and in the hands of lesser writers, the use of this method becomes horribly tedious; as tedious as *Romola* with its dovetailed 'Who's Who' of contemporary Florentine celebrities. The recipe, as now practised, is roughly this: write a biography of Marie Antoinette and give a description of her at the age of ten; then let it read: 'But four hundred miles away, in a little house outside Paris, in very different circumstances, the infant Robespierre is on hands and knees, cutting off the heads of dolls with a rusty knife; and further off still, in an old island in the Mediterranean, in Corsica itself, a mother is crooning to a little son; a mother who is afterwards to be known to all the world as "Madame Mère".' . . . Let Parliament decree a close season of ten years for the ghosts of the great.

29

ADULT FRANCHISE FOR
DOMESTIC ANIMALS

I T IS quite time that certain wrongs to the animal world
were remedied. The English, a race essentially of animal-
lovers (for, though they kill more members of the animal
and bird worlds than any other nation, they are surely—
except in the case of the fox, the badger and the stag—kind to
them until the tocsin sounds for their official massacre), yet
display, in the abusive or playful phrases that roll off their
rather unpractised tongues, the most profound misunderstanding of the various, even dumber, tribes that inhabit the
English and foreign countrysides.

The horse, by far the most imbecile of God's creatures,
and one which, apart from its brutal bad temper, stupidity and
annoying habit of holding up street traffic, contrives to give
any sensitive person brought into close contact with it an
attack of hay-fever, is, of course, our acknowledged pet;
with the dog, so well described recently as 'dirty and immoral',
ranking as a good second.

I do not object to such favouritism, such horrid injustice, when it errs, as in these two instances, on the side of kindness; but that the goose, which, as every motorist recognizes, is the only intelligent biped on the road, should be cruelly libelled, grieves me. 'You silly goose', indeed! The goose is wise, decent and economical in its private life, and has a beauty of speech rare in the animal world. 'You silly chicken' would be a much more apt description of a pedestrian who refuses to clear out of the way.

Who again has given the donkey, a favourite animal with painters of all schools, and an animal full of spirit and intelligence, its bad name? And then there is that pathetic poor relation of ours, the monkey, in whose behaviour—inquisitive, inventive, playful and humorous—we can trace every virtue, as well as every vice, of the human being. The monkey, it seems, is blamed for catching fleas; yet surely it is to the credit of our little cousin that he should strive after this almost unattainable and very clean dexterity?

But, rather than for all these, would I put in a plea on behalf of the cleanly and almost puritanical pig. A more moral, more thrifty animal has seldom existed. The tragedy of the pig-world lies in the fact that this creature is ever carefully and slowly saving up for a winter that never comes. Originally intended for hibernation, like a thrifty housewife, she accumulates her winter stores—only inside herself rather than within the household cupboard. Thus, as some would hint, after the fashion of a good Christian, her whole earthly life is regulated with a view to a future state which never comes to pass. A devoted wife, a good mother, the pig is possessed of every peasant virtue, in addition to every instinct that makes the capitalist so beloved in modern Europe. Nevertheless, even in France, a thrifty country, the word *cochon* carries an unpleasant significance. Why, then, in the name of justice, should 'pig' be a term of reproach, when the camel, notoriously self-indulgent, and equipped for gluttony with seven stomachs instead of one, is allowed to move amongst us free and uncensured?

Moreover, if the names of animals are thus to be taken in vain, why also are they not sometimes used as terms of commendation? Why, for example, do we not say, when we wonder at some mother's devotion, that she is 'a perfect kangaroo of a mother'? Has there ever been a better parent than a kangaroo, with all the ingenious fool-proof equipment for carrying her children; a machinery evolved, no doubt, from hundreds and thousands of years of acute maternal love and anxiety?

Finally, as a fervent democrat, I should like to advocate the granting of adult franchise to domestic animals. And of all these fine beasts, the backbone of this great country, not least of them could the pig be trusted to register an intelligent and cautious vote.

30

ON FOGS

THE sound of the word 'London' is magnificent; no better name could be found for a great city. Its simple, reiterative syllables evoke all the thunder of modern traffic, and there pertains to it a ponderous and exquisite dignity. Nevertheless, to most foreigners the word 'London' is merely synonymous with 'fog': a fact about which is something peculiarly appropriate, for, after all, the power of Britain blossomed from her coal, and fog is the aerial manifestation of this force. To them England lies in a murky mist, floats on the ocean, a heavy and impenetrable cloud of smoke. Foreign eyes can hardly pierce it, but, if they do, they find a strange country, peopled by inhabitants who seem as different from the Europeans as are the Japanese from other Asiatics. Something romantic always clings to islands in the minds of Continental peoples, and from the time of Caesar to that of Casanova there is continual comment on the strangeness of the life to be found here. And just as the Japanese are inevitably pictured under the snowy cone of a volcano, with the falling petals of plum, peach and almond flickering down over their golden faces and slanting eyes, so to others we remain subtle, inexplicable and morose, only just discernible through the dark and sinister screen of smoke poured forth from every chimney.

As we know, Continental nations can never comprehend us. To them our actions and the processes of our minds are as much enshrouded in mystery as the kind of lives we lead; we are a rich, proud, perfidious and intensely subtle people. Our Foreign Office, staggering from blunder to blunder in the past century, has achieved undreamt-of successes owing to the Continental inability to understand our lack of logic: the fact, for example, that our diplomats really say what they mean, though they often change their minds. With few diplomatic triumphs to our credit during the past years, it is still supposed that we pursue a policy, ingenious and diabolically subtle, and that all this is connected with the fogs through which we move and in which we exist.

Every Englishman, I think, loves fogs; both of an atmospheric and of a mental variety. The first memory of many a child is often of a fog; of walking, for example, through Kensington Gardens when the trees could only just be discerned, looming up suddenly, and the Palace was altogether hidden. All my life, indeed, fogs have been my friends. At school a black fog would occasionally visit us and supply a whole holiday; one was told that the railway lines attracted them, and certainly they rolled down them as far as Barnet. In this dark, delicious moment, games became impossible, and fortunately it was still more impossible to be made to watch them. When I was in the Army a fog, again, prevented parades; and the centre of fog-land still seems to me to be the Tower of London, in which my battalion was stationed for some months during the winter of 1912. It was my introduction to soldiering, and there was something very impressive about the havoc that fog caused to the military system. You might have thought that where so much mental fog prevailed, a little more of another, more material kind would not have made much difference; but this was not so. All parades had to be cancelled, bugles sounded out in the darkness and the barracks became hives of light and gaiety as the word went round, while the Tower of London itself seemed to be a lighted beacon in the centre of this enormous circle of fog which surrounded it for miles and miles in every direction.

During the 1914–18 War the fog was a firm and very valuable friend. The white Flemish mists that hung, like cotton wool, above the little dark pools and muddy fields made life more difficult, and yet easier, for both sides. They prevented sniping; but, on the other hand, any broken tree that showed itself suddenly was liable to look like the figure of a man, and fog seemed to invest these still things with movement. Sounds in the fog, too, became magnified and therefore more alarming; yet on the whole fog was an ally to friend and enemy alike. . . . But I imagine that the authorities did not approve of it, for anything that tended to check the pursuit of hostilities, and thus to make life more normal, was unpopular with them. Thus I shall never forget the rage that inspired our Staff when, during Christmas week, 1914, the Saxon regiment opposite my own put up placards with 'Why should Saxons and Anglo-Saxons fight one another?' and, in consequence, the men began to fraternize. It became quite obvious to those in command that if the rival troops found that they liked one another and the artificially manufactured enmity waned after this fashion, the war might end: and then where should we all be? . . .

Of course, there are different brands of fogs. There is the almost tangible, white fog which fills the streets of Florence and the neighbouring Tuscan cities in the winter. From the top

[159]

of one of the mountain ranges, indeed, I have seen the whole of
Tuscany, though I stood in bright sunlight, lying engulfed
beneath the frozen waves of this mysterious sea, out of which,
every now and then, there rose a hill with a castle on it, standing up as though it were an island. . . . But to the Londoner,
fog means either a yellow fog or a black one; a Dickensian fog,
a fog which creeps up from the river and hides all the black
wharves and mean streets, a fog in which the criminals can
pursue their business unhampered; bringing the sort of night
on which Fagin would have chosen to go out on one of his
nefarious errands. And indeed, fog takes you to another world,
the sort of locality and age which Dickens describes in *Oliver
Twist*:

> Near to that part of the Thames on which the church at Rother-
> hithe abuts, where the buildings on the banks are dirtiest and the
> vessels on the river blackest with the dust of colliers and the smoke
> of close-built, low-roofed houses, there exists the filthiest, the
> strangest, the most extraordinary of the many localities that are
> hidden in London, only unknown, even by name, to the great mass
> of its inhabitants.

Over such regions ever broods a fog, just as it always
fills the offices and rooms and the Court of Chancery in
Bleak House.

Some find a black, others a yellow, fog the more interesting.
It is a matter of temperament. If lazy, you will prefer the black:
for London can turn bright primrose yellow, and yet retain a
certain semblance of itself, because a fog of this kind—not so
much a blacking-out as a darkening or, rather, dyeing of the
atmosphere—enables the life of the city still to retain its shape;
whereas a black one closes down every activity. Eternal night
seems to reign, and in it you lose your identity for other
people, just as they lose their identity for you. It imparts a

strangeness to every street, and, if you have a good sense of locality, an additional pleasure to walking, for it alters distances, investing the town with more than its usual enormous proportions. It would be possible, it seems, if you had the strength, to wander through streets, on ordinary days familiar to you, for hours and hours without reaching their end or being able to identify your surroundings. . . . And it is to the vast blackness of this wonderful yet nightmare city that the minds of foreigners turn at mention of the word *London*.

31

BY TRAIN

Unlike the majority of my friends, who seem to be for ever regretting that they were not destined to live during the reigns of Cleopatra, Caesar Augustus, Queen Elizabeth I, Louis XIV or King George IV, often I repine at having been born into this world too soon. But, whereas the reasons which govern their nostalgia for past epochs are usually vague and indefinite (though not seldom founded upon a suppressed sentiment of self-importance, a belief that their talents would have guaranteed them a greater respect and position in ampler days) my desire for a later birth is, at any rate, in its foundation, simple and precise; prompted by an overwhelming hatred of railway trains.

For one who likes travelling—to whom, indeed, travelling is a necessity, almost a mania—this prejudice is unfortunate. Easy, you may say, to charter an airplane or hire a car; but airplanes are fortunately still expensive as well as dangerous (fortunately, because you can attribute your neglect of them to a love of economy, rather than to a morbid fear for your own personal safety), and motor-cars, too, cost a great deal of money to hire. Trains, on the other hand, are supposed to be quick, cheap and comfortable; while, moreover, quite a number of places—desirable places—are still inaccessible save by rail or on horseback; and however unpleasant may be the idea of a railway-carriage, the thought of even one hour spent on—or off—the capricious back of Nature's most ridiculous creation is yet more distasteful.

Trains sum up, to my mind, all the fogs and muddled misery of the nineteenth century. They constitute, in fact, so many slums on wheels. Think, first of all, on their dirt! No mere question of personal vanity instils in the wretched passenger his dislike of arriving at his destination disguised, apparently, as a collier or dustman; for, while no reasonable being can entertain any objection to fancy dress in appropriate surroundings, who, on the other hand, would wish deliberately to arrive at one of the large stations of the metropolis, where friends and enemies may be in waiting, with a face blacked like that of a nigger-minstrel? Or is it, I sometimes wonder, only myself who suffers in this manner? This may well be so; for, as the fields whirl themselves past into the distance, and the telegraph poles dance by with ungainly hops to the rhythm of a nightmare polka ground out by a discordant jazz orchestra, every scrap of dust, perhaps long treasured, every speck of soot and, worse still, every fragment of cinder, finds its way into my eyes, nose and ears—until I am blinded, choked and deafened—and the residue smears my face and enwraps my hands, the while I sit, enviously regarding from bloodshot eyes the clean and untired countenances of my companions.

And what of the noise, so far scarcely touched on? The engines of automobiles have been subdued to a gentle purr, a little soothing, even, in its monotony; the roar of the aerial engines sounds far overhead, a brave and leonine roar; but, even apart from the jolting thunder of its naturally ungainly and stilted movement, no train can ever either start or stop without an agonizing bump accompanied by a fiendish scream. Why, we demand, this convention of hooting and whistling, when the noise alone of an approaching train is sufficient to herald its arrival? Perhaps this sound is due, again, to that prevalent sin of our time, an 'inferiority complex'. Certainly the smaller the engine, the louder the screech; and I suspect that, as trains become more and more supplanted by other forms of locomotion, they will yell more loudly yet.

Then let us examine the problem of Hot or Cold. . . . In England, it is true, the question seldom arises, because in the winter a train is never allowed to be brought to a higher temperature than just above zero, unless it contains a restaurant-car, which is then scented with a sickeningly vivid smell of cabbage, bad Virginian cigarettes and stale smoke in tunnels, and brought to a steady temperature of ninety degrees. In the summer, too, the really clever railway can always arrange for a train to stand for several hours in the sun before starting on its stifling journey. But, on the whole, the compartments are cool. . . . On the Continent, however, it is otherwise, and I have been almost unable, sometimes, to discover a waiting train owing to the dense clouds of steam encircling it, but, having at last fought my way through this atmosphere, so painfully reminiscent of the last act of *Götterdammerung*, I have finally found myself in a torrid zone of overheated red plush, reeking with stale tobacco, while every cubic inch of so-called air is laden with the most lithe and vigorous of germs, which, after the manner of the hosts of Midian, prowl and prowl around, alert and waiting for new victims.

And what would you have me say of travelling companions? In the days of coaching they appear always to have

been either delightful, intelligent and considerate, or con-
spicuously, interestingly sinister; but the railway-chatterers
stand high on the list of public bores and liars. Only with long
experience can be acquired the technique of dealing with them,
for which it is necessary to develop an admirable terseness of
retort. In example of it, a famous professor, now, alas, dead,
who was an expert in the use of words, when questioned by a
fellow-traveller as to whether there had been snow where he
had come from the previous day, countered with the enigmatic
reply: 'I did not come from anywhere yesterday,' leaving his
interlocutor puzzled and silenced.

On the other hand, but only with rare luck accompanying,
the entire life-history of a fellow-traveller, or of some friend
of his who must for ever remain unknown to you, may be laid
at your feet. Thus it was Max Beerbohm, I think—or at any
rate one of those very few other fortunate persons to whom all
good stories are attributed—who was privileged to be present
at an occasion of this kind. Travelling in his compartment was
a couple, man and woman, who remained silent all the way
from London, until, as the train passed Malmesbury, the man
looked out of the window and remarked in an intensely meaning voice: '*Poor* Mildred! She had reason to remember Malmesbury,' and then lapsed into silence again for the rest of the
journey. . . . As to liars, I was once on my way to London in a
crowded third-class compartment, when the talk turned on
the murdered Tsar and Tsarina. The general feeling was with
them, until a mean, cringing little individual in the corner
suddenly looked up from his paper and said: 'If you people
only knew what *I* know about the Tsarina you wouldn't feel
a bit sorry for her; but I'm pledged never to tell.' This speech
produced a tremendous impression and the Tsarina at once lost
the sympathy of all those present except myself.

32

DOGS

I F Y O U admit to—or, it may be, boast of—a dislike for
dogs, then, in England, it is inevitably assumed that you
favour their being treated with brutality. Many people,
indeed, hearing you indulge in such a confession, would
demand your immediate impeachment by that fighting body,
the R.S.P.C.A. . . . It becomes necessary, then, to remind
yourself from time to time that you cannot, as yet, be prosecuted for an aversion from, but only for cruelty to, animals.

Therefore consider, and condemn, dogs and their ways. In
them, very few virtues of the animal world are evinced. They
are dirty and dishonourable, immoral—not amoral, as some
suggest—and, yet, teetotal; enemies, too, of beauty, of silence—
in itself enchanting—and of all lovely objects from Persian
carpets down to foxes and pheasants. They have no sense of
humour, only a vacuous and rather cruel grin. Above all, they
are cynical, supremely cynical: the very word cynic is derived
from the Greek word for 'dog', for cynics were supposed to

'grin like dogs', and, indeed, the dictionary definition of 'cynic' as a 'sneering fault-finder' fits all dogs to a tee. Finally— and this, too, is a serious objection to them—they are not even good to eat. . . . (Let me interrupt my dissertation here, to assure nervous dog-owners that I have no wish to eat their pets; but that, were I to do so, they would have no remedy. To eat an animal is, in English law, neither cruel nor illegal; though I, with no great fondness for brutes, should have deemed it both.) . . . They are not good to eat, I was saying, except to the very cultured palate of the Chinese; for it is stated that the word 'chow', which is the formal title of one of the proudest and most detestable of canine breeds, means 'good', merely in the sense of good to eat.

But worse, far worse than any fault that I have cried against them, worse even than their unappetizing inedibility, is the fact, plain for all to see, that they do not *know* when they are disliked: unless, perhaps, the explanation is an opposite one, and they do know it and revel in it? . . . In any case, they delight in adopting me, in following me on what I had intended to be a lonely walk through the countryside, disturbing my train of thought, tripping me up unaware, panting hotly after, so as to make me, too, feel hot and out of breath. . . . And then, any sign of wild life in vale or woodland, and, however fatigued they have pretended to be, they are out hot-foot to destroy it, snuffling, fussing, growling and yapping. And this brings another objection in its train: how ugly are their voices, whether gruff in anger or wheezy in contentment! Yet, in their self-conceit, it is plain that they think them tuneful, pleasing to all men. 'What can I do to comfort my master, for he is nervous and ill at ease today?', they seem to say, and reply to themselves: 'I will bark.' . . . Nor can man, his master, be altogether acquitted of lending a certain encouragement to this point of view.

Yet, though dogs, it may be, are popular today, were they always regarded with such approbation? Is this alliance between man and dog in reality such an ancient one, to be traced back, as the archaeologists have told us, to far times when, together, these two creatures were hunted, through lands which are now seas, by the sabre-toothed tiger? . . . Perhaps the idiom of our language, a frozen repository of knowledge of such a kind, can help us towards a conclusion on this subject.

The dictionary, certainly, informs us of no innate liking for dogs in our ancestors. To begin with, it defines the meaning of dog, when applied to a human being, as 'worthless or surly person' (and, in support of it, I may own that often, when reading some particularly stupid and ill-tempered review of a book, the description 'beastly dog of a reviewer' has risen involuntarily to my lips). Again, 'to go to the dogs' was wont, formerly, to be considered no desirable journey; 'a dog's life' was no good thing, 'dog-days' were days to be avoided, nor was a 'dog's death' an end after which to hanker. The baboon, called 'dog-faced', does not derive his name from the beauty of his countenance, neither is the 'dog-fish' a pretty object; nor, as far as that, is the word 'bitch' generally used in any sense even of empty compliment. And I notice, in the dictionary once more, that 'Dog-Fennel' is a name applied to 'Stinking Camomile'.

Of course, the explanation of so much dignified dislike and contempt may be that dictionaries are compiled by literary men, and that authors, as a profession, must be hostile to dogs (George Moore, for example, was a noted leader of the anti-dog campaign), since many are the books, good and bad, which dogs have prevented being written, many are the poems in embryo which their insensate yapping has strangled. . . . Yet it looks as though this antipathy rested on a firmer basis. Why, then, you may ask, are dogs, their names formerly a term of

[168]

reproach, so popular in modern England; who has conspired to give the dog a good name? . . . In modern England alone, for foreign races, more kind to children, are less kind to animals.

The reason, I apprehend, is because the dog is by nature dumb, inexpressive; incapable of speech and gesture, or the thoughts which these things transmit. . . . And this, of course, appeals to the Englishman, often in somewhat the same way himself. Babies, too, are loved in this our land until they grow old enough to be sensible, when, indeed, they lapse in favour; for, as a race, we loathe reasoning, or, as we call it familiarly, 'answering back'. The dog cannot answer back. . . .

In Latin countries it is quite otherwise. Parents adore children; children love parents. There we find never any need for a society to prevent cruelty to children. But animals certainly need protection. . . . Thus I remember sitting at breakfast on the terrace of a hotel in south Italy. The concierge, talking of animals, pointed to a waiter, and remarked, in a congratulatory manner: 'Michele is very good with animals.' 'You mean, kind to them,' I corrected, 'very kind, no doubt.' 'No, sir,' he replied, 'I mean, he can kick them very quickly, and as if by mistake, without attracting the attention of their masters.' . . . Now therein Michele goes too far for my taste: though often I, too, make horrible, frightening faces at these pets, when their owners are not looking.

To sum up, dogs should be neither seen nor heard; they should never be allowed to enter a house or city; nor should they be permitted in gardens, but only in parks and meadows. . . . From this proclamation of outlawry I would alone except the Pekingese, that arrogant but quiet race of palace-dwellers, and my personal friends. For I have friends in the animal world; and Carlos, who pants beside me as I write, is one of them; a fussy, woolly, self-important friend, but a friend none the less.

[169]

33

ANIMALS VERSUS CHILDREN

Let us now pass on to an examination of the British attitude towards other animals beside the dog: which brute, together with the horse, this strange race worships, as surely as ever the inhabitants of ancient Egypt ritually adored the hawk, crocodile and cat. Essentially a people with a tendency towards favouritism, out of all the animal world, horse and dog are the only two beasts to whom they grant immunity from the consequences of the rites which they term 'sport'. Thus a continual public clamour is raised against the traffic in worn-out horses, which are carried over to Belgium to be made into meat—though, leaving altogether out of consideration the point of view of the gourmet, why, you will ask, should it be more wicked to eat a horse than to eat a sheep? Again, the practice of vivisection is intensely unpopular because, firstly, a dog might be injured in the process, and, secondly, the results might be of benefit to mankind.

Yet, for the English, all other animals exist only 'to offer sport'. Fox and stag and otter and hare must, once their tracks are discovered, be pursued for panting miles, and, at the end of the run, if possible, be torn to pieces. (It is held, I know, that stags and foxes *enjoy* being hunted, but the instance of the stag which swam up the Channel as far as the Kentish coast constituted, surely, a disproof of this statement?) Bigger animals, elephant, lion and giraffe, were created only to be shot, just as the purpose of the wild pig is to be 'stuck'—in whatever that unpleasant process may consist. Thus in our free land, so long as it does not involve the two national pets, very little objection is raised against cruelty to animals. It is just sport. But directly a really magnificent and tremendous sport, like bull-fighting, is mentioned, some English sportsman will at once protest: 'But don't the poor *horses* run some risk of being injured? I think that is terrible.' Notwithstanding that 'poor foxes' are injured after every successful meet.

Yet we are apt to boast of our fondness for animals in general, blinding ourselves to our treatment of them. In order to avoid a plain statement of our feelings towards the animals we eat, we have adopted the equivocal practice of using two names for them; one when alive, the other when dead. And so skilfully facing both ways, we are kind to cows, sheep, calves and pigs, but devour those doubtless synthetic victuals, beef, mutton, veal and pork. The French and Germans, more logical and more blunt, care for these animals *because* they eat them: we pretend, when we face the matter at all, to eat, because we love, them. Nevertheless we expose our cattle, before they are killed, to the most horrible, nerve-racking ordeals in our slaughter-houses, the conditions of which are, for the most part, much more cruel to the victim, and dangerous to the consumer, than those prevailing in civilized foreign countries.

And yet I believe it to be really true that we are fonder

of animals than of children. . . . Especially, I think, would a visitor from another planet, were he to visit our country, conclude from the evidence round him that the wealthier classes were possessed by a morbid dislike—or, perhaps, fear—of their children. (And, indeed, antiquaries inform me that this was always so; that in medieval times the young nobles, pages in the castles of the great, were much more ill-treated, and made to lead a much harder life, than the children of the villeins—those Saxon untouchables.) The moment the poor little creatures are born, they are handed over to the fond attention of a succession of ill-educated and morose half-wits, to be trained by them during their most impressionable years.

Further, they are treated in the most extraordinary fashion in several directions: given horrible food to eat—sago, tapioca, rice and greasy meat; hushed whenever they talk—though talk must be their medium of learning; hurried away, whenever possible, from the living-rooms to the nursery; and, finally, sent to bed at six of a summer evening, by far the most healthy and agreeable hour of the whole day. This, of course, is defended on the assumption that it is *good* for children to go to bed early. But who is to decide, save their Maker? In Naples they are taken to the Opera, which continues until two o'clock in the morning, and you can hear them playing in the hot, summer streets of Barcelona until the small hours. Yet are there less of them, fewer survivors, than among our down-trodden, less lively children? . . . Abroad, too, they receive better food, and are not forced to drink barley-water and the like. They are nurtured on wine and water. . . . Thus an old Italian woman once remarked: 'I think it dreadful to give wine to very young children. Personally I never allowed one of mine to *touch* it until he had reached four years of age!'

Finally it must be acknowledged that, as soon as the male child of prosperous parents has attained an age when his elders

[172]

can be certain that by so doing they are not rendering themselves liable to a prosecution for cruelty to children, he is got out of the house altogether and dispatched to a preparatory school, where a prison-like system of life and discipline obtains. Henceforward the child is never seen again except during a paltry three months of the year.

Would fond, or even humane, parents consent to being thus parted from one whom they love at such an early age? They must know what schools are like; especially since most fathers have been to similiar schools themselves. Usually, however, they comfort themselves with the argument that material conditions have improved since their time; there is more jam, less dripping; more play, less Latin and Greek. But they know, surely, that human nature changes slowly, and that small boys, while often delightful and intelligent as individuals, are, in the mass, most barbarous and brutal?

34

ON STATUES IN GENERAL

PYGMALION and Don Juan are not the only persons to have been startled by a statue. One day, in a fourth-storey room in a hotel at Genoa, the author, already only half conscious after the utilitarian agony of unpacking, turned round towards the window and there beheld—its eyes gazing blankly in, its enormous features seemingly almost flattened by being pressed against the upper panes—a marble head as big as a small cottage. This pantomime ogre was no less a person, as he afterwards found out, than the famous Doria Admiral, here disguised as Neptune, naked and with a trident as his only attribute, but so much larger than life that with his feet firmly planted on the ground, he could thus easily soar up for four or five storeys.

Indeed, a quality that is a little alarming clings to these pale and motionless spectres, more especially when they are of great size. Even a better example of such an effect is to be found in the story of Cellini's 'Mars', for with this giant statue the sculptor, though unintentionally, contrived to frighten a whole city. In his memoirs he tells us how he set about its construction. He covered a 'framework of well-connected woodwork' with a crust of plaster, about the eighth of a cubit in thickness, carefully modelled for the flesh of the Colossus. Lastly, he prepared a number of moulds in separate pieces, intending to dovetail them together.

Having brought the head of the statue to completion by this method, he left it alone for a little, and indulged the vanity of creation by exposing it in a place outside his castle in Paris. Here, he says, so enormous was its size it could be seen by more than half the town. Indeed, his neighbours took to climbing upon their roofs to inspect it. Crowds came on purpose to have a look at it, but what was the surprise and horror of the superstitious to notice in plain daylight that there were various movements in its eye-sockets! Many visitors fled in terror, saying that a ghost inhabited the body, and was setting its eyes in motion and controlling its mouth as though it were about to talk. Even the more sophisticated, when they came to observe the phenomenon, could not deny the flashing of the statue's eyes, and began to declare their belief in a spirit, though 'not guessing', as we are told, 'that there *was* a spirit there, and sound young flesh to boot'.

The explanation was that the sculptor, in some rather unexpected frenzy of morality, had forbidden all his apprentices to bring any 'light women' into his house or within its precincts. But one of them, Ascanio, a very young man, loved a handsome girl, who returned his passion. Eventually contriving to elude her mother, she came to see him one night. At his wits' end to know where to conceal her, he suddenly hit upon the stratagem of hiding her in the framework of the statue of Mars. He made up a place for her to sleep in within the head itself: a lodging which she occupied for some time. But during her inhabitation of the giant's head she could not prevent some of her movements to and fro from being perceptible through the open eyes of the statue, and so was at length discovered.

But though this actual life is usually absent, the impression produced by such a skyscraper of a statue must always be considerable, even when the detail of it compares poorly with that of works of a higher order and less size. Moreover, it is in its essence a very different one: to overawe, and not to please, is its object.

So diverse indeed must be the aims of the sculptor as he works on statues of varying scales that it is convenient for us to divide these frozen tribes into three orders: colossal, heroic and life-size. Further, of course, there is that diminutive and elfin variety to be found dancing in the gardens of Salzburg, posturing on the walls of the Villa Valmarana at Vicenza, peeping out of Gothic nooks in northern churches or stiffly at attention in the galleries of early Greek sculpture: such pygmies we prefer for the present to ignore.

The colossal statue is necessarily rarer than the others, and the greatest one ever projected was never carried out—that figure of a giant carrying a village in his hands into which Michelangelo wanted to carve a whole mountain of Carrara marble. The ingenious mind of Flaxman, too, later conceived a somewhat similar, but more strictly patriotic, project. His scheme was to make a statue of Britannia, two hundred feet high, and place it on Greenwich Hill. Of this conception, which was never realized, a contemporary critic wrote: 'Flaxman is not contented with cutting marble into man; he wishes to hew Greenwich Hill into a woman large enough to graze a couple of goats in her lap—gigantic dame, of whom we may say with Virgil:

Like Eryx, or like Athos, great she shows,
Or father Apennine, when white with snows,
Her head divine, obscure in clouds she hides,
And shakes the sounding forests on her sides.'

Such gigantic schemes are by their very nature liable to defeat. Yet there are more colossal statues than might be supposed. There are many Egyptian monuments of this order, gods, sphinxes and pharaohs; and prominent among its more modern exemplars, besides the Doria Admiral we have mentioned—now so cruelly cut off from the garden he was intended to dominate and which, indeed, he ruled for so long—is the image of San Carlo Borromeo that menaces Lake Como, and the formidable, star-spangled harridan that acclaims American liberty and guards the harbour of New York. Nearer home, too, there are some to the scale of which familiarity has blinded us. Thus, when passing Buckingham Palace one morning, it came with all the force of surprise, all the shock that descends on one who is the unwitting witness of a sacrilege, to perceive a workman standing balanced with one foot securely wedged in the left nostril of Queen Victoria, while he stretched up to clean unfeelingly an august and marble eyelid above him. Such is the race of giants that dwells among us unnoticed. Even the white, nude nymphs that, like undulating soles or turbots, are disporting themselves flatly in bas-relief round the pedestal of Her Majesty's effigy must be of no mean size or weight—fit subject for any fisherman's story. Her consort, too, under the dim and distant gilding of his canopy in Kensington Gardens, is of more than mortal stature.

Now we descend to the heroic type. To this order belong statues of such size as Michelangelo's 'David', or the 'Achilles' in Hyde Park. But the most beautiful and romantic of this sept, which exemplifies all its possibilities, is the kilted effigy of the

M   [177]

Emperor Heraclius, who yet stands outside the cathedral of Barletta in southern Italy. This is the perfect monument to a leader, an epitome of military vices and virtues. The slow, cruel smile contains in it an air of Napoleonic force and confidence, of absolute and wise command; the whole expression is that of a man born to rule, proud to use his power.

Passing from such heroes to our third tribe, we find a race of beings dependent, apparently, only on their esthetic qualities. But though they appear as our petrified brothers, yet they are larger than ourselves and are set up above us on pedestals. It is with this everyday world of Palmerstons, Gladstones and Havelocks, so much more fantastic in their dry realism than the hawk-faced gods of the Egyptians or the large-eared Easter-Island giants, that we are chiefly concerned. But before considering them in detail we must examine the descent of this frock-coated and arid crew, for only thus can we fully comprehend the interest, even of the meanest contemporary image, the latent suggestions of magic or godship which it contains. Indeed, the history of the statue runs close to that of man, and, however substantial, is the shadow by which it is possible to measure his achievement.

The relation between the sculptor and the form he creates is, more obviously than between any other kind of artist and his art, a parallel to that existing between God and Man. For this reason it is, that the imagination of the people has so often played with the possibility of the image thawing to life, of Galatea standing stiffly in the studio until one day a gentle breathing is distinguishable in the silence, and her body is seen to glow with the first delicate, pulsing agony of life. Certainly there has always clung to the art of the sculptor a suggestion of the two magics. In addition to the likeness of gods, saints and holy men that exhale an odour of divine inspiration, there are the little waxen effigies of those they hate,

which the wicked of every age have burnt, broken or stabbed
with needles: a practice that is the theme of so many medieval
ballads, and which persists openly in the East to this day.

In early times, then, the sculptor's aim was religious rather
than representational. He sought nothing less than to create a
God—for just as the child's first instinct is to play with a doll or
toy soldier, so the primitive man's first effort was to make a
God, not merely for his own protection and for the discom-
fiture of his enemies, but that he could evolve round this idol
a whole system of order and ceremony. If we wish to know how
primitive man looked, or wished to look, it is to the statues of
his gods that we must turn, for invariably he made God in his
own ideal image, whether it was the bestial gods of the Hittites
or the lovely, silly gods of the Greeks. Moreover, to create a
god was for the sculptor actually more easy than to portray
a man. Nobody could question the source of his inspiration
or remark: 'But I don't think that's a *bit* like him.'

As he became more consciously an artist, he could diverge
from his man-god ideal, and, if an oriental, could 'throw in'
the face of a cat or hawk, multiply the angular but whirling
arms; or, if a Greek, could attempt a deliberate improvement
upon Nature combined with some difficult essay in technique;
for in order to aid the balance, and to free the new smoothness
that he had achieved from rough marble, he would add, perhaps,
an extra, an inspirational, toe or finger, should he so desire.

But while one origin of sculpture can be traced undoubtedly
to the necessity of primitive man to worship something
concrete, another is to be found fast-rooted in his self-conceit:
a quality of which many may be proud, for it differentiates him
from the rest of the brute-creation. An animal, for example,
knows when he feels well, but hardly when he looks well;
nor has any other creature but man fancied himself to be of
sufficient importance ever to have wished to leave to his heirs

[179]

or to posterity a record of his physical appearance. As the sculptor then sorted the gods from the men, there arose among his fellows a new desire, to have their flesh and blood translated into a more permanent form: magic, again; for what was portraiture originally save a wish to attain a spurious immortality through mortal means?

Portraiture, as we see, originally budded in the sculptor's, not the painter's, art. Except with the Jews and kindred races —and who knows but that in their case God's commandment may have been prompted by an esthetic rather than a moral motive?—it now ceased to be an act of boastful blasphemy to have made of oneself a graven image. Thus the desire which prompted Narcissus to his epoch-making exploit was essentially human. Flatteringly struck into a flower, he was the first to wish for a record of his beauty, and the image that blossomed down into the pool was in a sense the first portrait-statue, while the punishment meted out to him did indeed bestow upon its victim a sweet and perennial permanence.

Yet, though in the Greek and Roman civilizations it was quite common to put up a statue to oneself in a house or garden, how rarely it is in the England of today that a man bequeathes to his heirs a full-length sculptural representation of himself. The modern prejudice against this particular vehicle of Narcissusism is perhaps due to its intimate connection with the effigies on tombs, for few men in these times have the courage to lift up the lids of their own coffins. Besides, as a medium for self-admiration, sculpture is as demoded as the pool. The mirror, the portrait-painter, the photographer, have all swarmed to the rescue of the new Narcissus, whom no such floral fate now overtakes. Recently, moreover, the cinema and television have come, to bring with them the possibility of harnessing his failings and converting them into a wholly admirable and very remunerative profession.

In the ancient world, however, sculpture was the only refuge for Narcissus, and its chief art. And soon the habit of statuary had spread from the luxurious private houses into the public thoroughfares. With the gradual sophistication of the Mediterranean races there arose everywhere, in street and forum, a stony-eyed crowd of toga'd mediocrities. While the library of each private house was littered with marble likenesses of the owner and the busts of his favourite philosophers, the market-places and the public-baths positively bristled with statues.

Even in the highest period of their art outburst, the Greeks appear to have been unable to arrange the lovely things they created. It was impossible, apparently, to see the Parthenon because of the buildings round it. Rome always exaggerated Grecian tendencies: and when commerce succeeded art, and the little cities in Greece, Italy and Egypt swelled into those elephantine communities of merchants and slaves of which the later Roman Empire was composed, it can be imagined how much this crowding was intensified. Everything was huddled together at haphazard and piled up in confusion, so that it was impossible to appreciate any one feature to the full or to form an adequate conception of the whole muddled array.

To understand this phase of city-life, it is best to study that series of frescoes removed from Pompeii to the Museo Nazionale at Naples, in which you may see both town and country as it was, but under a blue sky that eighteen hundred years of interment have turned to a livid green. There are portrayed cliffs that are now deep under the sea, lakes that are plains, cities which are little but dust upon the wind. These are a jumble of offices, skyscrapers and granaries for the slum-dwellers, arenas, temples and triumphal arches, crowned with quadrigas drawn by prancing horses and crowded with figures too full of action, while over and above the whole city swarm a host of statues, little statues and big statues, statues on horseback, statues on roof-tops, statues on pedestals, statues on pillars. High in the air rises a forest of debauched emperors, laconic generals, verbose senators, all standing like storks or stylites on their columns that grow near together as blades of grass.

Without a knowledge of the paintings from Pompeii, one cannot comprehend the forest-effect that these pillared forums bestow on a city, or how much there is to be said in favour of them as a method of 'skying' the famous. If a city is forced to teem with statues, as Rome yesterday or London today—and of the same sort of person—the majority of them will be bad art. It is, therefore, better for the citizen not to be compelled to examine the detail, not to be able to see the tree for the wood, but to move as though through a forest of marble pillars, warned of the existence of the gesticulating but static army above only by the slanting and grotesque shadows thrown down among them by the hot Roman face of the sun. Yet thus occasionally to be warned was salutary, for the host of Roman greatness that swarmed aloft was possessed of another beside its purely artistic purpose. In a startling and symbolic fashion this cloud of witnesses testified to the greatness of the age; its presence inspired later generations to emulate their ancestors, called on them to stem the rising floods of barbarism. Indeed, these over-life-size supermen were so venerated that their welfare and preservation were entrusted to a civil servant, specially appointed for the purpose. They were his sole care; and his office was considered one of the most honourable and responsible in the government of Rome. Gibbon describes this official as the 'guardian of that inanimate people'.

To such an extent had this overhead population multiplied that it had in truth reached the dimensions of a 'people'. Cassiodorus, the last senator, so often and tediously described as the 'last Roman', speaks of the enormous quantity of statues and the immense number of stone and marble horses that still stood in the city of his day. Alas, the streets of Rome were before long to show more statues than people.

It is easy to imagine how this patrician order of being, their limbs composed of pure white marble or travertine stone, must have impressed the Roman citizen of that epoch, summing up for him more than anything else, and in a material way—the only one which he could appreciate—that grand estate from which he had fallen. The Roman blood had long been vitiated by the strain of a slave and slum population, and the dark, disconsolate and slothful little heir of so much greatness, as he wandered among the mute mob of statues that everywhere surrounded him or idly climbed up the winding and now rickety stairs within one of the bronze columns that supported the celestial majesty of the old emperors, to gaze on their stern countenances, could measure his own decadence by matching his puny physique, his weak, amiable but cunning features, against their giant frames, their resolute jaws and decisive noses. Yet Civilization, however decadent, was safe as long as those statues stood there to protect. With the overturning of them Western man renounced his birthright.

This first great experiment had failed. The old world began to perish: Gods and great men, poets and philosophers as much as generals or statesmen, were now lying face downward, slowly sinking into the earth, or were shattered into fragments. The broad, broken streets were becoming overgrown, as though an oblivion that was tangible and concrete were silently stealing upon them. Many a marble and stone arm could be seen raised imploringly from this tangle of weeds and wilderness of vine and creeper. As for the great sea-board cities, the blue of the Mediterranean became all the more intense for its new paving of parian limbs, and deep down

below, in a misguided search for food, huge silver fishes—
fishes that flashed through the transparency like a knife—
goggled at the hard, deceptive flesh and poked it angrily with
their beaks that were long and sharp as swords. Nevertheless,
this dumb and massacred host, dying away into the earth or
being swallowed up by the ocean, was in reality but awaiting
resurrection, destined to come forth again and to be the
progenitor of hordes still more infinite in number.

Soon, though, this solid army of statues had vanished, one
would have presumed, altogether and for ever, superseded as
guardians of learning, heirs of the past and prophets of the
future, by little groups of monks. These dwelt equally high
up in the air, but huddled in the twilight on hillside-ledges and
on mountain-tops rather than braving the full light each on a
column, while their limbs, far from flashing nakedly in the
sun, were concealed absolutely, swaddled in coarse, rough
clothing. Packed closely in their monasteries, they illuminated
their missals, and with a rare impartiality copied out Greek
love-poems and Latin scientific treatises just as laboriously as
they transcribed the beloved evidences of their own ascetic
faith.

In time their labour bore fruit, and a new light dawned.
Once more there were books, fine furniture and pictures in
houses of carved and intricate design. But the order of statues
that evolved was again at first restricted to religion. Idols
and images gleamed with a golden fervour behind their screen
of flickering candles, while the stiff effigies of knights and
ladies—ideal and hieratic creations—lay on their stone backs,
side by side, with their heavy gauntlets still holding the swords
of the Crusades. Only in the south, one or two favoured statues,
forgotten altogether or become the object of legend, still stood
where they had always stood, supposed to be the creation of
wizard and magician. And these now became the centre of a

renewed interest; artists and sculptors looked at them with curiosity, measured and observed. But now, as the light became day, and the Renaissance proclaimed itself, out of their damp and mildewed hiding-places a million statues leapt up like white flames to greet it. Every foot of the ancient soil teemed once more as this frozen mob fought its way back to life. So easy were these hidden armies to unearth, that the Borghese princes, who three times suffered the sack of their villa and the theft of those antique statues with which house and grounds were plentifully embellished, after each occasion were able to replace them merely by digging in their garden. The whole ground of the southern countries now showed itself to be strewn and littered with limbs of stone and marble, as though long ago rival forces of these immortals, their fury for a moment endowing them with movements, had engaged in ferocious contest, while yet the number of those uninjured, merely left motionless on the field, was so beyond counting that not only did every prince and noble fill his palace with them, but special barracks, or, as we call them, museums, had to be constructed for their internment: and there to the present day these hordes are to be seen, frozen and solitary and soundless, enclosed by four walls—a fate so little intended for them that they seem, in these dim rooms, spectres that materialize only to startle us.

This repopulation of the modern by the antique world continued for centuries, and though it need not be pretended that the larger groups of statues, which now writhe in the galleries of Naples and the Vatican, are the most beautiful, it must be admitted that to our forefathers the most sensational discoveries must have been the 'come-back' of that genial circus-giant, the Farnese Hercules, from his thousand-year retirement, the reappearance of the Laocoön, and the emergence of those various quadriga-groups in which wheels, horses, chariots and drivers are for ever wrapped in a confusion of whirling marble. The culminating point was undoubtedly reached after several hundred years with the distressing excavation of Pompeii, which in its turn exercised so baneful an effect on European sculpture and painting.

In the meantime, alongside this growing host of ancient and broken statues, there had been called into existence a competing army of modern ones, their children. Gods and goddesses, nymphs, satyrs and shepherds, soon found themselves postured in green enclosures of ilex, box and running water. To this confined and miniature Paradise was the mythological system of the antique world now condemned. But garden statues are an order by themselves. While the great of other days were thus prisoned in their green captivity, every city in southern Europe was determined to celebrate its contemporary great: in Italy, especially, the smallest towns were filled once more with heroes trampling on satyrs, bristled with a whole system of petty and mundane tyrants in the self-decreed guise of demi-gods. Even today one or two of these ruffed and verdigrised commanders are to be seen in the piazzas of the little cities of central Italy, places such as Cremona, Mirandola and Piacenza. Usually they are shown with ruffs, breastplates and pointed beards; their legs armoured, a lance or sceptre in one hand. To this clan does the statue of the 'Commendador' in the opera *Don Juan* belong. And, with his birth, this beautiful, if grotesque, conception enters into an art and moment greater than its own, for that dreadful instant when Mozart makes us hear the huge figure stiffly clanking and creaking up the stairs in answer to Don Juan's drunken invitation is assuredly the very zenith and climax of European music.

35

ON STATUES IN LONDON

THE armoured warriors, in bronze and stone, gradually extending their conquests northward, were installed in the market-places of Germany, France and the Netherlands. And then, after a long and tedious crossing, a representative of the sept found himself in England. In those times a man, if he were fortunate, spent twenty-four hours in journeying from Calais to Dover. Proportionately, it took an idea in art or literature one hundred and fifty years to travel from its home in Italy to this distant outpost. Thus the statue of King Charles I is, though a century and a half later in date, a relative of those bronze tyrants we have described, just as the monarch himself in his patronage of the arts and in his theory of government was akin to those iconic beings they represented. From his time onward, London furnishes us with all we need in the way of public monuments. As the cold religious fervour of the Puritans conquered England, the images which were being hurled out of the churches began, instead, to adopt lay costume and strike prouder attitudes in the market-place. On such a rude space, cleared in the wilderness of gabled, over-topping houses, and full as yet of rustic speech that well accorded with the warm lowing of cattle and the timid bleating of sheep, this aristocratic posturing produced so civilizing an influence that it soon acquired a new development and became a square, silent save for the pattering of running footmen or the rattle of coaches.

It is thus impossible to write of the London statue without a word as to the evolution, so intimately connected with it, of the London square; for that ordered but haphazard architectural arrangement, so typical and delightful a feature of our city, arose, as though preordained, to set off to perfection by its railed garden or green lawn the monarch, general or statesman who adorns it.

It was the fourth Earl of Bedford who, in a moment of inspiration, determined to evoke a 'piazza' on the Italian model in the centre of London, and for the carrying out of this noble but exotic caprice very happily chose Inigo Jones. The site selected for their enterprise was that upon which now stands Covent Garden Market. Doubtless it had been intended to lay out a paved and arcaded square, with a fountain in the middle, and perhaps with one or two of those statues at the end of it—on tall, wide-topped pillars (the ancestry of which, like that of our own Nelson and Duke of York columns, can be traced in direct line to the Roman forums) that are often so pleasant an evidence in a town of its former possession by the Venetians. It was to be a piazza, with a theatre, I apprehend, rather than a cathedral, as its focus. The character of London, however, and the genius of our greatest architect were too vehement to allow of any such dry copying. Instead of the frozen Italian importation that had been intended, there emerged, albeit always known as the 'Piazza', the first London square. This square boasted arcades which, though rebuilt and modified, to this day survive as a reminder of its descent and origin.

This new building experiment was celebrated in countless Restoration comedies, in which at least one scene, leading up to various misunderstandings, encounters and unmaskings, opens with a rendezvous under the arcades of the Piazza at Covent Garden. Indeed, the Piazza soon became notorious as a place of intrigue and assignation. The masked figures who strolled thus anonymously under its arches attempted all too successfully to reproduce the free or, as some thought, licentious atmosphere of Venice. And among many such meetings it was here or near by that Charles II met Nell Gwynne selling her oranges; an adventure perpetuated for us by a certain ducal family and, less intimately, by the beauty of the Royal Chelsea Hospital.

Once the Piazza had been built, the London square, as we know it, rapidly developed. St James's Square was one of the first. Then came Cavendish and Kensington squares to represent the early years of the eighteenth century, the Bloomsbury squares to represent a mutilated and uncertain middle epoch, Portman Square and Fitzroy Square, most beautiful of all, to embody those new views of architecture lately brought back from Dalmatia by the Brothers Adam, that little square in Chiswick, eyrie of so many stucco eagles, to illustrate an English Empire style, and finally Belgrave Square to sum up the last shoddy influence of decadent Italy—for, if you walk round it and examine the fog-coloured houses, you will notice that, though signed buildings are rare in London, one of them bears, to this day, at the side of its pillared portico the signature of the Italian architect who made it: 'George Basevi, Architect, 1827.'

Of all these squares, the best is St James's, where houses railings, garden and statue are equally appropriate and at their best. Yet the charming statue of King William III, which graces this square, and seems to contain in it every feature that belongs to the seventeenth century, was not made before the beginning of the nineteenth. It was erected in 1808, though the pedestal, on which the bronze horse now tramples, had stood there empty and unechoing for over a century.

But each of these squares, besides the old trees and lawns common to all of them, has its own charms of garden and decoration; displays a statue, a fountain, a classic vase or Chinese pavilion mounted like a jewel on its green-velvet cushion: while the railings that hedge and fence off each oasis offered the English an unparalleled opportunity for indulging their national vice of revelling in railings—though very nice railings they often are. Nowhere else in the world are such miles and miles of expensive and needless metal to be found. Indeed, one is almost tempted to think that the wealth of England, due to her supremacy in the iron trade, must have been founded on the insane demand on the part of her own people for this metal, out of which to make their railings. And yet these spikes and knobs are not here quite so unnecessary as one might suppose, for there have been many mysterious disappearances among London statues. Orderly as is her population, several have changed their places and others have been wafted away in a night, never to reappear.

Right up till after the construction of Belgrave Square, the tradition of railing, garden and statue continued; but with the 'Landseering' of Trafalgar Square it ceased. This national possession, know by name in every country, became merely an asphalt dumping-ground for bad statues. And as though to emphasize the degradation of our present condition, we are here within sight of the equestrian statue of King Charles I, and within a few yards' walk of Grinling Gibbons's King James II, two of the most beautiful monuments in London.

These, father and son, illustrate for us the fact that a fashion had already been established in men's statues as much as in their clothes—and, further, that the art of sculptural effigy was much influenced by costume and even by the contemporary manner of hairdressing. No two beings could be made to appear more unlike each other, and something must here be said of King James's dress. It is with him, and with his elder brother, also carved by Gibbons, that we reach the second great cosmopolitan fashion in statues. The Emperor Charles V was the first to adopt this Caesarian affectation of laurels, sceptre and abbreviated toga, and so swiftly did it spread over Europe as the 'correct gent's wear' for statues of monarchs and reigning princes that it reached London within 120 years of starting, a record journey for those days. Further, it is in the statues of Charles II and James II that we find the first emergence into English art of the toga, a garment which was yet to furnish another and much more strange compromise.

During the nineteenth century these laureate statues of the Stuarts were entirely condemned, characterized as 'stilted and unreal'. Yet it was this later age, which gave birth to those extraordinary toga'd figures with which, since they still form the main bulk of our stone population and dominate absolutely our great cities, this essay must be chiefly concerned. Indeed, from the opening of King William IV's reign until the close of Queen Victoria's, our statues proved themselves quite as prolific as the nineteenth-century Englishman: while now, with the declining birth-rate of the English, they threaten to follow the example of their Roman ancestors and positively to outnumber us.

But to understand how it was possible to put into the field—or rather into the city—this great army of nineteenth-century worthies, who can still be seen thus solidly disporting themselves on pedestals of an altogether incredible appropriateness, we must first a little retrace our steps.

[191]

Even in early Stuart times, then, the days of the old anonymous religious carvers were long over, and in their place reigned the makers of effigies and likenesses, of whom the best and first was Nicholas Stone. With the Restoration, statuary had taken a new turn towards prosperity. Busts and effigies were now, from being a luxury, a necessity of the rich. Soon to have one's own bust, with a periwig, in the parlour, or the gracefully reclining effigies of one's parents on a tomb, became a rage, a frenzy, and the output of the successful artist was not enough to keep pace with the fashionable demand.

Throughout the second half of the eighteenth century the tendency towards employing assistants increased, until each English studio became a factory, where the 'hands', young statuaries, did the work, and the famous artist supplied only the hallmark of the style he had made his own. Far from the work of so many assistants making their productions in any sense anonymous, it had the very opposite effect, strengthened the tendency towards stylization and mannerism. The output of each studio must be feverishly different, able to be recognized at a glance as the works of Banks, Flaxman or Chantrey. Moreover, size, vast size, became the object of ambition, a gigantic tomb, covered with trophies and crowded with allegories, the highest prize any firm of sculptors could carry off. For firms they now were. Sculpture had become a trade, the sculptor's studio must rather have resembled a shipbuilding yard, full of fragments of metal and timber and scaffolding, upon which crept little men, working on huge shapes that towered up into the gloom like figureheads. Yet, in spite of such methods, there flourished during these times sculptors as truly great as Roubiliac and John Bacon.

In this last sculptor we find the essence of the age, of the art and the processes by which it was carried on. The son of a poor cloth-worker, he was born in 1741 and died in the

[192]

ultimate year of the century. At first he was employed in painting figures on plates and dishes, then took to clay models for pottery figures, and finally became a sculptor. Unfortunately his works are too numerous, and are still further cheapened by the countless artistic progeny of his son and namesake, who altogether lacked his talent. For with all the ridiculous faults and failings of his lesser works, in his best, such as the monument of Guy in the chapel of Guy's Hospital, are to be found a grace, humanity and dignity that fall but little below genius. Just as he was the best business man of our sculptors, so was he the best sculptor of our business men.

Bacon actually invented a pointing instrument which had great effect in making easier the efforts of the sculptor's ghosts, so that inferior apprentices could henceforth be employed with safety. From this time forward modelling showed a steady deterioration, for when the statuaries, who, whatever their errors of taste, were masters, like Bacon and Chantrey, had passed away, the art was altogether in the hands of these feeble and untrained assistants. But what was thus lost, perhaps, in his art, was made up for in the mystery that attended Bacon's proceedings, and even his assistants were banned from the laboratories of his artistic alchemy. A few years later, however, the sense of mystery was dispersed by Westmacott and Chantrey, who, in an effort to attract people through an exactly contrary method, threw open their foundries to the public and there exhibited the casting of colossal statues twelve feet high. Bacon had rapidly become popular, though not with his fellow-artists as much as with the public. Banks and Flaxman charged his art with 'the want of antique feeling', and the sculptor, we are told, 'had little consolation save in his own good opinion of his works, supported by the almost general voice of the country'.

Concerning a sculptor's chance of making money, he lived

in an ideal age. So great was the rage for monuments, so large, fortunately, the number of deaths from patriotic causes, that for an artist with a name the field was limitless. Not content, however, with such opportunities, John Bacon actually attempted to extract a monopoly out of the Ministry, offering to execute each commission for them at a rate slightly under that of any of his rivals, on condition that he became the sole purveyor of allegorical figures to His Majesty's Government. In this spirited effort he failed, but, nevertheless, was in a good way of business. 'His studio was filled with commissions; his banker respected him for the weight of his deposit . . . and the India Company, seeing his shares in their company increase, thought that a sculptor who was at once eminent in art and strong in Eastern interest, might be employed in recording in marble the actions of their heroes.'

Thus Cunningham, who worshipped Chantrey above all other sculptors, and describes Bacon's style as 'unique and uniform, something elaborate and ostentatious, the postures a little affected—the action ambitious, the draperies graceful but redundant'. And here is his description of some of Bacon's best-known works: 'Truth tramples on Falsehood, and Honour presents the insignia of the Garter, in the monument of Lord Halifax, whose bust stands in the centre. Britannia places one hand on the medallion of Sir George Pocock, and with the other shakes a thunderbolt over the ocean where that eminent commander was so long a ruler. A figure of "Poetry" bends over the head of Mason the poet and laments his loss.'

It is clear that in addition to being religious, Bacon was both sensible and amusing. It can have been no easy task for him to devise these countless allegories, even for men who were remarkable in themselves as much as in their histories, but what was he to do in the matter of invention when he must celebrate men of dull intellect and no achievement, whose perfect punctuality and moderate but regular income were their chief virtues? 'On one occasion,' Cunningham relates, 'in the absence of Bacon, an order for a monument was left with the person who conducted his business: the sculptor, on being informed of it, said: "Well, in memory of a private gentleman? —and what price was mentioned?" "Three hundred pounds, sir." "Three hundred pounds—a small bas-relief will do—was he a benevolent man? You enquired that, I hope?" "Yes, sir. He was benevolent. He always gave sixpence, they said, to an old woman who opened his pew on a Sunday." "That will do—that will do—we must have recourse to our old friend the Pelican." ' Great, indeed, must have been the temptation sometimes to leave 'the Pelican' to his assistants!

However, these mystical fowls were prolific and paid well, for at his death, at the age of fifty-eight, he left to his family the sum of £60,000—a considerable fortune even for a sculptor in the eighteenth century.

Thus was the field prepared for the great mass of public statues to be turned out in the course of the new century. The studios were full and large, ready to undertake work of any description, the masters dead, the apprentices incompetent. This was the condition of affairs responsible for the birth of that whiskered and fantastic sept, one of which can be found in any town or village in England, disporting himself in a toga with a solid pomposity that declares a conviction of his own worth.

With Waterloo, a great change had come over Europe. Our country had finally tested the theory it had maintained for so long—that genius could always be defeated in the end by a combination of money, 'common' sense and obstinacy; in fact, that the genius of a people, successfully interpreted, would always triumph over the genius of a person, however much greater he might be individually than those pitted

[195]

against him. Other nations learnt the lesson. The world, it seemed, was now for ever made safe for plutocracy, and its ideals, religion and materialism. The whole wealth of the five continents passed as tribute through Victorian England. Nor was this all the riches that her triumph achieved. It had long been said that the streets of London were paved with gold, but now, as though a prize delivered by Providence itself for good behaviour, it was discovered that the streets of Sheffield, Leeds, Manchester, Newcastle, Durham and countless other provincial cities had all the time, and without their good citizens knowing it, been paved with coal and iron . . . so infinitely more discreet than gold, less 'showy' and yet at the same time more auriferous. Thus was a whole people bribed by Fate to reject that wave of new-fangled revolution that had threatened to sweep Europe.

But though the middle classes had to be paid in the solid cash of manufactures, the workman was foolish enough to be satisfied with payment by ideas. Just as a savage might be content to work for the glittering bribe of a bead necklace, a Sheffield knife or a penny whistle, so the English workman was first overcome by talk of the Vote—so scintillating a bauble, it seemed to him, that he was content for many years to work merely for the thought of it—and then, finally, by the actual gift of this strange weapon.

In a miraculously short time our country had adapted itself to the age it had created. Enough money passed through the England of the nineteenth century to have paid for cities of an unequalled beauty, to have bequeathed to the next age palaces, parks and gardens for the worker as much as for the owner. Instead, the old beauties, everywhere denounced as uneconomic or insanitary, were levelled to the ground, and there was nothing to put in their stead but these grotesque statues of which we speak. The adult workman, however, was too wrapped up and happy in the thought of his vote (equivalent to being given a latchkey at the age of twenty-one), his children too busy being sent down the newly opened mines, grinding away long hours in a factory, or being used as the living brushes of the chimney-sweep, to resent the changes or to regret the opportunity which they were thus losing. . . .

London, alone of all the great English cities, contrived to retain through the increasing yellowness and blackness of its fogs a certain and almost incommunicable quality of dingy grace. But for the child of poor parents in a rich provincial town there was nothing to indicate that such things as beauty or the arts had ever existed. No intelligence was visible there save that of Skinflint and Gradgrind. Architecture, sculpture, painting and books lay hidden away out of sight of this wilderness of gaslit houses, in the windows of which an occasional fern, dying for want of air and sunlight, asserted the pathetic claim of its owner to belong to a race bred of open fields and woodlands. Very seldom a concert, perhaps, would call them to a miserable realization that there might be other gods than iron and industry, other pleasures than football-field and whippet . . . and then, too, there were those legendary figures, hard-faced supermen of the golden age, striking their heroic but modest attitudes, prudishly clasping the marble toga in its place with one hand, as though it were a towel and they fresh and rosy from the bath, while in the other clenched fist they grasp the long roll of a folded speech, which apparently they are on the point of delivering, their lips already parted, their tongues already rolling over in secret the Latin tags and trite quotations, as though they were so many sweet pebbles in the mouth of a thirsty man.

The wealth of Greece has left us her treasures of sculpture, that of Rome, her baths, aqueducts and public buildings, that of Venice, her exquisite palaces and canals, that of France, at least the gardens of Versailles. But here in the realms of outward art only these thousands of fabulous, remote and incomprehensible figures survive in every square and market-place as the representatives of the English century of triumph, of a wealth that was boundless, beyond any dreams of past ages, sufficient for the creation of streets, squares and houses of matchless beauty.

Moreover, it is possible to estimate the character of this cultured age by the nature of the men it celebrated: never, scarcely, a musician, poet, painter or philosopher, but, instead, the inventors of engines and spinning-jennies, politicians and contractors, aldermen and plumbers, while its bump of veneration is attested by the invariable sprinkling and admixture of Royalty and the nobility, and towards the end, as it died away in a cheap flash of bloody [sic] imperialism, by the eruptions of scarlet generals on prancing horses that broke out in every city.

We must now consider more minutely the reason that made this toga-effect once so popular and necessary. Its causes were several: there was the conscious but muddled sense which we have attempted to sum up, that Britain was, as a state, the Rome of the modern world, with Queen Victoria as both its Boadicea and Vestal Virgin. Therefore was the toga considered appropriate to the age.

Then, too, a profound and delightful misunderstanding of antique statuary caused the most debased Roman copies to be mistaken for Greek works of the best period, to be held in high repute and copied. Moreover, patriotism assured the country that it was heir to the antique world as much in art as in arms—but heir of a world purged of idolatry, its somewhat unfortunate and twisted moral code straightened out, and for ever purified by the adoption of petticoat and trouser. Yet the trouser, sculptors felt, was more for drawing-room than for

[198]

pedestal. What was to be done? Thus, too, it can be seen, the sculptured toga was in part the result of an impassioned and quite justified desire to keep trousers out of art. Even more— and this is the fourth and most important reason—was it due to a desire to repel and banish an undesirable and alien nudity. Such fashions, they averred (and here, for once, public opinion concurred with that of the *cognoscenti*), might be suitable for flighty foreigners, mushroom princes and their like, but even for the five royal sons of George III such treatment appeared rather 'advanced' and unsuitable, while for English statesmen and bankers it was patently absurd. In addition, it might insinuate into the mind of the democracy a queer and quite mistaken notion of its rulers.

This pagan glorification of the body was founded on the gospel of Winckelmann, and it must be admitted that English artistic and religious opinion was—however unconsciously— right in opposing it. The productions to which it led—always, be it understood, apart from those of Canova—were more often than not deplorable. At first this unfrocking was confined more to allegorical figures than to effigies of persons. Thomas Banks, R.A., the 'poetic sculptor'—at once one of the very best and very worst of English sculptors—was perhaps the first Englishman to imbibe and express this doctrine. After working in Rome, Banks was employed for a lengthy period by the Empress Catherine, who presumably had no prejudice against nudity as such, working at Petrograd and Tsarsky-Seloe. The chief commission which the Tsarina entrusted to him was one for a large marble group to represent 'Armed Neutrality'! After this adventure the sculptor returned to London and was elected an R.A. He made a very good beginning with the British public, for in the august galleries of the Academy he exhibited an effigy even more pathetic than that of 'Armed Neutrality'. The inscription on it ran: 'To Penelope, only child of Sir Brooke and Dame Susannah Boothby, born April 11: 1785, died March 13: 1791. She was in form and intellect most excellent. The unfortunate parents ventured their all in this frail bark, and the wreck was total.' Cunningham says: 'The exhibition of this touching work occasioned much sensation in Somerset House. It was placed in the middle of the room, and obtained the notice of hundreds of mothers —the queen and the princesses stood looking at it for some time and were affected to tears.' So far, so good. But a few years later Banks was entrusted with the making of three monuments: to Sir Eyre Coote in Westminster Abbey and to Captains Westcott and Burgess in St Paul's Cathedral. The last two gentlemen were sailors, the first being killed on the Nile, the second in the battle of Camperdown. The monument to Sir Eyre Coote had been ordered by the East India Company, the others by the 'Committee of Taste for His Majesty's Government'. Of these creations, Cunningham informs us: 'There are no crowds of figures and emblems; all is plain and simple—yet with so few figures no sculptor ever contrived to give more offence. The two naval officers are naked, which destroys historic probability; it cannot be a representation of what happened, for no British warriors go naked into battle, or wear sandals or Asiatic mantles. . . . Having offended alike the lovers of poetry and the lovers of truth, he next gave offence to certain grave divines.' In short, Captain Burgess's drapery had to be lengthened.

Banks died in 1805, by which time such scantiness had been forgiven. Indeed, he was one of the first sculptors to be commemorated by a tablet in the Abbey. Two years before the demise of this artist, Prince Hoare wrote in a tone of triumph: 'A competition with the fine forms and beautiful outlines of the antique statues has banished the vitiated outlines of Puget's and Bernini's school.'

[200]

It appeared that the new mode must win, for in the meantime Napoleon's upstart princes and princesses had popularized this regrettable, if classical, fashion. In Rome the Emperor's sister, Pauline Borghese, had sat naked and unashamed to Canova, her statue boasting no drapery save that of her curls. Then in painting there were pictures of Murat's siege of Capri, in which the young Prince, his son and Napoleon's nephew, is shown without clothing of any description. Further, there were coins and vases bearing the image of this youth, boasting the same abandoned grace of body. Indeed, it seemed as if the more crowns the Buonapartes put on, the more clothing they took off. In Parma and Lucca, where there were soon to be similar princely statues, even the old régime was infected. The Duchess of Alba, too, had sat to Goya in the most unducal state of nakedness. Apart from other objections to such modes, the English climate would have prevented its spreading so far northward. Sitting under such conditions in an English studio would be both unpleasant and perilous to the constitution of the sitter. Even Rome was hardly hot enough for it.

Allan Cunningham, writing apropos of Flaxman in 1830, says: 'To the heathen sculptors, who represented their gods and heroes naked, anatomical and geometrical knowledge was much more necessary than to Christian Artists, who trust to mental expression and cover their figures with draperies. He who is acquainted with the general principles of anatomy knows enough to enable him to make a statue now, for the greater delicacy of our religion demands a costume which conceals all the muscular detail on which the ancients prided themselves; and the purer taste of the world forbids those statues and groups which, in their naked loveliness and vigour, were the delight of the Greeks.' Some conception of the difference between this respectable English ideal of sculpture and the one that reigned abroad is to be gained by a comparison of the work of the talented Flaxman with that of the genius Canova. Yet even in England the revived classicism for a time held its own, and attempted to sweep away the barriers of drapery. Benjamin Haydon, as pious as any painter that ever lived, apparently unable to start on a picture without praying for help and guidance, and for the sense of piety that should be infused into the HIGH ART OF THE NEW GOLDEN AGE, notes, in 1836, of a lecture: 'I told them all if they did not get rid of every feeling of indelicacy in seeing the naked form . . . taste for Grand Art would never be rooted amongst them.' He toured the country, lecturing and exhibiting naked wrestlers to the British public, in the provinces as much as in the capital. This perilous and subversive movement must, too, have made some headway, for, four years later, he writes: 'I have lectured on the naked model in London, in Edinburgh and Manchester, and lately had wrestlers to struggle before 1,500 people at Liverpool, with immense approbation.'

But British common sense again triumphed. For example, when, in 1830, Mr. Huskisson, leader of the Commons, met his death by being run over by the first steam-engine, it was felt to be inappropriate to represent him, in the monument that was to be erected to his memory, addressing a drowsy House in the likeness of a Greek athlete, however much such an invention would beautify the statue. Yet the Classic Age had come; trousers were 'taboo', so a compromise was, as always in England, adopted. The toga was taken as a convenient classical garment but lengthened a little for propriety's sake, and was given a more probable, more usual, air by being made on the model of a large bath-towel. Tombs and every sort of monument now rejected cupids and winged allegories and boasted instead a strict but variable affectation of the antique. Thus it will be seen that these toga'd statues of the early nineteenth century may be said to sum up to perfection the English virtues of their day (for national virtues are not immutable)—cleanliness, respectability and a love of public-speaking—that is to say, the bath-toga stands for cleanliness, the hand holding it in place for respectability, the folded speech for oratory. About them, however grotesque and occasionally repulsive, there is a sense of recognized infallibility, of financial integrity and benevolent, almost American, bullying, which still lingers on in the murky, yet comparatively soot-free, air of an impoverished England like the echo of 'Rule, Britannia' on a salty breeze.

Moreover, since this was the century of good fortune to our country, by an indescribable stroke of luck, just as these statues were being turned out by the thousand, Aberdeen granite was discovered to complete their effect: such a coincidence as must inculcate in us all the doctrine that each person gets what he deserves. Just as Swan was conjured up out of the void of words for Edgar, and Sankey leapt up to greet Moody, so it was with this porphyry of the north. Actually, we believe, the world had been cognizant of the brutal medium for several centuries; but not until 1801 had the technical processes been perfected by which so meaty and everlasting a substance could attain to that state of oily polish which interpreted, in such an accurate manner, the hardness, complacency and hypocrisy of contemporary commerce and politics. Only of Aberdeen granite could be wrought the appropriate setting for such artistic jewels.

Alas, Aberdeen granite was soon to be used for a more esthetic, yet even more perverted, purpose! Harmonious as it was as an accompaniment for leaden statesmen and generals, it was scarcely suited as a vehicle for all the gothic panoply of trefoils, quatrefoils, pinnacles, pointed windows, coats of arms, imps and angels that were now once more on their way

back to earth, to the strains of harmoniums playing Sterndale
Bennett's anthems, but filtered through the very feminine, if
fiery, mind of John Ruskin. The brief blossoming of our
truncated and well-draped classicism, purged though it was of
pagan ideals, purified and respectable as it had endeavoured
to be, perished at his touch as though consumed by hell-fire.
Piety and handicraft had henceforth to enter into the making
of gas-works, brewery and sewage-farm as much as into the
fashioning of a church effigy or a stained-glass window. With
the flowering of the Albert Memorial, that wistful, unique
monument of widowhood, the new movement reached an
unlooked-for climax. It is the highest point to which we could
attain in that direction. And, in all seriousness, that gilded and
pensive giant, on his dais, under the gothic canopy, strewn with
the white, mosaic daisies of a blameless life, has certain elements
of a beauty that is not altogether literary or confined to the
mirroring of an absurd epoch.

Ill-suited as we may conceive Aberdeen granite to have
been for the expression of the gothic spirit, yet it was at this
very period that peculiar stress was laid upon 'appropriateness'
as a quality of art. In indication of this, we can give the
following story. Queen Victoria's secretary wrote to John
Gibson, then resident in Rome, commanding him to send in
a drawing of the Rape of Europa, as H.M. wished him to
execute it as one of the numerous embellishments at the base
or corners of the monument, then in the course of construction,
to her Consort. The sculptor, who possessed, apparently, a
sense of humour, at once wrote back a letter addressed to the
Queen herself, asking her to pardon his temerity in pointing
out that the choice of subject was hardly suitable to the memory
of such a Prince and such a husband. Her Majesty, impressed
by this argument, and gratified that the perpetration of so
grave an error of taste had been prevented by the foresight of

the artist, at once wrote him a letter of thanks in her own hand-writing, and suggested as substitute for the offending, some other subject, of her own choosing, such as 'Learning yielding to Modesty'. Though ill-health compelled him to refuse the commission, Gibson was ever after much in the royal favour.

Appropriateness was once more to give way to fantasy. The Victoria Memorial, with its fat, floating mermaids and adipose, underclothed children, so unsuited to the remarkable Queen it celebrates, registers, as compared with the Albert Memorial, a sad deterioration, in this respect as much as in art and execution. But what could be done? Huge sums of money had been collected, hundreds of thousands of pounds must be spent and something that looked extremely expensive must positively be delivered to the public. Tons of allegorical females in white wedding-cake marble, with whole litters of their cretinous children, had, therefore, to be 'thrown in' with the gigantic effigy of the late Queen, beside water-nymphs and fountains, until the whole affair grew into a work that, if decorated with coloured candles, would be a source of justi-fiable pride to a firm of wedding-cake caterers, but is a disgrace to all the sculptors or contractors concerned in it. But even after every possible form of expensive accessory had been lavished on the thing, enough money was left over from the fund to spoil Buckingham Palace by covering over the old Blore façade, with its comic sky-line groups, and by refacing it with a mean, silly and pretentious Portland-stone front—the first and most dastardly act in what we may conveniently term the 'anti-Nash' hostilities, that culminated in the destruc-tion of Regent Street.

The art of public monuments, however, was to fall yet further. But before we approach more nearly to the present and the future, it would perhaps be courteous to address a few words of sincere commiseration to our Indian fellow-sufferers. If, between the Battle of Waterloo and the Boer War, the statues in England multiplied more swiftly even than the population, that at least was our own affair, of our own choice, however regrettable. Moreover, the persons represented were usually of our own blood, or, if not, had at any rate been adopted and set up there of our own free-will. Every sect and every party finds in English statues its stone or leaden champion. No voter is unrepresented. With an appalling impartiality we erect statues to Charles I and Cromwell, James II and William III, Pitt and Fox, Gladstone and Beaconsfield, thus honouring for each side the criminal as much as the hangman. If we are forced to wince at the result, we at least pay lightly the penalty of our own misdemeanours. But what excuse can be made to our Indian brothers for the ugly infamy that we forced upon their country?

Just as throughout the latter part of the eighteenth century India had been the paradise of the greedy fortune-seeker, so it was now to become the dumping-ground of the needy sculptor. There were to be nabobs of the arts as well as of commerce, and nabobs as much convinced of their own innocence and purity of purpose as ever was Warren Hastings. Mrs Damer, the fair sculptor—the cousin to whom Horace Walpole left Strawberry Hill for life—was the pioneer in this direction. A great hero-worshipper, she was, says Cunningham, 'far from confining her enthusiasm to those of her own blood. Fox was her hero in the House of Commons—Napoleon her hero on land—and Nelson her hero on sea. Admiration is too weak a word to express what she felt—she absolutely adored them.' Alas, later, at seventy-odd years of age, 'her heroes had all departed; Fox had followed Nelson to the tomb; the star of Napoleon had set for ever; and there remained none save the sons of little men, whom she considered unworthy of her hand. But the longer she lived, sculpture rose higher and higher in her estimation. . . . She had contemplated it as the auxiliary of government in Greece; she had seen it the handmaid of religion in Italy; and, turning her thoughts to the East, she conceived that her art might be made the chosen instrument of civilization and improvement there. . . . She conceived the design of substituting European and Christian subjects for those innumerable idols whom the natives adore. Understanding that the Rajah of Tanjore . . . had introduced civilization and science into his dominions, she resolved to aid him in his philanthropic attempts, and accordingly made a bronze bust of Nelson, whose victory of the Nile had given security to the British Empire in India. . . . But this was nothing compared to what she contemplated doing for our brethren in the East. The head of Nelson was but the first of a series of the busts of heroes and statues of kings which she proposed to set up in place of those false gods who had so long misled the people of India. . . . She did not live to make the experiment.'[1] Nevertheless, this remarkable woman was eighty years of age when she died! In her will she directed that her working-apron, hammers, drills, chisels and modelling tools should be laid with her in her coffin; perhaps a rebuke from the tomb to those spiteful persons who, during her lifetime, had unkindly insinuated that the works she displayed as her own were, in reality, executed by other and more skilful hands.

Yet Mrs Damer did not live in vain. The future fulfilled her dreams for her. If, as she held, Hindustan could be civilized with statues, that goal must by this time have been attained; for India, once the land of rubies, emeralds, pearls, elephants and palm trees, pullulated with statues of grim statesmen, viceroys, generals and missionaries, seen dimly through the hot veil of red dust raised by our industry. There, on their

[1] Cunningham's *Lives of British Sculptors.*

[207]

imported granite pedestals, above bungalows and stone
buildings, stand the effigies of men perhaps more popular in
England than in India. How should we English like it if
London were adorned with the Indian heroes of an English
mutiny, embellished with the forms, larger than life, of
Brahmin priests, Babu merchants, Parsee viceroys and Rajput
generals, who, having failed to make us eat of the flesh of our
God, the horse, had tied some of our countrymen to the muzzle
of their guns and fired them?

Yet even these statues have a charm of romance. What an
exotic picture will not the future excavator, ignorant of our
history, form of us? What fantastic conclusions will he not
deduce from the evidence before him as he uncovers these
strange, enormous cities so entirely overgrown by jungle?
Cutting down the scrub with a hatchet, hacking his way with
hot but breathless eagerness through the undergrowth, he will
find among those ruins, which so surely he will describe as
'extensive' and 'rewarding beyond his hopes', these toga'd or
robed figures, some even crowned with a sun-helmet. A
rattlesnake or cobra will uncoil itself from the neck of Have-
lock, Heber or Lord Curzon, and hiss venomously away with
upreared head into the seething darkness; parrots and macaws
will be shrieking, screeching and flashing their spangled wings
through the heat, securely perched on the nose and ears of a
gigantic statue of the great Queen-Empress, and the grey,
rugose bulk of an elephant will go dashing and trumpeting
down the broken, overgrown streets filled with our dead and
leaden heroes, riven by age and heat. This explorer will find
wild animals nesting in baths of rusty enamel, and many times,
too, will he cut his foot on a broken syphon, or upon a gleaming whisky bottle, opalescent from age—glass fragments
eagerly collected for their beauty by the esthete of the future.
Deeply will he ponder the mysteries of the Unchanging East.

Who, he will ask himself, were these dim native sahibs so different in their dress and manners from the present inhabitants, what these gigantic idols that they worshipped: and these granite pedestals, were they not, perhaps, the tables at some terrible, some unmentionable, feast? Cannibalism . . . it is possible . . . all things are possible in this extraordinary country . . . are they not blood-stains, those meaty streaks? And certainly baths, bottles, syphons, golf-clubs and polo-balls—the insignia of British civilization in India—will paint for him rites, libations and ablutions of an unknown and indiscoverable meaning.

Something like these, too, it seems to him, he once beheld in a ruined city on an island in the foggy, frozen and forgotten North. What obscure ramifications of an early people, once powerful and now buried in oblivion, does this imply? he wonders. To think that a race from this tropical peninsula should have penetrated so far and ruled for so long, stretching its dominion right up towards the snowy, polar wastes. This querulous, dark-skinned people, now so quiet and leisurely, must once have been a race of heroes, must have experienced a nomadic impulse unequalled in modern times, must have achieved exploits that even his own people and generation, with all their improved methods and instruments and weapons, could never attempt to rival.

36

EIGHTEENTH-CENTURY
DETAILS

I HAVE been reading a beautifully and profusely illustrated publication, which appeared some years ago from the Clarendon Press, entitled *Johnson's England*. To it the appropriate experts have contributed chapters on nearly every branch of English life during the period with which the book is concerned. And though, as a participant in one chapter, I perhaps ought not to allege this, a fascinating two volumes these make, full of information which every educated man ought to possess, and the previous lack of which he must feel, while he reads, to have been humiliating; full, moreover, of hints, all too tantalizing, of further information, of which, were he really educated, he would be cognizant; facts which lurk only just round the corner, and which, in his sloth, he may never now acquire.

Even in the man-in-the-street's realm of patriotic history, shame must overwhelm him who reads. Sir John Fortescue, for example, in his excellent essay 'The Army', writes: 'After all, even now how few Englishmen realize that those' (the years 1748 to 1781) 'were years of continuous fighting? How many battles are known even by name to the ordinary man who conceives himself to be educated . . .? Of Minden, one of the most striking examples of the prowess of the British soldier, of Warburg, although the elder Mr Weller's public-house bore the sign of the Marquis of Granby, of St Lucia in 1778, the most wonderful instance of success achieved against vastly superior numbers by perfect concert between Army and Navy, they have never heard, or at least could give no coherent account. . . . In India the early work of conquest was achieved principally by mere handfuls of British soldiers, serving under the command of captains, as spearheads to small bodies of sipahis: yet that is no reason why the names of Stringer, Lawrence, Knox, Forde, Adams and Caillaud be forgotten.'

And if our ignorance is thus profound concerning the historical background of the lives led by our not so distant ancestors, how much less still do we know of the miscellaneous details pertaining to them, details of social, artistic and everyday life, even of the startling events of the time! Were *you* aware, for example, of one incident during the American War of Independence, which a little illustrates the vagaries of transport in that epoch, and the difficulties with which commanders had to struggle: General Clinton was sailing from New York to Charleston, Carolina, with the force under his command, when a fierce gale overtook him, and two of his transports were blown clean over the Atlantic—one to Falmouth in Cornwall, the other to Cartagena in Spain? . . . Were you informed, again, of the circumstances attending Captain Cook's third and last voyage of discovery; things, surely, which we all ought to know?

The great Captain, on his return from his second voyage, had, in token of gratitude, and as some slight recompense for his immense services to England and the world, been granted an appointment at Greenwich Hospital. Almost at once, however, the Lords of the Admiralty found themselves in need of more information: as to the possibility, among other things, of a North-West Passage. Aware that he was the only man who could help them, they yet did not care so soon to disturb him. When their difficulty became apparent, he solved it for them by at once *volunteering*. And indeed, as Professor Williamson writes, 'being what he was he could not do otherwise. He was now the representative not only of England but of civilization, and civilization acknowledged it.' And in the method of this acknowledgment there is something for this century to learn, for when, during Captain Cook's last voyage, war broke out between England and France, the French Minister of Marine issued orders to all his admirals that 'Captain Cook shall be treated as a commander of a neutral and allied power', and subsequently the American and Spanish naval authorities issued similar instructions to those under their command. . . . In the last war, I fear, a special price would have been set on his head, and the enemy troops would have been encouraged to bomb him from the air and torpedo him from under the water!

Are you aware, again, of how your ancestors were buried, of the severe but costly ritual attendant on their funerals? 'Hatchments were hung on the front of the house and cards of invitation, adorned with all the trappings of grief, skulls, skeletons, coffins and gravestones, were issued by the undertakers. Women, known as Wakers, sat up with the dead. . . . In memory of the departed, mourners were presented with mourning rings, some of which were of a considerable value. The pall-bearers were given black-silk hatbands and black gloves, and servants in attendance received the same. The parson who performed the service was also presented with a hatband and gloves in addition to his fee, which varied with the rank of the corpse and the generosity of the relatives.' Parson Woodforde, in describing in his diary one funeral at which he presided, relates how before the service there was 'Chocolate and Toast and Cake with red Wine and white', and after it, again, cake and dried toast, chocolate and wine, and concludes his description: 'It was as decent, neat, handsome a funeral as I ever saw!' Nor was this ceremonial spirit limited to the richer classes; among the labouring poor burial-clubs were common, and at some pauper funerals it was customary to toll the bell and provide beer for the bearers.

A French contemporary traveller, Le Blanc, observed that 'the care the English take of all particulars of their burial, would make one believe that they find more pleasure in dying than living'. But herein, surely, he was wrong. Londoners, we learn from the pages of this book, were able to enjoy themselves then as never since, in their own way whether vigorous or quiet. There were constant scenes in the street, so that walking was a pleasure; and, in the fine weather, there were cool places in which they could find comfort. When next obliged to slink down the burning pavements of the petrol-laden streets of our great metropolis, conscious that no place exists in which we can sit, peaceful and contented, in the open air, we shall look back with regret to eighteenth-century London. Of the exist-ence of Ranelagh and Vauxhall, the resorts of the rich, we were cognizant; but what of Bagnigge Wells, Sadler's Wells, White Conduit House, Marylebone Gardens and Islington Spa?

The features of these London pleasure gardens, we are told, were walls, lawns, clipped hedges, shrubberies, as much ornamental water as could be managed, with a grotto, foun-tains and statues, vistas and views. 'Within the environs of the capital', wrote a German visitor, 'there is a prodigious number

of tea-gardens. The happy arrangement, the order, the cleanliness, the promptitude of the service, the company always
numerous and agreeable make these gardens as pleasant as they
are interesting. At Bagnigge Wells, in fine weather, it is surprising to find from ten to twelve hundred people taking tea.
. . . These places are frequented only by the middle and
common class; people of distinction come rarely, ladies of
quality never.' . . . What can be said now on behalf of the
sweltering London tea-shops, which cater for those of middle
income, in a 'new and elegant way'?

37

THE CONSPIRACY OF DWARFS

HEIGHT, like beauty, resides, I suppose, in the eye of the beholder. Sculptors, for example, invariably present Queen Victoria to us as a seated giantess, albeit the whole charm and dignity of her appearance consisted in her being so small. Every author, again, is imagined by the non-writing world as essentially tiny and insect-like. The height of Bernard Shaw came as a perpetual shock to those members of the public who had not seen him before: for his stature, together with that of his work, has been consistently minimized and mis-represented for over half a century. Again, caricaturists have always shown the writer of this essay as a thin, black dwarf, whereas, unless my mirror lies, I am not by any means either as short or as black as I am drawn. The tape-measure supports the testimony of my mirror; somewhat over six foot. . . . Nevertheless, today that is no great height; many, especially among my friends, overtop me by several inches—for the truth is that, though we may not be much wiser, we are certainly much taller than our ancestors.

The cave dwellings reveal the traces of a small, if wiry, people. And, in medieval times, armour crushed and contracted the physique of the governing classes, wrong feeding, that of the governed: since a winter diet of salt fish, once every twenty-four hours, year in, year out, without ever a sight of fruit and vegetables, was their lot. No vitamins worried the heads, and none ever figured in the food, of the Middle Ages. . . . Height, of course, varies singularly with the generations. It is said that, after the decimation of the French race by the Napoleonic and Franco-Prussian wars, the average Frenchman lost two inches off his stature: it may be too that the Romans were taller than the Italians. Perhaps, spread over a century or more, the trend of politics affects height. (And here we may notice, in parentheses, how curious it is that the citizens of a free democracy should be tall, for surely the essence of democracy is that all should be short and of the same size? Height should be rationed and equalized. And, indeed, we find the acknowledgment of this ideal in the contemporary newspaper cult of the Little Man, of which I attempt to treat in a later essay.)

Why, then, when the young everywhere are so tall, and when height has so much increased, is the modern world entirely constructed for the benefit of the dwarf? . . . Looking round, it is indeed hard not to believe that there is in process a conspiracy of dwarfs. It is all very well for the poet to sing—

How jolly are the dwarfs, the little ones, the Mexicans!

but they are not as jolly as they seem, being a cruel and malign race. Everywhere you go—'you' signifying any ordinary person of ordinary size—you are compelled to walk almost on all-fours; a penalty comparable to that exacted in medieval times, when sinners, or persons who had made vows, were induced to crawl up the aisles of cathedrals on hands and knees. . . .

Take, for example, the National Galley. The rooms are lofty and old-fashioned; but before the war you had only to attempt to look at the pictures! The bigger, more important works were hung just below the level of the collar-bone, though the whole of the space above them was vacant, so that this must have been done on purpose, was by no means merely accidental. By craning and straining down—though even this gave one, as the saying is, 'a pain in the neck'—it might be possible to see—though not to enjoy—so much of the canvas as the reflection in the glass allowed; because the image of a custodian sleeping on his chair, or of lines of empty benches and skylights, was invariably superimposed upon the artist's conception of Mrs Siddons or of Bacchus and his Pards: while to catch a glimpse of any fragment of the second row of pictures, hung an inch above the wainscoting, it was necessary to throw yourself, after the manner of the Moor in *Petrouchka*, at full length upon the floor, and then push upward with the arms. But this behaviour, though essential, unfortunately worried the attendants and embarrassed any spectators who chanced to be in the room—though most of these, since they came here to 'do the sights', were not perturbed by the fact that under no circumstances could they see the pictures. . . . The dwarfs were indeed triumphant.

Possibly, gentle reader, though tall, you may be one who prefers the picture theatre to the picture gallery, and therefore doubts the truth of this particular conspiracy. But consider the facts; the patron of the picture theatre, too, is victimized. In the winter the building is over-heated, so that he must catch cold when he leaves it; in the summer, icy-cold currents of air play on him so that he is obliged to catch a chill while he sits there. At first it may *seem* as though there were plenty of room, as though this time the dwarfs had been defeated; but just try to get up—for each seat clasps you tightly round the waist—to push your way between two rows! . . .

As for hotels, they are constructed entirely for the midget tribe. Endeavour in any modern hotel bedroom to wash your hands; only by going down on your knees, that terrible classic attitude of submission, is such an action practicable; only thus can you gain quarter. The wardrobes, whether let into the wall or boldly jutting out from it, are made too shallow for suits and too short for dresses. If the cupboard is not built-in, its cornice will knock out an eye every time you pass it. . . . But, worst of all, try to unpack your suitcase on the special stand which the authorities provide for this purpose. Often the wretched victim must remain there for ten or fifteen minutes before he can straighten himself out again. Only a long series of Dalcroze eurhythmics or years of practice in the gymnasium can teach him to perform this feat.

The old style of private house, it is true, is less dwarf-ridden than the hotel: but, ranged in the enemy camp—a powerful weapon in tiny hands—are the blocks of modern flats, with their equalized, low-ceilinged storeys, pressed in a sandwich-like manner between others. 'Who lives in all these new flats?' is a question often asked—but nobody knows the answer, for an entirely new race of fur-coated flat-dwelling pygmies has apparently been called into being. . . . Perhaps we have reached a new stage of evolution; perhaps the flat-dweller has come at last to supersede the house-dweller, to take his place for many thousands of years, until a newer type has been evolved; just as in ages past the dweller in stone houses superseded the troglodyte. . . . Certainly this heir of all the ages will be a dwarf, the contractors and builders have seen to that. . . . To prove this, select any flat in any block of flats you like—or don't like—and try to wash up the cups and plates at the sink. Your least reward, the lightest penalty which the dwarfs decree for you, is a sharp attack of lumbago. And what of the aluminium chairs, which it seems may clasp you in their cold embrace for ever, without your being able to rise?

Let me counsel you, then, as you pass these endless, ugly, built-in Mappin terraces that, piled one upon another, climb towards the skies, sheltering at each level their dwarfs' broods, to feel no envy for the labour-saving tricks they contain, but instead to reflect, with some feeling of superiority, that you are on your way *home*, going to your *home*, a thing which their inhabitants will never have, though if quarrels and noise are what these hop-o'-my-thumbs want, they can most easily find them here, in these reverberant, machine-ridden egg-boxes, among their own malevolent septs. . . . Let us avert our gaze.

Three motors pass by: we notice again the same show of favouritism; even the largest vehicles are nowadays constructed solely for dwarfs. In them only a manikin, a midget two feet tall, can be comfortable. . . . To reach the further seat is a torture to anyone over that height, while to leave it, to get your feet on the step, you are obliged to adopt the position of dancer in the famous Cossack dance—is it called the *gopak*?—arms crossed, one leg doubled, the other straight out in front of you at right angles. 'Ai, Ai, Ai!' you must shout. 'Olla! Olla! Olla!'

In one single instance are the giants victorious. . . . The tube trains must have been designed to avenge our sufferings, and as they rush shrieking through the burrow at thirty miles an hour, you may observe the poor little people swinging, like so many monkeys, from the straps, or, in some cases, looking at them wistfully: for they are out of reach.

38

THE BANQUETS OF TANTALUS, 1942

*To the memory of Viola Tree, who gave
the author much help and information.*

For the morning of 14th July 1941 *The Times* republished
from its issue of precisely a century before the following
account of a suit that had just been brought in a French law-
court:

M. Clary, a 'useful actor', on being summoned by his manager
for most impassible obstinacy in being of no use, pleaded that his
manager's feasts on the stage were no less than sheer matters of
famine; that when playing the parts of princes, marquises and the
like he deemed himself entitled to treatment conformable to his
temporary rank and the spirit of the part. 'Pray, M. Clary,' said
the Juge de Paix, 'explain yourself.' 'I mean, Monsieur le Juge, that
in almost all pieces we figurantes have a dinner or supper; in truth,
we reckon upon it—we poor devils at 600 francs a year! Well, we
are treated like the veriest beggars.' The manager protested that he
treated his actors as he ought. 'Yes,' interrupted M. Clary, 'you give
us Seltzer water instead of champagne, and yet expect us to sing—

Qu'il avait du bon vin
Le Seigneur châtelain;
Buvons encore
Pour en être certain!

And the other night in the *Dîner de Madelon*, of what country was the turkey? Pasteboard, by all the gods!'

Reading an outburst so heartfelt as that of Monsieur Clary, it is impossible not to feel a profound sympathy for the 'useful actor' who made it—more especially because he plainly possessed temperament and, in addition, belonged to that European nation which has for long been the most famous for the interest it takes in meals and the genius it expends upon the cooking and serving of them. These tantalizing banquets, of which he makes so loud a moan that it carries easily and with full volume across the hundred years that divide us, these cruel feasts where bread turns inevitably to a stone and every—or almost every—chicken to a property fowl could, no doubt, assume a dream-like quality of horror to those compelled every night to partake of them. But, just as there is always, to the members of the audience, a glittering wonder attendant upon theatrical jewels, the marvel of their high lights, how they are composed and what magic makes them real, so, in a similar manner, the food in that bright world of illusion—the dishes seeming as though the curtain, when drawn up, left behind it a mirror that reflects with precision the items of food familiar to us—exercises a considerable fascination upon the minds of those who are not initiated and cannot interpret each symbol into its equivalent upon this side of the footlights. It is to us a miracle, and one that never loses its power to astonish. We can go to the play five nights running, until we become tired of it, but the properties never lose their enchantment for us; *our* eyes can, during dull moments, find occupation in examining the delicacies spread out for the actors, though beyond the proscenium it is far otherwise. Many people have been known to grumble if confronted with the same dish two or three nights running; try to imagine, then, what it must mean to be faced with it every night for two or three months, and, besides, even when obliged to put up a pretence of eating, to know it for a sham, a lie, a flint-hearted dissimulation, a piece of hollow, hard and sticky pasteboard, dizened so as to look appetizing at a distance.

I write, moreover, in years of war and shortage, when all things that we can eat appear to possess more than their actual value, and this, in turn, bestows on their counterfeits upon stage tables a corresponding increase in the apish mockery of their enticement—yet these meals continue, withal, to this very day, and constitute, indeed, almost the only kind of feasting that a strict system of rationing permits to exist. . . . There are, for example, those banquets set for kings and princes in ballet and pantomime, where processions of girls, dressed as boys in tights, bear aloft vast dishes, holding them at the captivating but improbable angle which their substance allows—because, since plate and apparent contents are in this case one and indivisible, no accident can occur; things that we seldom encounter in real life but which are yet recognizable, boars' heads, roast swans or peacocks diademed in their finery. In addition, during the course of the last thirty years, these feasts have increased in number and attained a further pitch of verisimilitude by means of photography; thus have they entered upon a new world, and conquered a fresh dimension. But this development, the long meals of Hollywood, its tables scintillant with silver and wisecracks, the crooks' supper-parties in cellars, with a revolver laid for each guest, these Imperial Roman banquets, couched in the idiom of the cheap illustrated papers, but graced, here and there, with tags of tradition and fragments of Latin, these sumptuous repasts where those partaking eat their

> ... broaths with spoons of Amber,
> Headed with Diamant and Carbuncle.

and have

> The beards of Barbels seru'd instead of sallades;
> Oil'd Mushromse, and the swelling unctuous paps
> Of a fat pregnant sow, nearly cut off,
> Drest with an exquisite, and poignant sauce;

or those strange transatlantic meals of the small hours, held in an idealized mixture of night-club, casino and Versailles, where, hidden beneath palms and scarlet trumpet-lipped hibiscus, from islands pitched on lakes, Caribbean bands knock out upon the skulls of beasts perpetual rumbas, and only the Marx Brothers spoil by their capers and ingenious tricks, their ladders and ropes, their flying trapezes and falling pots of paint, the nostalgic decorum of the scene, or, again, such a supper-party as I once saw represented in a Soviet film, wherein the domestic animals broke, unsuspected, through the French windows at the back of the dining-room, and seized the dishes and the glasses of champagne from the resisting hands and under the protuberant eyes of the assembled convivial plutocrats; all these, then, form a new path, which is too broad and too long for me to follow within the space of a few pages, and I will therefore, apart from the short discursion that follows, and a sequel to it at the end, confine my reflections and revelations to the compass of the old-fashioned stage.

In private life such properties as I have described are rare, with one exception: those shimmering but dismal replicas of

Victorian wedding-cakes, which were to be seen in many London streets, but more especially behind the steamy plate-glass windows of Oxford Street caterers and confectioners; plaster ghosts in two or three diminishing cylindrical storeys, terraced and set back after the constructional manner of a Chinese pagoda or an Aztec sacrificial pyramid, while across their counterfeit coating of spectral white (no wonder that Herman Melville in his *Moby Dick* enquires rhetorically why the mention of white should raise 'such an eyeless statue in the soul'!), enlivened at each cornice with elfin touches of pink, pale-blue and lily-green pseudo-sugar, trail discon-solately sprays of white artificial flowers. . . . Do these edifices, aged and glittering, alluringly phantasmal in their bride's attire as, in *Great Expectations*, was old Miss Havisham when first Pip saw her, do they, more dusty yet, still survive the bombing behind broken windows?

To these cakes, towering up into their London fog, I will revert later; they are nearly the only relations in the outside world to theatrical-property food, and it may be that their appearance provides an answer to something that we shall ask: we will now return to the dishes on the stage. These are of two kinds, those which are made of pasteboard, and those which are genuinely edible, but composed of some other substance than what it seems. And we may note in passing that both of them will be in the keeping of 'Props', who keeps all food and drink and other dummies in his charge. As a rule he is the most dependable, and often the most popular, person in the company, no Oxford or Cambridge novice, enthusiastic about the theatre, but a stage hand of wide experience and all-embracing, if rather nonchalant, sympathy.

Pasteboard plainly cannot be eaten, and therefore presents comparatively little difficulty to the actor; but of all the illusions of reality which the Western theatre demands, no effort costs him more in the way of achievement than the semblance of consuming food. We Europeans worship truth to Nature with a passion that is purely occidental; eating *on* the stage must be made as much like eating *off* it as is humanly possible. In the East, no doubt, it is otherwise. Thus in China, though I can at the moment recall no instance of a meal being served upon the boards—albeit every member of the audience in the gaily painted wooden theatres of Peking drinks tea noisily throughout the performance, of four or five hours' duration, and after he has finished one cup, wipes his face, in order to be ready for the next, with a steaming towel which the attendant brings him, and then proceeds to roll this up and throw it across, for his use, to a friend at the other side of the stalls; though, I say, I can recall no instance of it, nevertheless it can be deduced by a process of analogy that a dinner-party would be represented by some brief and exquisite convention executed by the chief star. In the same way that a journey of a hundred miles undertaken by a score of people is portrayed by a swift circling of the stage on the part of a single figure with long, fluttering sleeves, a gliding movement, with a special angle and tilt of the body, at a particular pace and, as it seems, on a level a little above that of the rest of the boards: in the same way that the cuts and direction of a warrior's sword intimate the victory or defeat of a whole great army; so, no doubt, the principal male impersonator would convey the effect of, let us say, a host and forty guests enjoying a banquet, by a graceful grinding of the mandibles or a peculiarly expert and elegant manipulation of chopsticks.

Such conventions, however—except when presented at long intervals to illustrate the 'quaintness' of orientals—would not satisfy an English audience for one matinée, let alone a run of nights. It insists, to the contrary, on the sight and sound of *real* flesh and blood eating *real* food—not, I apprehend, that it

P [225]

requires a higher degree of culinary excellence to be represented beyond the curtain than upon its own dinner-tables, but the material, if it appears at all, must seem incontestably prime and demonstrably genuine. . . . And this, in its turn, calls for a special technique because, natural though it may appear to us in our everyday lives to talk with our mouths full and at the tops of our voices, yet on the stage it is by no means easy to manage in a way that will ensure that every word, at the same time, shall carry to the most distant places in the auditorium. To be able to play such a part at all, the actor has, perhaps, been obliged to accustom himself for years to a considerable degree of physical suffering, so as to gain complete control over his appetite. He must, in short, have trained himself to be an ascetic, a role that in private life seldom suits an actor. He may, for example, be numbered among the majority of the members of his profession, the working of whose nervous systems prevents them from eating until after they have finished their performance before the footlights; then, if such be his case, and unless he has most carefully accustomed himself to the sight of food, the glimpse of even a counterfeit meal will stimulate the salivary glands in such a fashion as to interfere with the correct delivery of his words and in this way ruin his interpretation of the whole part. The reader may ask what training could possibly qualify the actor for such an ordeal; and in reply I would suggest that régime of deprivation which Augustus Hare, the author of so many guide-books, tells us was inflicted upon himself, at the age of five, by his adoptive mother and her associates of the Maurice family. 'I was not six years old', he writes, 'before my mother—under the influence of the Maurices—began to follow out a code of penance with regard to me which was worthy of the ascetics of the desert. Hitherto I had never been allowed anything but roast-mutton and rice-pudding for dinner. The most delicious puddings were talked of—*dilated* on—until I became, not greedy, but exceedingly curious about them. At length *"le grand moment"* arrived. They were put on the table before me, and then, just as I was going to eat some of them, they were snatched away. . . .'

Of course, there are occasions upon which actors are allowed, encouraged even, to eat upon the stage, but people connected with the theatre are notoriously superstitious and, in consequence, producers and backers are apt to eschew plays which necessitate the serving and consuming before the audience of an entire meal, since an ancient tradition of ill fortune attends them. The stage manager, on his side, dreads the idea for more practical reasons, foreseeing, as he does, the heaviness of the task laid upon the hands who have to clear up the ensuing litter and debris. Moreover, albeit the success of a book, especially a work of fiction, is said to depend largely on the amount of description of food that it contains—Dickens, for one, enters into considerable detail on the matter, and, indeed, almost the first novel ever written, or at least the earliest that has come down to us, the *Satiricon* of Petronius Arbiter, is chiefly concerned with a feast, the Banquet of Trimalchio—yet the sight of food it cannot devour is held to divert the attention of an audience from the play in progress. But if this be so, it would seem most unfair when one remembers how much the noisy rattle of hard and crinkly paper in chocolate-boxes, and the subsequent munching of chocolates, must distract the hungry actors who have themselves enjoyed no dinner.

English playwrights and actors, then, tend more to favour upon the stage between-meal refreshments. Formerly the ceremony of tea constituted the perpetual refuge of the mediocre dramatist, but in the two decades that separated the wars the cocktail-shaker supplanted it, and the ice-cold rattle that now prevails matches the fizzle of platitudes, dressed up as epigrams, in progress. But there are also soda-water in syphons, port in decanters and cigarettes in boxes. To help, the actor's case can be taken out of a pocket—preferably a hip-pocket—opened and a cigarette chosen. The cigarette can then be tapped on the top of the case, and lit, and the case can be snapped shut again, to the accompaniment of a tense face, at the critical moment. Indeed, authors of modern comedies or thrillers appear to be unable to get through three acts without turning for aid to these adjuncts and, similarly, few actors of the Snack-and-Run-School—a type of technique invented and carried to its highest pitch by the late Sir Gerald du Maurier—can bestow an illicit kiss or even commit a single murder without having recourse to them.

To manage even these things properly requires, however, a great deal of experience and technique. The crunching of an apple, for instance, in which Miss Elizabeth Bergner indulged when playing Rosalind in *As You Like It*—that startling *crackle! crackle! crackle!*—can by no means have been as casual and unpremeditated as it appeared. Lucien Guitry, again, as protagonist in *Le Grand Duc*, imparted to his always magnificent presence the further needful touch of hyperborean splendour by the barbaric extravagance of eating great spoonfuls of caviare—real caviare—as, talking all the while, he strode or lounged about the stage. . . . Again, I remember in 1909 seeing one of the famous Grasso family of actors achieve a tremendous feat in the way of eating upon the stage. This member of the Sicilian clan was young, about twenty-three or -four, and undoubtedly would have been acting within a few years in all the world capitals had he not been drowned a very short time after, while crossing with his Sicilian company to South America. At the time I saw him he was playing in a disused church which had been turned into a theatre. The performances, which every night included a drama, followed by a farce, and ended with music-hall turns, continued until two or three in the morning. The audience was entirely male, except for foreigners—for no Sicilian woman ever then permitted herself to be seen in a café or a theatre—and consisted of peasants, shopkeepers and waiters, who cried and laughed and cheered, and must, indeed, from the point of view of an actor, have been a perfect medium upon which to work. The setting, too, the makeshift platform for the stage, the footlights, hastily improvised, the shadowy roof, the plaster angels and cupids and coats of arms, falling into powdery dust upon the shoulders of the audience, all these form an unforgettable picture in the memory, but one which Grasso, by the power of his art, still dominates. I was fortunate enough to see him on many occasions, and several times when he was acting the role of a worker in the sulphur mines, and throughout one intensely dramatic and moving scene, added to his part a touch of sullen melancholy, alternating with a farouche and flaring gaiety, by eating macaroni, picking it out of an enormous bowl with his fingers, which he made to seem thick and swollen, and cramming the strands clumsily into his mouth. He would sit down, get up, walk about, still munching, still talking. Every word was audible.

Other great actors, again, aid themselves in the matter of eating by thinking out devices beforehand. Thus in *Gringoire*, the late Sir Herbert Tree, playing one of his most famous character studies—that of a penniless poet at the court of Louis XI—found himself faced with the problem of being a starving man on whom a meal is suddenly bestowed. He had to eat, for he believed in realism; he *had* to tackle a whole chicken, with his hands. He solved the difficulty by causing to be constructed for himself a fine, plump, hollow pullet of papier mâché, the breast being composed of two lids. He then filled it every night with real slices of excellent cold chicken and was thus able, when the moment came, to fling himself on the bird, tackle it with his fingers and eat it with a proper relish and abandon in front of an enthusiastic audience. In addition, he concluded this banquet with a whole bunch of genuine grapes. The wine, however, which accompanied all this food, consisted of coloured water—except when one evening, by mistake, turpentine was substituted for it. Unfortunately Sir Herbert swallowed a great gulp from his glass before he discovered the nature of its contents. With remarkable fortitude, however, he continued to act, although he was all the time suffering the greatest agony, until the end of the play.

This meal was a feat, but how much endurance, coupled with an equal art—and more appetite—it must take to have an entire dinner served to you upon the stage, and to consume it. Yet, in spite of the difficulties, in spite of superstition and stage managers, it has several times been successfully accomplished. Thus, in that popular play *The Man from Blankley's*, the late Sir Charles Hawtrey devoured his way right through the menu of a normal burgess dinner of pre-war days, with the customary number of courses—soup, fish, chicken, sweet, savoury—served in the traditional manner. Notwithstanding the apparent ease and enjoyment with which he ate, and for all the smoothness with which the scene was presented, this was a triumphant achievement—but then Hawtrey and his stage manager were both accomplished technicians.

Such repasts, such single dishes, that are what they pretend to be, constitute nevertheless a rarity in stage history. Though we may have listened with sympathy at the beginning of this essay to the complaint of Monsieur Clary, it was never, in fact, justified, and we come back to the two great categories already mentioned, into which the generality of theatrical food is still divided; pasteboard, and one edible material masquerading as another. When we see actors or actresses eating, un-doubtedly eating, we can, if we hold the cypher, translate the outward semblance of the food on their side of the mirror into its reality on ours; just as, to take another sense, that of sound, instead of taste, if we see a stage crowd in riot or panic, the faces contorted, the air full of shouts, we wonder what the words are that they utter, and then recall that the answer is 'Rhubarb!', 'Rhubarb!', or Rhabarbet', as some say; for that, I know not why, is the convention. Similarly caviare on the boards turns into blackcurrant jam off them, and meat—a partic-ularly difficult substance to swallow while talking—is always represented by a kind of pink mousse or jelly. The part of wine is nearly always taken by coloured water, though ginger-ale, as a rule, passes for champagne. (Admirers of Miss Tallulah Bankhead will, on the other hand, remember with pleasure how often they have seen her drink *real* champagne in one of the plays in which she appeared in London.) There are, how-ever, common exceptions: tea is always tea, hot and plentiful, but weak; and chocolates are chocolates all the stage over—the contents, it can be confidently stated, of no box, however vast in size, ever seeing the light of the following day.

Now we approach another matter, an abstruse and abstract question indeed.... It has been said that the first thing a Chinese asks himself, whenever he sees a being or substance new to him, is 'What would it taste like?'; so it is surely permissible, too, for an Englishman to speculate on how property foods *would* taste, were we—or those on the state—obliged to eat them. . . . And I believe that the property bridal cakes, des-cribed some pages back, provide us with a clue to the answer, indicate, indeed, how all property comestibles would taste; like ordinary wedding cake.... Be that as it may, these white, but unleaning towers of Pisa, these pipeclayed dwindling ghosts of drums, placed one upon another, pale spectres, like Ophelia, cheated of bridehood, trailing their flowers, would surely possess the same flavour, the same brittle crust of sweetness, the same soft edging of almond-paste to guard the dark, subtle, dank nothingness within. . . . Perhaps all combinations of sugar and almond, indeed, share a tendency to beget ghosts, or how else explain the similar fate of confetti, sugared almonds, smooth-coated in various light colours, which are still given away at wedding receptions in southern Italy and Sicily, and were formerly thrown after the bride and bridegroom as they left? Equally, they were used as things with which to pelt one another by the revellers at Carnival time. . . . But these sweets have disappeared, like Carnival itself, from most of Europe, leaving behind them only vestigial progeny, in the purely conventional confetti, the circles of coloured paper that we know, still seeing them littering the pavement outside churches. . . . But we wander too far.

Many actors, I intended to say, are hungry throughout a play: but fortunately more often because they refuse to eat than for involuntary reasons. At least the stage meals of today, however tantalizing they may seem sometimes, lack the poignant, terrible sense of irony which formerly they possessed. Already, in the time of Monsieur Clary, the status and condition of the actor had visibly improved from what they had been a hundred years before—or perhaps members of the French stage were never so pitiable and abject as English actors and actresses; perhaps it was the Commonwealth and the long Puritan blight which were responsible. But certainly in England of the early eighteenth century those who feasted on the stage in their apparently fine clothes very frequently starved in rags at home. Vagabonds outside the protection of the law, they were often obliged after the performance to slink off to bed, cold, miserable and starving, and, worse, when there, to hear their children—who, if above two years of age, would probably have been on the stage with their parents, and would, before long, be given a part—crying aloud for something to eat. Or they avoided going home, borrowed a few pence so that they could spend their time in the festive, aromatic atmosphere of Gin Lane (for the Whigs had seen to it that gin was cheap). Here at least they could temporarily lose the memory of their homes, or lack of them, could forget even themselves. . . . Yet it was this background which produced Mrs Siddons and her brothers, and David Garrick and Edmund Kean!

39

SAVE THE OLD SCHOOL TIE

ONE of the attractions of war to the middle-aged and safely placed is to be found, undoubtedly, in the release it offers to many long-felt but hitherto suppressed inclinations. Things that have been wrong for a lifetime—starting with the taking of human life itself—suddenly become morally right, and matters of national urgency as well. Those of us who have always wanted to wear old clothes, can live in them; those of us who have been misers, scraping and paring, find our vice a present obligation; those of us who felt repressed by railings, and ever longed to smash them, can tear them down to the applause of all who love their country; those who have always hated art, can rejoice in the bare walls of the National Gallery; those who hate books, can pulp them. And those who have suffered from a lifelong hatred of public schools, can attribute to the training these afford all the defects of our leaders. It has almost become a patriotic duty to hate the public schools.

I detested mine. I loathed playing games and the company in which I found myself. Even the pleasures of school life, the feasts and concerts, only made me long still more to be elsewhere. I well remember, incidentally, how depressed I was, during my first half at Eton, to hear boys and old boys roaring out together at a concert the words of the famous 'Eton Boating Song', for I misunderstood their sense, and as they bellowed 'We'll all *swing* together, and swear by the best of schools', I imagined the hangman at his grim task, and the band of juvenile criminals, myself among them, crying out, in a final contemptuous gasp, as the noose tightened round each neck: 'Floreat Etona!' Moreover, the words which followed, if I am not mistaken, in one verse: 'With our bodies between our knees', only added to the fate I pictured to myself, a final touch of physical degradation, comparable to being torn down from the gibbet after execution and being drawn and quartered. . . . The short career of nameless crime to which the song must refer, was not, I felt, one to which a boy should look forward, or that masters and parents should thus unite to urge upon him. . . . I was surprised at them.

When I left I was one of the first to attack the system, continually, with justice and without it. I saw that the cult of games and good form was inexpedient in the members of a nation mentally lazy. I dared to suggest—a suggestion that would be even more unpopular today—that intelligence, and especially ability of an original kind, was more to be admired and encouraged than a nimble foot or a correct style in batting.

Among the happiest moments of my life, therefore, was when, returning home one spring, after six months spent in a distant country, I found that, during my absence abroad, the old tie of the public school had become Public Joke No. 1. It seemed to me to register another advance in the conscious-ness of Everyman; a consciousness which, in England, so often registers by means of humour its new advances. . . . I remember, too, how I became aware of it. It happened thus. The porter at Victoria Station, who had, before his proper turn, attempted to take charge of my bags, was greeted by one of his mates with the rebuke:

' 'Ere, remember the Old School Tie, 'Arry. They don't be'ave like this at Eton, whatever them may do at 'Arrow. . . .'

Never, then, in those peaceful days did I expect to have to enrol myself under the banner of the Old School Tie. . . . Yet now that it is attacked from so many quarters, and for so many different reasons—nearly all of them bad—I feel an inclination to come to the rescue of these antiquated but still barbarous institutions.

Softness, for example, is not born of a public school. The hardships of which an ordinary man complains, bad sanitation, no baths, cold baths, insufficient, unpalatable and infrequent food, physical suffering of all kinds, including being flogged, an utter lack of amenities—to public-school boys all these were, and still are in the majority of cases, a part of the usual concentration-camp curriculum; so much a matter of course that they seldom even made complaints of them to their parents. These establishments were the ferocious nurseries in which the chiefs and founders of the Empire were reared; a glance at the *Dictionary of National Biography* soon confirms it. . . . No, the softness, the messy softness, the addled, sympathetic thinking, the belief that all was for the best of all possible worlds, these sins were born in other places and of other sires.

In a country where everyone is still free to lay the blame on whom he likes, on whose shoulders, I may be asked, do I place the burden of feather-weight wits? . . . Well, I think the systematic cultivation of whimsical silliness in children—a silliness encouraged in the first place by the late Sir James

Barrie, and very swiftly taken by up the uncles of the daily Press and the B.B.C.—has done an incalculable amount of harm. This influence was much worse in the south than the north of England, and never spread to the real poor, and seldom to the public-school class.

All the children affected by it, for example, had to wear badges to show that they belonged to some society of 'little ones', and this fortified the imitative qualities always so unfortunately strong in children. They caught the tone of current silliness from their teachers, and at the same time— perhaps for the only occasion in the history of the human race—became, consciously and self-consciously, children. Further, the badge business, and the waves of popular toys that succeeded one another at regular intervals, encouraged them to believe they must all be the same, all copy, in everything, other children of their own age, have the same manner, the same accent, the same toys, the same parties, the same thoughts, the same kind of parents with the same kind of thoughts. . . . In consequence, Peter Pan never grew up. He merely aged into the fussy, unaspiring, unthinking, uncaring, half-baked, semi-educated, ugly idol of the Press, the Little Man. . . . In his hordes he was the heir to the greatest Empire in the world, hacked out of chaos by such men as Drake and Raleigh, Marlborough and Pitt, Wellington and Nelson.

The Little Man was in charge. The world was his, and the illusion of power—though, since he was too silly to make use of it, his teachers and those who fattened on the instalment systems invented to please and entangle him, wielded it on his behalf. He was the *roi fainéant* of a vast Empire of which he was ignorant, and in the building of which he and his kind, only brought to birth in the last generation, had taken no part. The Empire had been built up, explored, wrested from the former owners, reclaimed or colonized—and even vast territories

beyond the Empire, such as the southern states of the U.S.A.—
by small armies of Old School Ties, younger sons such as
Trelawny describes them to be, at the head of large armies
of countrymen, adventurers and even criminals; but the
well-ordered herds of the cities had not been present. All those
men shared the same blood; but the Little Man has neither
blue nor red blood in his veins, but only red tape. Once
outside the confines of his office, he is lost, for he cannot consult
the rules. He—and she—meet every suggestion with: 'I'm
sorry, but we have no authority. You have to go to the other
ministry first, obtain an authorization; after that, come back
here (we shut at five), and if the regulations have been com-
plied with, we may be able to stamp the form for you, so that
you can go back next door.'

The Little Man, though irritable, is slow to anger. He acts
largely in accordance with the instructions of his prompters;
though constant flattery is the *quid pro quo* of power. He
welcomed a policy that laid emphasis on the necessity of
General Interference combined with Total Disarmament. He
was not pugnacious. Those who wore the badge of the Old
School Tie, on the other hand, were always longing to have
a scrap, perpetually grumbling, in spite of the enormous
taxation to which they were even then subject, at armaments
being cut down, saying 'We shall have to fight the beggar
sooner or later!' . . . But they had no power now: and the
papers were extolling the Little Man again, telling him to
'count his blessings' (chief of which was the vote he did not
know how to use): there would be no war. So he settled down
comfortably to sleep, in a cocoon of red tape spun on the
city's outskirts.

Let us discard, then, the talk of Old School Ties; and only
insist that, after the war, their disadvantages should be open
to all: for they do not breed mediocrity or herd-likeness to

quite the same extent—though still in more than sufficient quantity—as do other places of education. I hope to see the Little Man's Son wear the Old School Tie. . . . But meanwhile the daily Press must stop flattering its customers and telling everybody who has a penny to spare that he is the equal of Leonardo, Shakespeare, Napoleon and Pitt. He is not.

40

A ROSE BY ANY OTHER NAME

BEING A DISCOURSE ON THE
IMPORTANCE OF BAD ART

To MANY people, especially during a war, art signified nothing. It may be that the Englishman at any time regards it as being of little consequence; at best, a recreation. Moreover, frequently misled either by false prophets or by his own untrained faculties in this respect, he is usually inclined to prefer bad art, and to pronounce it of greater importance than good. . . . But, then, the Englishman is a political animal, and perhaps, in a sense and from a political angle, he may be right. Perhaps a worthless book, for example, can achieve more ill than a good book can ever achieve good. . . . At any rate it is upon this seeming paradox that I will now dwell, in the effort to demonstrate, beyond the power of any scepticism to disprove, how a bad writer, by means of his bad writing, can influence the fate of a whole country, and how, by advocating false ideals through the medium of cheapened words—and thereby still further debasing the verbal currency—the author of a fifth-rate romance can, years after he has written it and many years after his own death, become responsible for the destruction of a flourishing and famous land.

Bohemia was a country which we all knew. Every English child had read the story of the capture, single-handed, of the old King of Bohemia by the Black Prince; as a result of which the shield of every Prince of Wales since that time has been surmounted by the three ostrich feathers and has carried the motto 'Ich Dien'. Shakespeare himself deigned to pitch scenes in this realm and—another instance of how, throughout the ages, the English have plotted against a virtuous Germany— added to it a sea-coast. It may be that a vague knowledge of the fjords and rocky islands of Croatia had made him confound it with this inland country of mountains and of castles balanced upon conical hills, of vast forests and monasteries fattening in green valleys. At any rate, his description, for example, of Act III, Scene iii, in *The Winter's Tale*, runs: 'Bohemia. A desert country near the sea. . . .' And always for English children the name of this nation blended beauty, tradition and romance; the word itself possessed in its sound a high and chivalric ring.

The gypsies made their first appearance in England during the early sixteenth century, and were well established—though looked upon with no very favourable eye by their involuntary hosts—in the reign of Queen Elizabeth. Throughout Western Europe they were known as 'Bohemians', because when they had first entered it they had passed through Bohemia. But, in spite of their dirt, their lies, their vermin, they did little harm to the name they had appropriated; added thereto, indeed, a certain ragged lustre, associating it with scenes of wild and improbable beauty, of droves of horses, of sneering, handsome faces and of exotic dances by the light of fires blazing out on the darkest nights from strange encampments. . . . Then, two and a half centuries later, came Mürger and, with his triumph, the name of this ancient country entered on its decadence.

Born in Paris in 1822, the son of a German concierge and tailor, Mürger became secretary to a Russian nobleman, wrote several books and published his greatest success, *La Vie de Bohême*, in 1848. (Himself featured in it under the guise of 'Rodolphe'.) He it was who put across to the curious middle classes the idea of 'Bohemianism', café-gypsies of the bed and board, sharing everything—and everybody—with everybody. As his pattern of the artist, he set up the old crook and crank of the café, who, in the sacred cause of Intoxication for Art's Sake, would sit up all night in good companionship (with the result, of course, that he would be unable to work next day).

In time, the word 'Bohemian' became an excuse for almost any sort of moral obliquity or lack of manners. Anyone who never paid a debt, or lounged about the world never doing anything and getting in the way of those who did, was called a Bohemian. And, alas, attracted by the popularity of the book, and seeing in it the possibility of a popular opera, Puccini later lent his genius to this debasing process. *La Bohême* must have sullied Bohemia even more than *Carmen* tainted the idea of Spain. In time, therefore, the name extended from the improvident to include the rich; any rich young man who wasted his fortune and sat up till morning in expensive night-clubs, any girl of the 'Bright-Young-Thing' period, who possessed her own flat in a mews and had learned to live on cocktails or take drugs, was a 'Bohemian'. The name became a reproach equally to the genuine artist, to the Bohemian by nationality and to the gypsy; to the first because, if he is to learn his craft, whether painting or writing or music, his life must be devoted to it, and not to drinking in bars and cafés; to the second because he is the most respectable and hard-working of men; to the third because, after all, he belongs to a virile and open-air race, and cannot afford to sit smoking and drinking for days together, still less to take drugs.

The results of this debasing of a word have been tragic and amazing.

When Bohemia recovered its independence after the war of 1914–18, the provisional government very naturally shied at the implication of the word 'Bohemia'. Mürger, though dead since 1861, had rendered it impossible as the name of a country. ... And so the citizens of the Bohemian state were now called 'Czecho-Slovaks' (as if the English and Scottish had been obliged to describe themselves as 'Brito-Picts' and England as 'Brito-Pictonia'). The Czechs and Slovaks showed all their historic virtues of industry and imagination; they produced great statesmen, remarkable writers and musicians; their country became the most prosperous small state in Europe. ... But when old national enmities were able to assert themselves again owing to the rise to power of the Nazis in Germany, these foes to the Bohemian nation were able to say to the masses in Europe with some show of justice: 'Are you going to involve yourselves in war in order to fight for a nation that never existed until twenty years ago? Are you going to bring on your countries all the horrors of war for a composite, hyphen-ated race of whom no one has ever heard?'

If Bohemia had then been called Bohemia, the peoples of the world would have known where they stood; the banners of history would have unfurled themselves in their minds. We should have remembered '*Ich Dien*' and the proud panache flowing in the wind about it. And Bohemia might, perhaps, still be its ancient Christian self.

Thus the work of Mürger was completed, a nation passed into servitude because a bad author had written a cheap romance.

When the old state of Bohemia is reconstituted let us hope

that its rulers will decide to defy Mürger and return to the old name of Bohemia, and that the old name will then redeem its value and beauty. . . . Meanwhile you and I can help the cause by never using the word 'Bohemian', except of an inhabitant of the country Bohemia, and by calling a waster 'a waster', and a drunkard 'a drunkard'—or, if you like, 'a drunk'.

41

THE EYE WITHIN THE EAR

For Samuel Courtauld

'SIMONIDES', Plutarch tells us, 'calls painting silent poetry, and poetry, speaking painting.'[1] Yet, in spite of this close connection between the two arts, it seldom occurs that a great painter shows himself to be a great writer as well; the perfect equipoise is to be found only, perhaps, in the drawings and notes of Leonardo da Vinci—his entries, for example, about the Deluge, on the shape and effect of waves, or on different forms of cloud and vegetation, and his sketches for them. William Blake, too, maintains a remarkably fine balance between the poetry of his *Prophetic Books* and the drawings that accompany the text. Through his achievements in both mediums there sweeps a terrible and equivocal music; the sound of the rippling of great harps played by rank on rank of Immortals, who, risen from the age of the Old Testament, but armed with the full druidical powers of the Stone Age, combine the flowing beards and flaming orbs of the prophets with the staring

[1] From 'Whether the Athenians were more Warlike or Learned'. Plutarch's *Morals*: various translators revised by William Watson Goodwin.

wide-open eyes of extreme old age. . . . On the other hand, his pictorial work seems to offer no precise counterpart to his lyrics, to such poems as *Auguries of Innocence, The Tiger* or *The Little Black Boy.* D. G. Rossetti, again, manifests a similar genius in drawings and poems. But though poet-painters are rare, nevertheless, the similarities existing between the poetry and paintings of different great individual poets and painters— a similarity that often oversteps the spirit of the works they create, and extends, so far as this is possible between diverse mediums, even down to matters of technique—opens up a no less interesting realm of speculation. Here a whole new world lies ready for the investigator, the lover of beauty, thus able to explore the great and fruitful valley of the spirit that lies between the two vast ranges of poetry and painting.

In early times, poetry—I write of English poetry—lagged far behind the art of painting. For the equivalent of the Italian or Flemish primitive we must wait a full century, or even a century and a half. . . . But let us begin.

In the mysterious beauty of the lines that follow, can there not be detected a likeness to Piero della Francesca?

> The maidens came.
> When I was in my mother's bower,
> I had all that I would.
>> The bailey beareth the bell away;
>> The lily, the rose, the rose I lay.
> The silver is white, red is the gold;
> The robes they lay in fold.
>> The bailey beareth the bell away;
>> The lily, the rose, the rose I lay.
> And through the glass windows shines the sun.
> How should I love, and I so young?
>> The bailey beareth the bell away;
>> The lily, the rose, the rose I lay.

The actual *feeling* of the words, infiltrated by some meaning that can never be grasped, is, it may be true, absent in these paintings, which are more simple in their significance. But Piero's pale maidens, as they wait, young and grave and comely in their robes, so finely sculptured, and beneath their garlands of spring flowers, are set in the same light of a golden dawn, the same hush that can never be broken save by the songs, sharp as the first summer fruit, of the earliest thrush and blackbird.

To the work of Chaucer it is difficult to find a precise counterpart; though this may be because his great poems, with their burden of warm human feeling, to our modern eyes resemble the novel more nearly than the pure poem. Notwithstanding, some affinity is, I believe, to be detected between his *Balade*

> Thy faire body, lat hit nat appere,
> Lavyne; and thou, Lucresse of Rome toun,
> And Poliscene, that boghten love so dere,
> And Cleopatre, with al thy passioun,
> Hyde ye your trouthe of love and your renoun;
> And thou, Tisbe, that hast of love swich peyne;
> My lady cometh, that al this may disteyne.

and the most beautiful of French primitives, a saint by Froment or Fouquet's picture of the Madonna, guarded by those flying angels of red sealing-wax, at Antwerp. The flowers in Chaucer's poetry are Italian flowers, though, the same blossoms that spring from the verdant pastures of Botticelli. . . . But you would expect an Italian influence, as well as a French one, for he had visited the two countries. Again, *In Honour of the City of London*, attributed to Dunbar, displays all the flat and strongly coloured beauty of a cassone-front: any one stanza chosen at random will underline this resemblance:

Upon thy lusty Brigge of pylers white
  Been merchauntis full royall to behold;
Upon they stretis goth many a semely knyght
  In velvet gownes and cheynes of fyne gold.
  By Julyus Cesar thy Tour founded of old
May be the hous of Mars victoryall,
  Whos artillary with tonge may not be told:
London, thou art the flour of Cities all.

When we begin to approach the High Renaissance, painting still marches far ahead of poetry. We may look in vain, until the latter half of the sixteenth century, for an exact equivalent in verse of the work of any great painter. Where, for instance, can we discover the precise counterpart of Giorgione? The nearest we can approach him is by indirect paths, through those painters in whom his influence is to be felt (and no artist ever existed who, with a less body of work, though not of achievement, of his own, was able by means of his genius, clear and transparent as the elements, to affect plainly the whole trend of Italian—and through it of European—painting). Thus, in certain moods, Edmund Spenser, an altogether lesser artist, shows a dim reflection of this pervading glow; occasionally a gleam of distant genius falls on his work, in the same way that it illuminates momentarily, and at times, the canvases of such a minor painter as Dosso Dossi, whose pictures are often full of an umbrageous, fugitive poetry hidden under the not seldom coarse and superficial flatness of his brushwork. His *Prothalamion*, with its exquisite refrain of

Sweet Themmes! runne softly, till I end my Song,

and with such lines as

Eftsonnes the Nymphes, which now had Flowers their fill,
Ran in all haste to see that silver brood,

[248]

As they came floating on the Christal Flood;
Whome when they sawe, they stood amazed, still,
Their wondring eyes to fill;
Them seem'd they never saw a sight so fayre,
Of Fowles, so lovely, that they sure did deeme
Them heavenly borne, or to be that same payre,
Which through the Skie draw Venus silver Teeme;

possesses the identical summer calm contained in brooding
heat, the same flat leaves carved out of the golden, translucent
mass of air, the same mysterious sounds of voices and of lutes
coming from under them, that we find in work of this painter,
and in that of Giorgione with how much greater a degree of
poetry.

The most spectacular, however, and, in a sense, the most
unexpected of such analogies is to be found in the work of
Shakespeare. But first we must note that Giulio Romano,[1]
the curious Giulio Romano, is the only painter mentioned in
his plays. In *The Winter's Tale*, Act V, Scene iii, the Third
Gentleman relates how the princess heard of her mother's
statue: '. . . a piece many years in doing, and now newly
performed by that rare Italian master, Julio Romano, who, had
he himself eternity, and could put breath into his work, would
beguile Nature of her custom, so perfectly he is her ape.'
Thus the poet seems to go out of his way to pay the painter a
tribute; and those who like to argue out such matters may
wonder what examples of his art Shakespeare had seen, whether
there were then—as there are today—pictures by him at
Hampton Court, or perhaps at Greenwich. . . . But we might
well—because of the predominant background of the world
at that time, and because of the Italian atmosphere of so many
of his plays—expect to find in his lyrics a likeness to Italian

[1] B. 1492; d. 1546. Raphael's best pupil, to whom the painter left by his will
many of his implements and works of art.

painting; but, on the contrary, the most evident case of similar imagery, and of a kinship in essence, is to be discovered in Flemish painting, as it seems to the present writer an almost perfect coincidence.

> When icicles hang by the wall,
>   And Dick the Shepherd blows his nail,
> And Tom bears logs into the hall,
>   And milke comes frozen home in pail,
> When blood is nipp'd, and ways be foul,
>   Then nightly sings the staring owl, Tu-whit!
>   Tu-who!—a merry note,
>   While greasy Joan doth keel the pot.

These lines have the very life and movement of Breughel the Elder, the same queer, elusive perspective, the magical fore-shortening and airy view of snow and red noses and bare trees, that are to be examined in such pictures of that great northern master as 'The Months' in the Vienna Gallery. Occasionally, there is—as in *Antony and Cleopatra*, or sometimes in *Romeo and Juliet*—something that reminds us of Tintoretto or Veronese; but not for long, for the light is not the same. Indeed, when we notice Shakespeare deliberately introducing into his poetry a Mediterranean element, as in the lovely

> Come away, come away, death
>   And in sad cypres let me be laid;

the lines seem, notwithstanding, to lack the vivacity and strangeness and movement of most of his poems. Further, Breughel—or one of his descendants, the Teniers—is very evident in the same clown's other song:

> When that I was and a tiny little boy,
>   With hey, ho, the winde and the raine;

> A foolish thing was but a toy,
>   For the raine it raineth every day.

Webster, it may be thought, presents a similarity—though here the comparison is far less satisfactory, for it has only a likeness of spirit, none of treatment—to Mathias Grünewald:

> Sin their conception, their birth weeping,
> Their life a general mist of error,
> Their death a hideous storm of terror,

such lines resemble one of the great panels by this master at Colmar, though his palette and certain of his forms recall William Blake. . . . On the other hand, Donne approaches, by his deliberate and compelling use of distortion, by the wild and death-charged imagery of his love, the painting of El Greco. In these two worlds of pen and brush, these two tremendous kingdoms of the spirit, flickers the same delusive light of candles, meaning so much more than it says or can illumine, the same faceted depth of jewels, rendered, not because they are sumptuous or precious, but for their quality of magic, a capacity to catch the future and hold it for an instant in their scintillant depths.

With others of the Elizabethans, however, no comparison is to be found, and though an influence—or, at any rate, a reaction—from Italy is plainly to be seen in the work of Ben Jonson, it is of an entirely different order. That which, for example, stands out so obviously in *Volpone*, and from the following lines of Sir Epicure Mammon's in *The Alchemist*

> The few, that would give out themselves to be
> Court, and town-stallions, and each-where belye
> Ladies, who are known most innocent, for them;
> Those will I beg, to make me Eunuchs of;

And they shall fan me with ten Estrich tailes
A piece, made in a plume to gather wind.
We will be brave, Puffe, now we ha' the Med'cine,
My meat, shall all come in, in Indian shels,
Dishes of Agate, set in gold, and studded,
With Emeralds, Sapphyres, hiacinths, and Rubies.
The tongues of Carpes, Dormise, and camels heeles,
Boil'd i' the spirit of Sol, and dissolu'd Pearle,

is the English moral suspicion of the Italian Renaissance, even though, for all its grudging admiration, it may bring to mind some great fresco by one of the Venetian masters.

The lesser Elizabethans appear to have their counterpart in the native plastic arts rather than in Flemish or Italian painting. The wonderful painted plaster frieze of the Boar Hunt at Hardwick, the figure of 'Ceres' there—albeit they may be the work of a Fleming—or its stone chimney-pieces, on which are sculptured all the conceits of the contemporary poets, stars and flowers and suns and dolphins and unicorns and sheaves of wheat, these are the equivalent of Peele and Nashe. In the poems of Sir Philip Sidney, for example, we might expect to discover traces of his friendship with Paolo Veronese; because friendships between English poets and great Italian masters have been very rare, and when one such relationship occurs, we should hope to find some influence from it, some concrete token of it. And, indeed, in this connection it is pleasant to wander further along the lines of conjecture, trying to summon up for our own delight the series of magnificent frescoes which Veronese would have been called upon to execute for Sidney in the royal palace of Warsaw, had that epitome of Elizabethan virtues accepted, as he was asked to do, the throne of Poland. But *Rural Poesy* and his other finest poems have none of the pictorial sumptuousness of his friend's paintings.

With the great figures of post-Elizabethan poetry a

comparison is difficult; albeit those lovers of Italian painting
who estimate Guido Reni at his true worth may think the comparison to be drawn between his pictures and Milton's poems
more exact than one between Milton and Michelangelo. . . .
Towards the end of the seventeenth century, however, the
relative positions between poetry and painting were completely reversed; poetry raced ahead of the sister art, and
remained there. Thus, with many of Dryden's lines, with those,
for example, from *Absalom and Achitophel*, beginning

> Now stop your noses, Readers, all and some,
> For here's a tun of Midnight work to come,
> Og from a Treason Tavern rowling home. . . .
> Round as a Globe, and Liquored ev'ry chink,
> Goodly and Great he Sayls behind his Link;

and with a great deal of Pope, too, a very manifest equivalent
is to be obtained, but it is with the best of Rowlandson's work,
a hundred years later, with Daumier's dark canvases, almost
another century on in time, or even with the paintings of our
contemporary, Rouault.

In the eighteenth century Gray and Richard Wilson have a
great deal in common, the same lakes, catching the light's eye,
the same ruins inhabited by melancholy; and in the late nineteenth some may observe a similarity of spirit, and even of
technique, between Verlaine and Whistler, between Baudelaire
and Gauguin. But, on the whole, comparison becomes more
difficult, since from the time of Chatterton onward a consciously archaistic spirit begins to betray itself in poetry. Of
Keats, perhaps, a reflection shows in the groves and nymphs
of Corot, but as I have suggested elsewhere, the domes of
Coleridge's *Kubla Khan* are to be found mirrored in architecture
rather than in painting. We must look for the 'stately pleasure-
dome' and for the 'gardens bright with sinous rills' in the

grounds and buildings of the Royal Pavilion at Brighton or of Sezincote in Warwickshire, rather than in the painting of the time; for Coleridge's great poem is therein reflected as surely as the dream that gave it birth was rooted in the *Travels* of Marco Polo. . . . Nevertheless, even today, when poetry and painting are more conscious of themselves, of their bodies and minds, than they have ever been before, the same untrodden land, its territory only a little diminished, still lies between them, a kingdom hard to reach, and over which rules that most incorporeal yet dominating of tyrants, the Spirit of the Age. Perhaps he is a god more than a tyrant, the messenger, the Mercury, of the Time God. His is the power to come down from Olympus and blow life into innumerable works of art that, without his inspiration, would swiftly wither and die. He seems, too, to be a god whose direction is seldom clearly seen, or indeed to many visible at all, at the moment of his descent, while the results of his visitings are not to be mistaken. For this god can make the same blossoms flower at the same time in places the most remote from each other, and in climates the most diverse; for example, he caused the pre-Raphaelite painters to flourish, poppy-fed, in their ivory towers among their blue-and-white china, and poor Richard Dadd, forlorn, immured for whole decades in Bedlam, to paint in those identical years almost in the same style, but yet without any knowledge of the contemporary work in progress outside his besieged world of delusion.

42

THE ART OF PAVEL TCHELITCHEW

(1897–1955)

I HAVE long been of the opinion that Tchelitchew was a great painter, and it is for this reason that I take up my pen to write about him. . . . But there are two kinds of great painters, and it seems as well to decide to which order he belonged—though of the two divisions, who, finally, except the person content to mouth the contemporary modes of thought, is to decide which is the greater?

One group of the masters—painters such as Giotto or Titian or Ingres or Raphael or Cézanne—leads us through the rich open pastures of pure painting. Their personality provides no veil to darken the subject here, and to lighten it there, no film of light interposed between subject and spectator. . . . But there are the others, such as Giorgione and El Greco, Simone Martini, Rembrandt or Seurat, who conduct us into a closed garden full of mysterious forms merging into shadows to listen to the sound of voices coming we know not from where, but from beyond the wall that bounds us, and carrying in their tones the most elusive intimations. In these works it is as though the silken strands of cobwebs, hitherto unsuspected, glitter for a moment in the sun.

There are, then, I think, these two divisions, and in my opinion Tchelitchew belonged to the second and more mysterious of them. Nor is this distinction I am trying to draw but another formulation of the old difference between classic and romantic; for even when Tchelitchew purposely discarded all the old cloak-and-sword effects that would come so easily to such a hand, even when he forbade himself to use his own most brilliant and personal effects of form and colour, and limited himself to a bunch of grapes or a shape as severe as a map pinned down at the corners, even then the voices still whisper their hints of immortality from behind such apparently dry and dusty curtains.

Tchelitchew was, of course, from his beginning a 'success'. He met with no difficulty, ever, in finding admirers and people who would buy his productions. Nevertheless, he suffered, I apprehend, from the fact that his work was so varied, and that he was never content to serve out the same dish every day in the year: which is the ideal, unfortunately, of most collectors of painting. His talent was infinitely varied, and showed as many successive phases as that of Picasso. . . . I wonder, at times, then, whether the contemporary world can yet correctly estimate the enrichment which he brought to it; an enrichment comparable to that which accrued when the first Spanish painters joined themselves to the European tradition, or when the first Russian novelists became engaged in the writing of the European novel. He was, in fact, the first Russian painter of Western power and originality, and counts in the same way as does El Greco as a painter, Dostoyevsky as a novelist, as a European.

There was in his work a curious and primitive horror; and

[256]

yet, this strange imaginative line, new in European art, was not far removed from certain traits in Chinese painting. It may be that here we again tap the source of Tchelitchew's power, and that we feel, in the vibration of these paintings, the oriental strain that influences all Russians. But the imagination resided in the treatment as much as in the conception. Take any of his great oil paintings, and remark how unusual and original were the textures and surfaces which he created.

Moreover, in this, as I have said, the only twentieth-century painter who could rival Picasso, he continually experimented and passed on to new modes of expression, throwing them aside afterwards. Each phase as it came, I suspect the painter himself considered to be final: but subsequently, in its turn, he rejected it, and then deemed it to be for ever discarded. It was at that moment that the jackal painters and decorators of the Art World pounced on his refuse and produced it as their own. . . . Thus, there are often exhibitions, derived solely from the example of this painter, in progress at galleries in fashionable streets, just as there are to be seen in the theatres several ballets similarly founded, without acknowledgment, on his work. Indeed, Tchelitchew's richness of imagination, the strangeness and newness of its quality, was quite as much in evidence in his designs for the theatre as in his drawings and paintings. If you had ever come across the merest scrap of a drawing by his hand—a head, for instance, scrawled on a piece of blotting-paper—and were then to be presented in the theatre with any scene which had been mounted by him, it would, however different in execution and conception, have sounded at once for you the same pealing bells that announced his personality as a painter.

A power almost of hypnotism inhabited the forms he made, so that a little mound of sand became a mountain, and a head became a sphere embodying the whole world of space as well as its own world of thought. In instance of this, take one of the giant babies he depicted for us. These infant Titans, related, despite the passage of infinite centuries, to the stone progeny of Ancient Rome, and, more nearly still, to that Children's Crusade which Michelangelo, or such an artist even as Correggio, caused to march round the walls of churches and fly up under the heavy heavens of their domes, are full of intimidation, because full of their own power to grow; infant Napoleons and infant athletes; the progenitors of some mighty brood of warriors.

I choose these heads to talk about, since the subject itself is one devoid of strangeness. The heads, in a sense, are ordinary heads; the quality of their imagination resides entirely in the treatment of them, in their presentation. But the bulls and matadors of Spain, standing so sturdily in their vast golden plains, or the bull-headed figures he drew for us elsewhere, the actors and the clowns, the singers and the strange inhabitants of that lost planet which he depicted, are full of visible as well as invisible imagination. Imprisoned in their cages of blue air stand the prima donna and the actor, the dwarf and the clown: it seems as though they would be there for ever, unable to escape, moving with the terrible slowness of a slow-motion film. All these beings seem to have a reality of their own, to stand in space, with a quality that belongs as much to the everyday world as to the world of nightmare upon which it so often touches. And thus it is, too, with Tchelitchew's later work, with the great pictures he painted in America, those huge, fecund continents that turn to naked women, those mountain ranges that are human, those trees that have the limbs of men, those masks of prophecy, caught for a moment in the spherical and opalescent perfection of a soap-bubble, or the pathetic and artful foetus, immeasurably old for all its immaturity, and comprehending within itself the whole secret of animal birth and growth, as well as the music of the choirs of angels.

43

A GRAIN OF SAND AND
A GRAIN OF SALT

O NE of the advantages pertaining to a democracy, in time of war, is that, when no definite public catalogue of war-aims or peace-aims is pronounced by its leaders, every citizen feels free to set up his private list in his own heart and fight for it. But this apparent multifariousness makes, as I hope to show, for national unity. To the contrary, the peoples of the Totalitarian States—the great Paupocracies, to coin a bastard but serviceable word—possess no notion of the perverse ideals on behalf of which they have really been obliged to sacrifice themselves. The only thing of which any single individual belonging to those countries can be confident is that, whether winner or loser, he will not be permitted to have his own way.

In Britain, on the other hand, we are sure, each of us, that our personal prescription for human ills will be adopted after the war. Some groups are engaged in a struggle to build a new civilization, others, in order to guard the old from change or to preserve their right to maintain that wars achieve nothing; some are prosecuting a mystic crusade, on behalf of nameless, mysterious but Christian ideals, occasionally led by Lord Halifax; others fight because they refuse to believe anything; some are fighting because they thought Nazi-ism to be the same as Bolshevism, others, because they hold it to be the opposite, and, at the lowest, a few are fierce in battle because two million dogs are said to have been liquidated in Germany —and, since dogs do not possess political principles, no man can be found here willing to defend this enforced liquidation and/or pronounce it to have been 'an interesting experiment'. Many, likewise, are under arms because they are British Israelites or look forward to the prophetic interpretation of the measurements of the Great Pyramid, give credence to the prognostications of Nostradamus or find comfort in the more homely couplets of Mother Shipton. Every man fights, therefore, to protect his own right to believe in what he believes, and thereby asserts in general the rights of the individual. . . . And the rights of the individual include the rights of the amateur—using amateur in its English, rather than French, sense.

In lesser matters as in greater, we insist on the rights of the amateur, and like to pay but scant attention to that which the professional says concerning the things within his own province. We even have a disparaging word for it, 'shop'. Equally, the public is never-endingly curious to hear what Sir William Dobbie or Lord Gort has to say upon God, and is much moved to know the opinion of the Archbishop of Canterbury about banking and poetry. The Director of the National Gallery was sent not long ago to the Ministry of Information to supervise the making of films (at which, being a man of talent, he no doubt proved his worth), while, equally, any film director is popular with the crowd if he lectures them upon the esthetics of Leonardo. There are continual picture exhibitions by firemen, and a wireless concert has just been given, I notice, by the Band of the Post Office. Moreover, the phrase 'freedom of the Press' impels its writers to tackle every subject that does not concern them, and perpetually to put forward madhouse or crèche schemes in finance and diplomacy, as well as in tactics and military. Only lack of space now puts a limit to their kaleidoscopic ambitions.

This system, at which it is so easy to mock, nevertheless possesses certain advantages. . . . In his declining years the Duke of Wellington is said to have summed up the virtue which had enabled him to overcome a Napoleon in the metaphor: 'Bonaparte made his dispositions in wire, I made mine in string.' And something of this same looseness and flexibility (which renders his nickname of 'The Iron Duke' so unsuitable to him) will no doubt animate, too, our present improvised war effort at its fullest; just as it inspires our conception of religion: for our national religion is apt to be hastily reassembled and mobilized, and the help of its patron constantly implored, in times of stress. On the other hand the 'good old German God', whose character never varies, who was once Thor or Odin, and was so often invoked in the last German war, still creaks down the immutable steel rails of Time to another of his recurrent tumbles.

Our danger, contrarily, transpires to be that of too much flexibility and versatility, of the public being *too* easily and variously gulled. In normal epochs the citizen is more interested in profits than prophets, but now, rather than dwell on the unhappy present, he turns to the future, and so becomes the prey of charlatans in the spiritual realm and of delusive hopes in this. For, though it may well be that a true prophet lacks honour in his own country, a false prophet is none the less honoured here because of the continual and patent failure of his prophecies. To realize the truth of this, it is only necessary to read week by week those columns that deal with the military situation. Obversely, a single false prophecy based on apocalypse and insight fatally damages a prophet of the *mystical* category, except to his own flock, bound by *espirit de corps* to support him.

For the most part, however, men and women constitute in war-time their own diviners. Patiently they tot up the figures, and find that the letters in Hitler's name, given their equivalent numerals or whatever the trick may be, amount to 666, the Number of the Beast; just as their fathers applied the same mystic stratagem, within my memory, to the Kaiser, or their ancestors, before that, to Kruger, Napoleon III and Napoleon I. Indeed I have just read a similar calculation, which worked out beautifully, applied to Louis XVI in the pages of Mrs Piozzi's *Thraleana*. William Blake wrote:

> The bat that flies at close of eve
> Has left the brain that won't believe.

And it may be that bats, in that sense, are fewer today than in time of peace.

When a friend informs me that Nostradamus foretold the calamitous advent of Léon Blum to power in France, I am not averse from believing it, for certain of his references to earlier periods—notably to the flight to Varennes—seem, but always after the event, to have been singularly apposite in a mumbo-jumbo way. Similarly I always find Strindberg's attitude to domestic portents comprehensible, albeit unattractive. . . . In my childhood, however, in remote Boer War days, my teachers used continually to stress that, while it was the 'right thing' to put my trust in every fancy incident of science, and in every supernatural occurrence related in the Bible, I must not believe in anything of the same sort that took place outside its pages. Only 'uneducated persons' and fuzzy-haired savages were superstitious, they pronounced. But I knew in my heart that, were I given the chance of it, I should prefer the company of fuzzy-haired savages to that of fringed governesses and neatly groomed tutors, and should learn more from them. As it was, I cultivated my friendship with the servants, who were then less highly educated than they are today, and in consequence possessed much greater knowledge. Their gossip was both more racy and more full of omen and portent and ghost. And, in tribute to their wisdom and character, it may be remarked that in the whole panorama of Shakespeare there occur no governesses or tutors, though there are countless memorable and typical servants, of whom Juliet's nurse is chief. . . . But the educated, I noticed, though they did not believe in ghosts, were frightened of them. In fact, they altogether neglected the psychic side of life. Not theirs

> To see the World in a grain of sand,
> And a Heaven in a wild flower,
> Hold Infinity in the palm of your hand,
> And Eternity in an hour.

My own experience, in no way, I imagine, unusual for an artist, who must possess highly trained senses, has proved them wrong. On more than one occasion in the last twenty years I have caught a glimpse for an instant of what men call a ghost— though, of course, I have no idea of the nature of the manifestation, whether subjective or objective—and three times during the last six years, but only three times altogether in my whole life, my dreams have outwitted the trained Viennese truffle-hounds of the late Professor Freud and, in their old-fashioned way, have very accurately and precisely foretold incidents in the immediate future: a winning number at roulette, the death and burial of a cousin, and the death of an

acquaintance. . . . Perhaps these episodes can be explained on
the basis of Dunne's theories, but their mystery is thereby for
me in no way dispelled.

Even the superstitious, however, should be selective. A
grain of salt must be taken to the grain of sand. And, indeed,
the growth of a certain kind of credulity in the last three or
four years has often greatly enraged me. I refer to that 'Leave
it to Old Moore' attitude which saves so much thinking, and
avoids the making of so many preparations. . . . Thus in latter
years, whenever you asked any prominent English politician
how he thought international affairs were shaping, instead of
beginning to expound his views, or those of some expert,
he would at once start his reply with 'Well, Old Moore says'
or 'Lyndoe leads us to believe . . .' Nor were these answers
founded in discretion. . . . In Germany it would have been
'The Führer is said to think . . .'; though, of course, Hitler
himself was a confirmed star-gazer.

Again, why read Old Moore and Lyndoe when you can
read Blake? What more strange and accurate indication was
there of the future than that contained in the couplet from

> The strongest poison ever known
> Came from Caesar's laurel crown.

That the poet no doubt based this prophecy upon the contemporary facts of Napoleon's career, in no manner invalidates the
predictive quality of the lines. Yet Englishmen still prefer the
star-gazing of the Sunday Press to such poetic illumination,
still rely on the spirit voices of mediums rather than on their
intuitions. . . . Myself, while remaining unregenerately
superstitious, I find the hocus-pocus of modern spiritualism
unconvincing and distasteful. When reading of mediums who
hear the voices of dead airmen, and of all the other current and

tragic psychic trash, I recall with pain the many cruel cases of deception and self-deception practised to my knowledge during the last war.

From a factual point of view, moreover, I find it difficult to put much faith in the 'controls' (as they are termed in the technical jargon) of those mediums prone to trances. Why, for example, should these controls invariably claim—according to the mediums—to be the disembodied spirits of negro, Red Indian or Chinese children? . . . Indeed, my confidence was shattered from the start: because the first time I visited a celebrated medium in order to investigate a little for myself, she at once tumbled into a trance and, falling under the influence of the little Zulu or Hottentot child whom she stated to be her guide, began to talk very quickly, whining in broken English, between really terrifying snorts and grunts, and finally, wishing to tell me that I must produce something for her to hold that belonged to me, my latchkey, if I had nothing else, said: 'Massa gimme key of wigwam.' Insinuatingly she repeated her request and with no sense of incongruity, or any feeling that, while from a negro child the word 'kraal' might take in a beginner, the word 'wigwam' would never deceive the merest tyro.

This psychic fondness for piccaninny and papoose is due, I apprehend, to the serviceable ambiguity of their childish utterance. Their lingo, that particular pidgin in which their vehicles presume them to indulge, imparts to the sentiments expressed a more than delphic equivocation. 'No-Go-Africa' may be interpreted, according to later events, as 'You are not proceeding to Africa', or as 'Please do not proceed to Africa', or as 'You would be wise not to proceed to Africa', or as 'Africa will prove a disappointment'. . . . In spite of all this, I am willing to believe that great mediums from time to time exist, and are able, though infrequently, to use their real

[265]

powers; that they are forced to eke them out with fraud in ninety-five out of a hundred cases through the continual strain of their profession and the need for them to produce results; that these gifts, usually in abeyance, are at present useless to the world, inexplicable, and in no manner connected with the spirits of the dead, being based upon some atavistic principle long forgotten by civilized man, some great natural endowment that has been allowed to run to seed and in its essence belongs to a world we have outgrown, inhabited by witch-doctor and shaman.

Strangest of all facts concerning modern man, however, is that he appears equally to despise the psychic and the physical. He believes in nothing he does not see, and yet he does not trust his eye. He seldom dares to say: 'This man must be a villain, or a fool, for he looks it.' He believes in no link between flesh and spirit, and neglects the half-tones audible from another world, no less than the poet's warning:

> We are led to believe a lie
> When we see not thro' the eye.

44

LONDON, 1943

For H.L.D.

For the last four years, London, especially during autumn and winter nights, has seemed to many of its citizens a place they had never seen before. Yet to others it may have revived memories of a London of which they have read; of London in the age of Elizabeth, or at times during the seventeenth and eighteenth centuries. In the words of Dekker, as 'soone as ever the sunne was gon out of sight . . . darkness like a thief out of hedge crept upon the earth', and 'the Banckrupt, the Fellon and all that owed any money, and for feare of arrests, or Justices Warrants had like so many snayls kept their houses over their heads all the day before, began now to creep out of their shels, to stalke up and downe the streets as uprightly . . . as if they meant to nock against the starres with the crownes of their heads. . . . The serving-man dare walke with his wench: the Private Punke (otherwise called one that boords in London) who like a Pigeon sits billing all day within doores, and feares to steppe over the threshold, does then walke the round till midnight, after she hath been swaggering amongst pottle-pots and vintner bags.'

During all the war period this great city has been at night a secret, apparently deserted, hive of darkened streets, of glimmering torches that dare not give so much light as Dekker's candle; of corners where footpads, too brutish to be conscious of their ancient ancestry, lurk once more, and where the prostitutes are bolder again in the pursuit of their dreary trade, jostling, laughing, talking loudly in broken English. Looked back on, it seems that the nights have always been dark and cold, with a soaking, all-pervading drizzle. People hurry down the streets as if they were haunted. They appear with a startling suddenness out of the darkness, and are swallowed up again by it as swiftly. Shapes are discerned for an instant, but not faces, unless a passer-by strikes a match for his cigarette. Even the searchlights, those glittering instruments that continually probe the darkness of the sky, reveal to us nothing; great domes in the sky, certainly, and golden roads of light, changing, shifting patterns, effected with diagonal lines that afford strange revelations of perspective, making us realize the immense distances above us in the heavens, so great as to have no distance; but nothing here, nothing down here below, on our own creeping level, as we scurry along, borne on a keen wind. The last buses, with their small blue lights, are starting —they seem always to be starting—and a perpetual bleating sounds from the pavements and the black doorways of apartment houses and hotels: Taxi! Taxi! Taxi! But not a single cab answers the call; each one approaching is watched by anxious groups on each side of the road; but it speeds on through the mud, unheeding. Sometimes groups of men and women in uniform, wardens or members of the A.F.S., stand in the dark gulfs that are the openings to houses, watching the interminable calculations of the searchlights, thinking of the end of their term of duty, wondering perhaps when the war will finish, and what London will be like in the years that follow.

Even as I write, London is changing again; a different sort of city, very confident of victory, has been brought into being before our eyes. Its people walk with a new ease and swagger. Many buildings have gone—yet this could be no city but London. . . . And it is at least appropriate that the background should vary, for the essence of London is change, and, in turning my half-century, I have seen and can remember at least five Londons. . . .

The earliest was the London of the late nineties, when I was a small boy; a London of vast railway stations for ever full of golden fog; a London to which the trains that came were lit by little yellow gas-flames flowering like *immortelles* beneath an inverted and steamy glass bowl. Outside, the carriages, the omnibuses, the hansoms, waited in line: but the 'growler', or four-wheeler, with the inevitable smell of oats and beer and leather within its mouldy interior, was the chief method of conveyance. First came the drive through the endless mean streets, and then the West End, the old Regent Street, lying in front of us, gas-lit, with the curve of some sickle-bay in a Greek island. . . . At night there was little traffic, the clop-clop of an occasional cab, the bells of a hansom and the forlorn and desultory whistling that served as its enticement. The daylight, when—and if—it came, revealed a city of yellow plaster houses, continually repainted, a modest city of crumbling caryatids and vases—though always, of course, there existed as a background and a culmination the splendid exteriors of Wren's churches, to show to what heights of genius, and even of magnificence, the English art of good manners and the plain statement of humane facts could rise. It showed, too, a city of paint and varnish and of glitter, transient in its impeccable finish. The brief winter sun flecked its red-gold on every kind of shining object, brass plates, plate-glass windows, elegant balconies, newly painted and varnished doors, and upon the royal coats of arms, and supporting lions and unicorns that embellished certain favoured shops, and drew out of them, though in a subdued and most respectable manner, a thousand muted sparkles. In spite of the high lights, there was no ostentation. The top-hats of the wealthy and of the hansom-cab drivers, with their polish and dark shining glitter, might well have stood for the symbol of this world now perished; but the clothes of the women, rich and poor alike, were complicated, fussy, designed for richness rather than for beauty or for smartness; fashions that remained the costume of Cockneys on gala days even until the outbreak of the present war. This London that I first remember was the capital of the world, whither the Thames bore its tribute of the spices of the East; delicacies responsible for as many wars as, since that time, has been the gold of South Africa—also conveyed here regularly, and over which hostilities were even then about to break out. Cattle from South America, leather from Russia, endless objects from China, wheat from America and Canada, all were brought hither, while some of the cargoes, no doubt, were of the most unexpected and almost fabulous character—humming-birds from the West Indies, hundred-year-old eggs from China for the colony in Limehouse, sea-shells from the coastline of Arabia, fruit from South Africa, turtles for Lord Mayors' banquets brought from the South Sea Islands or the islands of the West Indies. And the great fortunes that resulted from the commerce in these and other outlandish goods were to be lavished on such temporary, homely things as paint and varnish in a city so dark and foggy that one could seldom see the effect which they were attempting; thus the little sparkle that could be obtained ranked as a moral, rather than a material, aim.

The next London I knew was the city of stilted Edwardian

baroque, when the full tide of riches and materialism was sweeping over Victorian London, submerging it. The old Nash houses of Park Lane, so modest in their luxury, many of them rising to no more than two storeys, country villas set down on the most expensive sites in the world, were making way for riotous excesses, for flights in the Chinese Gothic manner, and for fantasies in the Hindu and Arabian styles; the capital of England was becoming a cosmopolitan city. Everywhere you looked the stucco houses were beginning to be torn down, and the monotonous, swollen palaces of commerce and of the newly created bureaucracy were replacing them. Only the lodging-houses and the slums remained the same. London, formerly, in the last century, renowned for its dullness and decorum, was now the pleasure capital of the world, and for the first time conscious of its mission. Triumphal roads, arches, stone balustrades, had been constructed. Blore's old plaster front of Buckingham Palace, chocolate brown, and with the statues of Britannia and the Lions decorating its roofline, was soon to be hacked down, and a rather mean and featureless Portland-stone façade, a kind of gigantic prophecy of prefabrication, was to be erected in its place. Portland stone constituted an ideal, to be worshipped rather than used. This was now a city built for processions, called into being to challenge the Rome of the Emperors; these great streets were built for visiting monarchs and for semi-captive princes to ride down, potentates who must be cheered enough, but not too much, on their way to Guildhall banquets. The Guildhall itself, and those who governed it, were still unique in their civic consequence, as when Dunbar had praised them five hundred years before:

Thy famous Maire, by pryncely governaunce,
With swerd of justice the rulith prudently.

[271]

No Lord of Parys, Venyce, or Floraunce
In dignytie or honoure goeth to hym nye.
He is exampler, loode-ster, and guye.

At night, as during the day, the din of motors, of lorries
thundering along the roads, was overwhelming. In the day-
time, horse traffic had almost disappeared, except for the vans
of a few obsolete, obstinate tradesmen, yet clinging to old
ways and deathlessly determined to block the traffic; though at
night the slow, clumsy market carts, with the carter asleep,
still lumbered along Piccadilly. But by 1912 there were not
more than a hundred hansoms left; one of them was the only
three-wheeled cab in London. In addition to the two enormous
wheels of the ordinary hansom, it boasted a small third wheel
tucked underneath it, the purpose of which remained obscure.
This cab was owned, and had been invented, by its driver,
who wore a black bowler hat and a black beard. He was a
man of marked originality, and a delightful and untiring
conversationalist, and I used much to enjoy a talk with him
after the opera, for normally he plied outside Covent Garden
Theatre.

The hotels, previously discreet and even muffled places of
comfort, given over still to muffins and stone hot-water bottles,
had now blossomed out into cosmopolitan centres, created in a
universal Louis-Quinze style, and each, despite the impossi-
bility of telling it from the next, famous throughout the globe.
The opera was the most celebrated in the world, mounted on
an unusually extravagant and ugly scale, until Sir Thomas
Beecham came to reform it. But even if the stage often left
something—or rather less of something—to be desired, the
audience was certainly the most astonishing spectacle in
Europe. The glitter of the jewels and the general splendour
could not be matched elsewhere, and the talk, during the

music, was louder—if not more entertaining. (The story of the well-known hostess who cancelled her opera-box on the grounds that she had a sore throat, belongs to this period, though it is said to have occurred in later years.) Indeed Edwardian London rivalled for gaiety that of Elizabeth I or Charles II.

Nevertheless, in this genial Edwardian climate, the arts too were beginning to be respected, and there were among the rich some who had begun on occasion to wonder whether the clever were not more amusing than the dull. They would perhaps experiment, invite one or two of them to their houses. . . . Indeed a ferment was to be felt in the art world. Shaw's plays were beginning to be popular; Augustus John's vast and impressive pictures of gypsies squinting in their camps were attracting much attention, and, finally, Russia, represented by Diaghilev and his band of painters and dancers and musicians, had taken artistic London captive with a genius for music, dancing and stage spectacle new to Western Europe. Russian ideas now influenced fashion and spread even to house decoration. The ballet *Scheherazade* alone was reponsible for innumerable lampshades and cushions that blazed in barred and striped splendour from the shop windows; and a more exotic style began to banish the drawing-room wall-papers trellised with roses and water-lilies, and the early Edwardian wood-panelling, that had seemed created as a background for long cigars, or perhaps even fashioned out of the fabric of their boxes. For the rest, in the warm long summer evenings, dance music prospered in the golden air of the squares, and striped awnings rose like mushrooms in the night to shelter the international herds of the rich. For more rich people congregated here than anywhere in the globe; and more poor—but the poor now had their diversions, mammoth football matches and cricket matches, and newspapers which, on Sunday, served up at

S

great length every species of moral delinquency in order to shock the intense and abiding sense of respectability and responsibility, dwelling still in the hearts of the majority of the citizens of London.

This glittering city of lights ended on 4th August 1914, and for the next four years a different London, a London in transition, came into being. . . . Now it had become a place devoted to officers and to men on leave. We were perpetually surprised at the way in which this darkened city, ever bleeding from the immense losses in process of being suffered just across the water, kept up its spirits. Lights were low, and bombs—though few and feeble compared with the bombs that fall on cities today—were yet sufficient in number and strength to be intimidating; but the cheerfulness was maintained, even when there was no manifest reason for it. Indeed, the First World War came in and went out in a blaze of popularity. I saw the vast crowds cheering it in front of the Palace in August 1914; I saw them dance it out in every paved square and open space on the night of the 11th November 1918.

Within a few years of the Armistice, one London the more had come into being—a new city which largely depended on the ruin of the old. The clouds of dust, rising from street and square, now added the same peculiar glory to London sunsets that the volcanic dust from the erupting mountain of Krakatoa was previously said to have produced. The age of destruction, which had originated in 1914, was continuing. Concrete was beginning to replace Portland stone; and the country itself, within a radius of thirty miles, was becoming part of London. A vast new economic class had been called into being, and the individual members of it were being housed in the red bungalows and villas on the city's edge. There was a new tendency to extravagance in life and morals, and the acts of a few rich young people, who, endowed with an idiot persistence, set themselves to enjoying life in their own manner—culminating in the celebrated exploit when they, literally, 'set the Thames on fire'—attracted more attention than the steady conduct of the mass of reputable citizens. But the mass of reputable citizens loved, nevertheless, to read of these antics in the papers.

The ferment in the arts continued, but there was never quite the same feeling as had existed in the former decade, that we stood at the edge of a great art revival. The fact that the stupid had been once again proved right—for they had been the only people to foretell the war—had set a further premium on general stupidity. It became the rage. . . . All the same, in spite of the complacency, in spite of the smugness, in spite of the vulgarity, it was an epoch of hope and accomplishment. People were happy. . . . But at the end of the pleasure-loving twenties, a difference was to be sensed in the air, a certain imponderable dullness, typified by the new fashion in house decoration; there was, it seemed, a rush for the vacuum, for negation, for nothingness, for beige and cinders and ashes; for white, and more white, and white on white, and near-white.

Now came the desolate London of the thirties, a disconsolate and apprehensive city; the City of the Slump, when all wondered what lay behind the curtain—for everyone could feel that it was on the point of rising. An intense and dreary earnestness blighted the arts. The newer buildings were less vulgar but more boring. There must be no trimmings. Life was to be a matter of wrestling with facts in a continual struggle, and economics began to take the place of religion. (Soon it would be impossible to distinguish the speeches of an archbishop from those of Lord Keynes.) Wren and the great builders had not, it was felt, looked life in the face, or come to grips with it. A wave of spiritual desolation engulfed literature, architecture and painting, and the voice of Lord Elton began to be heard in the land. I am not trying to say that the painters were not in themselves good, but a nightmare brooded behind their minds, and poetry—leaving even the marvellous world of nightmare aside—became acrostical, argumentative, a matter of addition and subtraction plus moral fervour. But artists are always right, always initiate, always inspired ahead by the years to come. . . . Outside, apart from the looks on the faces, which had indeed altered, the life of the West End remained much the same, except that hotels were fuller, the food in them richer and worse, the motor-cars more numerous. And when a reigning monarch—so much rarer a figurehead now than in the London I have previously described—came to visit us, he was still received in a style with which no other place could vie. . . . At night, though, a difference was to be detected. There were lights, neon lights and electric signs. The news, nearly always bad, wound itself in letters of fire round the squalid cornices of large Victorian buildings, yet, in spite of the greater illumination, the life of the streets had grown less vivid, partly, perhaps, because of the various purity campaigns, fiercely supported by the police, and partly because the suburbs offered the same form and quality of entertainment. The night was dull.

The London that followed was the darkened, sublunar London that we know today, and that I have attempted to describe at the beginning of this essay. Yet, as I have said, this war-time London itself has varied widely enough. . . . Compare, for example, the city of dropping bombs in September 1940 with that of 1943. Both are alike only in their darkness. On the second night of the 'blitz' I walked from Charles Street, Berkeley Square, to my home in Chelsea. It took me half an hour, and I passed hardly anyone on the way except constables on duty, in steel helmets. There was no traffic; a few buses, dark, black and deserted, drawn up in small lines at the sides of the roads. The noise then came from falling bombs, not from our gun-fire, for, in those times, we had few guns with which to fire, few aircraft with which to give battle. That kind of night has gone; only the black-out persists. . . . Now, as I write, the long summer evenings are beginning, and we are no longer confined to the primitive darkness of the Stone Age. The streets, during the long twilight, are crowded with soldiers of every nationality, French and Dutch, Greek and Polish, American and Norwegian. Some talk gaily, others are musing, thinking perhaps of the vast endless wheatfields of Canada or the States, that roll their golden waves over a whole continent, covering it with the sign of the sun; others are remembering sadly the tobacco-stained air of the cafés of provincial towns in France, the quiet talks and the games of chess, or the inns, where workmen sit outside under a trellised vine, above a river, and drink coarse red wine. Others, again, recollect scenes in Poland and Bohemia, pictures that suddenly flash into their minds, memories of their families, a chanting in a church, a bear trundling out of a wood into the snow.

In the day-time the city blazes with life, in spite of the ruined buildings, now tidied up and finished off like newly made graves. The flat lawns of water, installed where once were the basements of houses, reflect the light, and people—because of the deadness of the winter nights—cram into these hours of summer daylight an unimaginable pressure of life. The parks, too, trampled and without any railings, are fuller than in peace-time. Airmen, sailors, soldiers are lying and sitting on the grass, sunning themselves, and in some parks, where formerly duels were fought, groups of sturdy young Americans are playing baseball. The streets round Piccadilly teem with men in uniform, especially Americans. Everything is very bright, flamboyant and sure of itself. And the spring of 1943 provided an unequalled setting for this gaiety; it favoured the Americans, who must have been granted almost as many hours of sunshine here as they would have enjoyed at home. Flawless day followed flawless day, alike in its golden rind, until finally, in April, the whole city burst into flower; apple and cherry blossom, prunus and peach and lilac, in a thousand delicate, egg-shell varieties. The suburban gardens, the gardens of Hampstead and Chiswick, and such outlying districts, became comparable to tropical jungles. You could scarcely see the walls dividing them. The new shrubs introduced into common use some twenty years ago—and every Londoner is a gardener—had now grown up. Never had there been such a profusion of blossom. Even in China, even in Central America, with its jacaranda and coral and flamboyant trees, even in Spain, during the spring, when in the orchards of Andalusia, almond, peach and orange burst simultaneously into bloom, never have I beheld a scene which suggested an equal force of flowering.

It was such weather as caused you to look out of window every instant, and called on you to walk whenever you got the chance. . . . I used every day in those weeks to go by the Green Park, and thence into St James's Street, making my way there by means of what had formerly been a dark, narrow passage, pressed between high walls of old and grimy yellow brick but was now open to air and sky. On one side, below a wall a foot high, I passed every time, a floor of white marble, with an inlaid circular pattern, in the antique manner, of porphyry and serpentine; a floor now identical in appearance with those from which originally it had been copied a hundred years before, those pavements that have been uncovered by archaeologists in the Roman Forum, or in the Golden House of

Nero. Thus one night of modern high explosive can be seen to have produced the same effect as the rolling past of two millenniums, including numberless incursions of old-fashioned barbarians, and numberless outbreaks of old-fashioned wars. . . . But what imparted to this floor for me a particular interest arose, I deduce, from my egotism: this was the hall floor of a house in which I had often dined; it was here, standing on these designs in inlaid marble, that the butler and footman had waited deferentially to take the top-hats and coats of the guests. On the staircase above had stood the majordomo after dinner, posted there to call out the names of those who were arriving for the ball; names that he called portentously, as though trying to evoke an echo out of a tomb. The rooms that lay beyond were, when I knew them, always full of people, gay with flowers and pictures, and with tapestries that seemed from their colour to have been fashioned from rose petals. . . . When next I see the floor of a villa uncovered in some meadow or by the classic sea I shall be able to picture better than before the life of which it is the surviving token. And the smaller floors, those wooden miles of flooring that have gone, completely vanished; they meant as much, and are no less our gage that London shall be rebuilt, and yet remain her own self, only more splendid.

Of all the cities in the world, the future calls upon London, when the hour strikes, to rise from her ashes with a magnificence transcending even her own tradition in that respect. For, indeed, ashes are nothing new to her; like the Phoenix, she soared up from them once before, in a splendour born from flames. This historic city, already of 'high renown' in the Middle Ages, bore in it, even then, the traces of a legendary past and the seed of a no less fabulous future. Moreover, it was the prototype in Europe of the great modern cosmopolitan centres. As early as the first years of the Hanoverian dynasty, it possessed—apart from Naples—the largest population of any Western city, and by the middle of the eighteenth century it had come to contain its enclaves of Chinese, French, Indians, Italians. And this fact, more than any other, illustrates the nature of London. As with Imperial Rome before her, the very character of the place is complex in its essence, varied and variable. And we must, therefore, be most careful not to rebuild it in a way that will restrict it to one particular facet of its genius.

London, then, is not one city, but a noble group of cities, united by the waters of a river—the Thames, that tranquil and seemly river which, with its dark, quiet flowing, has made our capital one of the world's treasures.

> Above all ryvers thy Ryver hath renowne

wrote Dunbar, for the importance of the Thames was recognized from the first moment that London began to flower, and, instead of trying to hide it, we should undoubtedly strive continually to lay emphasis upon it. It is the Thames that quickens London every day with a breath of sea-air, and the Thames through which the blood of the Five Continents beats. These unsensational waters, with their typical lack of glitter, with their effects of beauty dependent upon surrounding mists and darkness, and a sense of purpose, are yet more important than any of the great historic rivers of the world. The Thames is, indeed, the one permanent feature of a shifting scene, for London changes with each decade. It was always a lavish, always a spendthrift city, tearing itself down and building itself up, apparently with no purpose but commerce and a love of change. We Londoners have destroyed, or allowed to be destroyed, even in the last two decades, far more of our historic heritage and architectural wonders—take the great squares of the West End alone—than the Germans could ruin in several years of war. During each raid that I experienced in London I was able to thank Heaven that we had been permitted to enjoy the sensation of destroying these things ourselves, and that if, for example, the Germans were blowing up the present Regent Street, at least the damage to the arts would be negligible. Nor must we forget that the clearing process effected by the German planes has, esthetically, its good aspect. If it has destroyed little of military value, it has rid many of the classical churches of their hideous Victorian coloured-glass windows, which defaced entirely the interiors of some of them. Similarly, in certain instances, the glass roofs of buildings have been injured, and we can see how unsuitable they were and are. Those condensers and preservers of fog and darkness are no longer apropos. Time, moreover, heals the wounds of a great city very quickly, and, for example, many who knew Paris intimately would be amazed if they realized how much of it perished in the Siege and the Commune, how much has been patched, mended and renewed. The unforgivable scars in that city, the boulevards and the vulgarization, were the work of the inhabitants themselves; Haussmann's wholesale reconstruction, regardless of tradition, made Paris hard and mean and featureless, and long ago, moreover, its great arcaded alleys had become the centre of the world's traffic congestion; which nullified their whole purpose.

What sort of city, then, are we to build to make a capital worthy of the people of London? (. . . I do not intend to write about London here from the angle of hygienic housing, but from the esthetic point of view, for bad housing will no longer be tolerated. Moreover, one cannot live in one's bath; we must have a perspective outside it.) . . . First, let me offer a word of advice.

[281]

Never trust architects; they are the most untrustworthy of artists, and have now become entangled with interior decoration and the various stages of fashions. Some would like to make the City of London into a garden suburb; others, under the spell of a tardy but grandiose Edwardian ideal, into the sort of thing we have lately seen at the Royal Academy; others want a cement hive for busy bees, a Middle Western city or mid-European, a concrete cobweb of flat-faced, flat-roofed houses. But we must avoid constructing a city in which each house resembles an airplane. There is no need for it, any more than there was a need, in the nineties of the last century, to build a city in which every house resembled a bicycle. The airplane is only a method of conveyance. We want none of these schemes, no excesses, old or new. . . . What we want is a new *London*, not just a new city.

Therefore the characteristics of the place, inherent in the nature of the various districts and its inhabitants, must not be denied. . . . London is, and must continue to be, a conglomerate city, what in botanical terms is called a composite. We must uphold the ancient—what little of it remains—as much as build another London. Modelling our new capital we must yet take as a model the old. Above all, we must remember the classical tradition, the hundred spires and shell-like turrets of Wren and Hawksmoor, so dignified and beautiful, and so unlike any other system of architecture in the world; a London that could only be London, austere and solid and reasonable, for all its imagination. We must never again haggle for years over the rebuilding of a bridge, but build with certainty, create bridges that are a hundred times more lovely and more effective than those that stand today.

Let us examine the proposed semi-Edwardian scheme, for it has the greatest popular support since it entails the spending of the most public—by which is meant private—money. We saw plans and models of gardens and fountains and arcades built with arches too wide apart to give us shelter from the delights of our climate. . . . Fortunately, London is London; even when we abolish a great part of the fog by abandoning the use of coal fires, it—thank God—will still be a lovely and a foggy city. . . . I imagine that, when the first Romans or the first Britons came to the site of this great metropolis, what they beheld on the marsh each side of the river banks was— a London fog. That, too, is what our most remote descendants will see.

It is a special and a very lovely robe of pearly smoke and mist in which our capital thus arrays herself. It possesses every attribute of poetry, and has been lauded, in their various mediums, by artists as dissimilar as Dickens and Whistler. It may not be easy to breathe, but it is the native atmosphere, and so there can be no purpose in introducing into it those vistas created for sunlight in Florence, Paris or New York. London should—and always will—be a Gothic city, true to its soil, a place of surprises, in which you come upon things suddenly, and not a town in which you can see at great distances. In Rome the superb twin colonnades of St Peter's enclose, above its fountains, stretching high over domes and towers, a vast arena of blue sky, piled with Roman clouds, like the trophies of conquered nations; but here, in London, we should not, if we are wise, plan to see too much of the sky, or it will fall on us in rain and snow and soot. We need arcades, certainly; but to protect, and not to expose, us. If you open up a vista of St Paul's, what you will see will not be St Paul's, but more fog, and, perhaps, a policeman looming up out of it from near an island. . . . The people of Bologna created, against the rain and cold of their winter, a special city of narrow arcaded streets, giving shelter. We must, similarly and obversely, be

[283]

true to the tremendous fogs that have been granted to us as a birthright. We must remember that both Inigo Jones and Wren, though it was then a so much smaller city, understood London. They gave it those precise towers and spires round which London fogs wreathe themselves with a peculiar splendour, suddenly releasing, as it were, the vision of them, so that they are unexpected, magnificent. We must remember that Nash's stucco and Wren's Portland stone were the most admirably suited mediums for building in this atmosphere, for the first could be—and must be—continually repainted, and the second acquired, from being smoked, a perfect texture and colour. We must try to invent new building mediums with the same qualities. We must never seek to emulate other cities, but only to transcend our own. We must not, for example, embank our river (alas, it has already been done), hemming it in as if it were some paltry ditch, because continental cities have treated their rivers in this way. We must avoid making another and more heartless cosmopolis; a poorer edition of some South American city copied from Paris or Vienna. We must remember that the people of this city are a people full of heart—and that is what the teeming irregularities of London have always shown and represented.

The seasons may vary, and with them the aspects of London; a fresh London may grow up and disappear, but the character of its inhabitants never changes. They are, indeed, the citizens of no mean city, and prove themselves worthy of it every day; royal in their politeness, ostentatious—even the poorest—in their generosity, unequalled in their courage, unsurpassed in their originality. In spite of the immense foreign influence brought to bear on London for so many centuries, the people are the very essence of the country. Rich and poor are alike in their courage, in the continuity of their conduct and in their determination. The rich accept countless inconveniences without a murmur, resolved to bear, without flinching, everything to which they are accustomed—bad food, little food, cold, walking in wet streets for miles, no servants, disagreeable servants—all because the war must be won. You can almost hear them repeating under their breath the public-school commandments: 'Do not let the side down, you can't do it, don't-yer-know.' The poor remain equally steadfast, working harder than ever, and taking little advantage of the position in which they now find themselves. Like those formerly more fortunate than themselves, they have little to which to look forward, but they are as resolute, unbeaten and unbeatable. And although the rich members of society may be more staid in demeanour, there is a feeling of irresponsible gaiety and *élan* about true Cockneys, as can be remarked during any Bank Holiday on Hampstead Heath. City-bred, they have the country-man's humour, identical, sharpened only by an additional tolerance and quickness. An immense love of liberty, a feeling for the best of life, inspires them. In their humour there is a sort of wise gravity that no other people knows, a consciousness, too, of the sacred idiosyncrasy of every human being that is typically English.

In this connection, I often recall an occasion before the war, when I heard a Covent Garden porter, as the crowd was coming out of the opera, hail a taxi in the street for an elegant young man in white waistcoat and top-hat, and open the door for him with the words 'In with you, Norman!' . . . Or, again, I think of the time when I passed some navvies in the now destroyed Lansdowne Passage. One of them dropped a paving stone as I passed, with a tremendous crash, and, noticing that I jumped at the noise, remarked—with a true observation of character, for he plainly deduced that I was not a devotee of night life, but an artist, possessed of a delicate nervous system—'There, sir! . . . That's the worst of them night-clubs!' . . .

What a mistake Hitler made to provoke these people, the inhabitants of this city, let alone of Great Britain and of the Empire! . . . How is it possible not to love Londoners, with their understanding of life, their want of envy?

45

A BUNCH OF SNOWDROPS

For those who are no longer children, Christmas, whether they enjoy it or not, must inevitably be a brief season of nostalgia—and this is all the more to be savoured in a foreign land whose habits at this season greatly resemble those one knew at home. (*Foreign* is a word inapt to describe how an Englishman feels in the States or, I hope, how an American feels in England.) In Italy, on the other hand, Christmas is very different from ours: there are the old, indigenous customs, many of them pagan in origin, others touchingly and tenderly Christian and medieval, as when the *Pifferi* come from the mountains to blow their bagpipes in front of the lighted images of the Virgin throughout the length of Italy. But the American Christmas so greatly resembles our own—or let me qualify that by saying the English Christmas of thirty years ago—that it is bound to bring back memories. In an age of catastrophe and dissolution, these memories, albeit they may in themselves be happy, are bound to give life to old regrets.

One Christmas, then, I passed at Boston—and, as might be expected, the occasion itself was happy. To one fresh from the splendours and exaggerative beauties of New York, which I so greatly love, Boston seems as English in its architecture, in the houses on Beacon Hill, and the shell-like spires of its churches, as does its climate at Christmas. The actual eve of Christmas I spent in the house of my two dearest friends in Boston, and in the atmosphere of pervading hospitality and affection which they evoked—and under the influence, I may add, of the delectable society and excellent claret they provided—all feelings of sadness were quickly forgotten, and I enjoyed every moment of the evening, the company of the people in the room, the crowds outside, the lighted candles in the windows, the carols. . . . Only in the darkness of the night, when I woke up, a sudden scent of snowdrops assailed me—are snowdrops also an American flower?—and it seemed to me suddenly that I had come a long and tiring way from the point at which I started. I was now, I believed—but how could one ever be sure?—a celebrated writer, I was certainly delivering lectures in a great and distant land, at fifty-six years of age. In a way it sounded comforting. By today's standards, fifty-six is no great age: but the people I knew as a child were dead, the world in which they lived was dead, and even though I had not liked all of them or it, it was borne in on me how quickly life could change its surface.

As I lay there in the darkness, the Christmas Days I had spent in my childhood loomed up at me like beads on a chain, or snowdrops gathered in a bunch. . . . The first I remember was spent under the hospitable roof of Ganton, the country-house of the Legards in Yorkshire, and a name known to all lovers of memoirs because of its frequent occurrence in the pages of the Comtesse de Boigne's reminiscences. Sir Charles Legard, portly and affable in the manner of the Prince of Wales (for we are still in Queen Victoria's reign), wearing a bowler hat and a dark suit, and Lady Legard, my godmother, tight-waisted, charitable, dressed in lilac and white, are drawn for ever in my memory against a background of snow.

There was a famous frost that winter, and they were forced to walk delicately when they went out, as if walking on ropes—and I remember that the cold had obliged the rabbits to nibble every morsel of stick or leaf left above snow level. The memory is sweet, tender and bitter as the smell of the bunches of early snowdrops from Renishaw, which reached us when we returned to our house at Scarborough; and which remain for me ever associated with the festival.

The first snow must have gone at Renishaw, or the flowers would not have come out. It was early for them. As they lay there, before my nurse took them from their damp box, I well remember my rapture at seeing those delicate, green-veined, frosty flowers, gothic in shape and edged with green, and with a particularly evasive and enticing scent; indeed, invented for what reason except to please human beings, because assuredly no insects are present at that season to be attracted?

After that first festival to be recalled, when I was three or four, came a Christmas spent in London. At that stage of infancy, the fact of mortality was still beyond my understanding, and I remember wondering what my father meant as, looking at a letter received from his father-in-law, Lord Londesborough, he remarked to my mother: 'As they've been invited, the children had better spend Christmas in London, with your father and mother. They're growing old, and may not be here much longer.'

What, I wondered, did he mean, and where would old people like that go to, at their age? (About their destination, perhaps, a doubt still lingers in my mind.) However, I entered enthusiastically into the idea of spending Christmas in London.

It meant, I knew, that we should be taken on the night of Boxing Day to the opening of the Christmas pantomime at Drury Lane—an occasion for which all children longed—and see the great Dan Leno as the Widow Twankey in *Aladdin*.

The atmosphere of London at Christmas proved overwhelming: the moment we reached the station, after a journey of five unheated hours, it came at us. The station was a cavern of iron, with a glass roof, crammed with the fog and smoke of eons: from its menacing, dark shelter, full of shouts and bustle, we stepped into a four-wheeler, bitterly cold and smelling of oats, beer and fog in equal proportions. Even the hoarse voice of the red-nosed cabman carried out, as it were, the same stupendous epitome of the season.

We drove to Grosvenor Square, where was the family mansion, and in it an exotic air of warmth, excitement and Christmas delights and surprises; which prevailed, too, in the day-time in the near-by streets, in the bouquets of sweet-scented flowers in the windows, in the toy-shops, crowded with ingenious mechanical treasures, and the fruit-shops, now full of southern fruits, such as tangerines, Elvas plums, starred with coloured paper, dates and raisins.

The size of London, in its thick muffling canopy of white or yellow fog, was immense, imposing: a fog lit by flares and torches, and through its often impenetrable texture would sound perpetually the cheerful, faintly contaminated Cockney vowels, as the shoppers at stalls and small stores called, one to another, and spoke of the weather, and of Christmas.

Yet, in spite of that urban experience of it, Christmas remains for me essentially a rural feast. Only a few Christmases did we spend at Renishaw—and these were overshadowed by my father's disapproval of the whole occasion, and by his fear of 'getting the children into extravagant habits by giving them presents'. (He hated to give presents to people who expected them, or when they expected them, and I still recall, with tremors of discomfort, the Christmas I spent with him in Venice some decades after, and how, when the amiable Italian waiter remarked to him: 'Good morning, Sir George, and a happy Christmas!', he replied in a tone of disillusioned comprehension: 'I know!')

My mother certainly made up for our lack of amusements as much as she could: yet Christmas at home remained a rather barren festival. But when I was about eight, my grandfather died and we began to spend Christmas every year in the house of his son. And it was this series of ten or so Christmases, spent under the roof of my uncle and aunt Londesborough at Blankney, that have subsequently conditioned and defined my ideas of Christmas, it horrors and pleasures.

It was perhaps not a typical Christmas, being more international and exotic, and scarcely Christian, except for brief desultory, purely formal appearances in church. No, pleasure, comfort, warmth, sport were the objectives, and these were obtained.

The large house was always full of relatives of every age, from second childhood down to first: some were in bathchairs, others in perambulators, some remembered King George IV and the great Duke of Wellington, some remembered nothing, from having left off remembering, others had not yet begun to remember. There would often be foreign connections present as well as English.

As for the children, we were tied to compulsory pleasure, as later, at school, to compulsory games. We took part certainly in the feasting of our elders. We watched them hunting, shooting and engaged in other diverse and repulsive sports, such as clubbing rabbits on the head, but we were, on the other hand, made to perform a French play, under the tuition of a whole platoon of governesses. This would be given before villagers who understood no word of French, and were there by a kind of corvée.

But, above all, Christmas was henceforth to be associated for me with my giant and genial uncle and his two passions, for music and mechanics. In the passages he had accumulated some twelve or fourteen mechanical organs; cases with glass fronts that revealed trumpets and drums that, when set in motion, could be seen indulging in an orgy of self-blowing and self-beating. This elementary, if expensive, form of juke-box greatly pleased the children, even if it acerbated the nerves of our elders, who did not like their favourite selections from Verdi—for such they usually were—played in this fashion.

But now the music is stilled, the machines are obsolete; the fashionable beauties and the plain, poor relations are equally unfashionable, for they are dead, even most of those who were young children fifty years ago—and the dead are always unfashionable.

As I look back, I see the vast tents of the rooms, lighted during the day's dark as well as the night's, shining out for miles over untrodden fields of snow that ended beyond our vision in the white-fringed sea; rooms that were filled with the contemporary symbols of luxury, palm trees of exceptional stature, poinsettias that seemed to bear as flowers stars cut out of red flannel; a fragrance of wood-smoke, and jonquils and freesias, hung in the air. . . . But, framing all these and bringing them back to me, is the more rustic smell of snow-drops, edged with a few prickly green leaves, their stalks tied roughly, inexpertly, with thin, damp string, lying in a damp cardboard box that has just been opened.

46

A LETTER TO MY SON

For my friend Duff Cooper

My Dear Boy,

O NE thing at any rate we share in common—an un-
common laziness. We both of us, I know, hate writing
letters—especially long letters. You will, therefore, when you
receive this, and count its pages, at once comprehend how much
energy it required for me to take the decision, and make the
effort to overcome in this single instance that mutual diffidence
upon which, I fully realize, a sound father-and-son relationship
must rest. But some apology from me is surely due to you for
the condition of the world in which you find yourself—more
especially because, before you were born, I foresaw the probability that the present conflict would ensue. And, above all,
I feel that you should know what I *really* think upon a number
of matters, for, when we meet, the joy of discussing family
affairs, and what we have each of us been seeing and doing,

is apt to banish talk of more serious things, even if our relationship did not make us dubious of approaching too near to them. It is true, of course, that being a generation older I can give you little direct help in your career, but, since we are both artists—and here I may pause to congratulate myself, for I expected a butcher, a house agent, a general as a son, but never another writer—I can, moreover, tell you, out of a long, tedious and at the same time enlivening experience, how to save yourself trouble in pursuit of your goal. Because it is vital to both of us that we should realize that the war is only the Great Interruption, and that your career *must* continue.

In spite of the talents you bring to your profession—and of them I entertain no doubt—it would be idle to pretend that it now offers you much prospect of an immediate success. The centre of the arts has shifted from Paris and London to New York, perhaps for a few years, perhaps for a generation, perhaps for centuries, and we find ourselves in consequence stranded upon an inimical shore, the members of a despised and maltreated sept. Sometimes I blame myself, indeed, for your sake that I did not go to America many years ago, as my friend Aldous did, and make your home there, but I am glad, too, that we stayed at home, because both you and I come from a stock not easily uprooted. In America we should not have felt at our ease, should have remained visitors. Yet our position here is not easy, for not only are we both artists, but we come of the privileged—formerly privileged—classes, and therefore are shot at by both sides; since the kind of people amongst whom I was born and brought up are still uneducated in esthetics, only respect pro-consuls and big-game hunters, and, worse still, have been infected with middle-class conventionality and worship of money, while the great majority, the voters, are unlettered, can read only the columns of the daily Press, and are now every day flattered into thinking themselves the arbiters of all excellence in the arts. As well tell every daisy that it is a rose!

I must cease generalizing now, though, and descend to the particular and the personal. . . . Those who do not know you well would say you were bitter, for you can express yourself pointedly: indeed, I have always been struck, ever since you were a boy, by the ease with which you formulate your opinions and the clarity with which you express them. You cannot have been more than fifteen or sixteen when, for example, you said to me—perhaps I paraphrase it—that it seemed to you that the embryonic writer possessed two enemies, the schoolmaster and the captain of the games; the writer, two enemies, the critic and the politician. And I know exactly what you mean; the same feeling, the same belief in authority's instinctive aversion from genius, is focussed in a story I once told you. . . . Let me recall it. . . . When I was about twenty, I used often to go and have luncheon with some surviving friends of my grandfather's and grandmother's. They were a picturesque and entertaining couple. The old lady was subtle and beautiful, with an affectation that was a work of art, the old gentleman—he was ninety—was imposing, with features carved out of rock—the last man, incidentally, to have his winged, starched collars and striped shirts made in one piece. He was a staunch upholder of the belief that everything was for the best and could not, indeed, have been bettered; a faith which, moreover, providence had paid him a regular thirty thousand pounds annually for more than seventy years to maintain. One day, he said to me: 'As you know, I have no patience with fellows who find fault with the world as it is. If they don't get on, *they're* to blame, entirely. . . . I remember when I was at Eton—it's nearly eighty years ago now—the Captain of the House sent for all us younger boys, and, pointing at a tiny chap with a tangle of red hair—a regular bookworm, always readin', said: "If you're ever near enough to him, kick him, and if he's too far away, throw a book at him." . . . Now that's the proper way to treat such people.' . . . A reflective, reminiscent look came into his eye, and he added: 'I can see him now; nasty little feller. . . . Swinburne was his name. A. C. Swinburne. . . . I often wonder what happened to him.'

That, I admit, is one kind of critical attitude—but there is another. The position which I occupy as a writer is entirely due to critics whom, naturally, I think discerning. All the help I have received in my career has been from critics. Yet I know there are many who, like yourself, assert that the critic's job is to kill creative art, just as the politician's is to kill those who produce it. Chekhov would have supported your argument—even Chekhov, gentlest of all creators—for Gorky[1] tells us that one day he remarked: 'Critics are like horse-flies which prevent the horse from ploughing. . . . The horse works, all its muscles drawn tight like the strings on a double-bass, and a fly settles on his flanks and tickles and buzzes . . . he has to twitch his skin and swish his tail. And what does the fly buzz about? It scarcely knows itself; simply because it is restless and wants to proclaim: "Look, I too am living on the earth. See, I can buzz, too, buzz about anything." For twenty-five years I have read criticism of my stories, and I don't remember a single remark of any value or one word of valuable advice. Only once Shabichevsky wrote something which made an impression on me . . . he said I would die in a ditch, drunk.' . . . So much for a certain kind of criticism, which always grows more rabid during a war, when, as I shall try to show you in a moment, a special kind of critic, attached to the politician as a crocodile-bird to a crocodile, come to the fore.

[1] *Reminiscences of Tolstoy, Chekhov and Andreev*, by Maxim Gorky. Authorized translation from the Russian by Katherine Mansfield, S.S. Kotelyansky and Leonard Woolf. (Hogarth Press, 1934.)

As for the politician, this is his hour. Important as the clown in the ring, he struts about as though he had contrived the situation intentionally, instead of having merely precipitated it, and by his folly made himself and us its joint victims. No worlds are too large for his ambition. Just as a clown is clothed in trousers and jacket much too big for him, so does he parade the stage togged out, as it were, in words and sentiments that drag round his feet and encumber his limbs. Yet, in spite of the recurrent calamitous tumbles in which he involves supporters and enemies alike, it is impossible not to feel sorry for him when you compare his lot with that of the artist. Every minute of the day pricks a balloon he has blown, and it collapses with a whimper; whereas the words that artists speak live after them in fire. The politician's words are memorable only when he approaches the rhetoric of the poet; yet a word or two from Blake, in a casual diagnosis of political ills, is worth all Burke. The couplet

> The prince's robes and beggar's rags
> Are toadstools on the miser's bags

is, for example, a more inspired and inspiring statement of the Socialist outlook than volumes of Marx, while the lines

> The strongest poison ever known
> Came from Caesar's laurel crown

foretell the rise of the Fascist empires with a singular and apocalyptic precision. For one casual remark of Swift's, we would give all Bolingbroke; one broken fragment from a poem by a great master tilts the scale against even the finest peroration. A country is worth dying for, as it is worth living for, because of the flowers its soil produces. Shakespeare outdistances Waterloo as an English triumph. Yet a link may

[297]

exist between the two: it is possible that had we always been a nation that preferred crossword puzzles to poetry and the cult of the body to that of the mind, we should not have produced either of these victories. Similarly, it was the writers and painters of republican France, and not her generals and statesmen, who, after 1870, by their splendour dragged the reputation of their country up from being that of a second-rate power to the leadership of Europe.

Perhaps it is only fair compensation that the lies and pretensions of the politicians should die on the air in front of them with a minute explosion, for invariably when, either through their policy itself or through the lack of one, they have landed us in a war, and entangled us for the rest of our lives with death and poverty, even if they do not succeed in killing us outright, it is others who get the blame. Always at a crisis—and I speak from the experience of two great and many lesser such times of suspense—there will be found a body, hitherto concealed, of critics only too eager to rush upon the stage and wave a number of truculent red herrings in order to divert suspicion from the real authors of the prevailing disaster. In normal times, no one would heed them, but war spurs them on, and by the vigour and falsity of their unfounded denunciations they are able for a year or two to usurp a brief, almost biblical, authority. In an hour of anxiety, the public will for a moment listen to any and every diagnosis, except the right one. And so it is that that denigratory band, Our Betters, who have perhaps for years been waiting for a cue that nobody would give them, step boldly out from the ambush of their own mediocrity, thick as sheep's wool.

You asked me in a letter a year ago 'Who is Lord Elton?'; an unfair question to put to a writer. I did not reply. Instead, I looked for his name in a book of reference. He wrote a book—as you know, for that is why you asked me—entitled, appropriately enough, *St George or the Dragon*. The dragon, from a perusal of the book, I take to be the modern artist. . . . This is a work of a kind which, in times of hysterical self-accusation—for the various papers and journalists accuse themselves of past blunders with all the enthusiasm of witnesses at a Russian state trial—readily becomes a prime Christmas favourite with the book-hating public; always a large body. Lord Elton resembles a methodist parson engaged on a witch hunt, the consequences of which he refuses to face. There is a lot of talk of 'the *dégringolade* of the cultured few'. 'Imitations of negro sculpture, engineering diagrams, drawings which suggested the scribblings of children or lunatics, patterns framed upon chance blots or the natural shapes of stones, all these followed one another with bewildering rapidity.' . . . Is Lord Elton unaware that to find the design latent in natural shapes is one of the chief manifestations of an artist's natural bent? Does he dismiss as artists Leonardo and Michelangelo— it is true, I fear, that they were Italians, and even belonged to 'the cultured few'—who placed so great a dependence upon the aspect of the material, or who derived vision-like inspiration from marks on a wall? Is he ignorant of the extreme importance in Chinese sculpture of such intrinsic design; or does he dismiss the great Chinese tradition as being 'chink'? . . . 'It was usually possible', he pronounces in the next sentence but one, 'to examine an exhibition of the work of these schools, without discovering, if one had not already known, whether they were the products of England or Thibet, of the twentieth or the twelfth century.' At one moment he accuses the intellectuals of being esoteric, at the next he denounces them because some of the doctrines they propound are not to his liking. . . . Well, what is the answer?—unspoken, for Lord Elton is a gentleman. . . . The answer is: 'Burn their books and paintings, put them in a concentration camp. Throw over the European tradition;

[299]

renounce Voltaire and Rousseau, and all the writers in succession from them. Do not tell the common man the truth; tell him only what you think is good for him to know, and at the same time flatter him continually with the assurance that he is the supreme arbiter of taste.' The whole book, in short, reeks with prejudice, and is full of a line of argument usually associated with those who denounced and overthrew the Weimar Republic.

Who, you ask, is this god descended to enlighten us? . . . He is the crocodile-bird of Ramsay MacDonald; his biographer and, I believe, his friend. Surely he could have whispered, or hissed a suspicion, into that statesman's ear, in those times when we were going 'up and up and up', and our Navy, for example, was going 'down and down and down'? Lord Elton, in *Who's Who*, proclaims that he was expelled from the Labour Party for supporting Ramsay MacDonald: why, in this book, does he denounce so many pacifists, and never MacDonald, chief of them in the last war? We turn over the pages in vain. . . . No, it is the poets and the painters and the sculptors who are to blame. They *made* the war, just as the German musicians made the war in 1914; just as the English Catholics were responsible for the Armada, the Spanish Jews for the ills of Spain under the sixteenth-century kings, and American negroes for all crimes of violence in their continent. James Joyce, Huxley, Shaw and others (including Gertrude Stein, who is not even an Englishwoman), were responsible for all the mistakes of the last twenty years, for the inadequacy of the Army, the fact that no British generals had been afforded an opportunity of training their men under modern conditions, and the terrible mass unemployment. Not for a moment were the vapid and unimaginative public, drugged regularly by cinema organists and their like, the incurious bourgeoisie, the herds of little men, now promoted, in view of a death to come, to the status of gods, not for a moment were these, though equipped with the vote, to be held responsible for any calamity that ensued. No, it is always the painters and the writers. In fact, in the words of Nashe's *Lenten Stuffe* '. . . no more winde will I spend on it but this; Saint Denis for Fraunce, Saint Iames for Spaine, Saint Patrike for Ireland, Saint George for England and the red Herring for Yarmouth.'

Let us now turn for an instant to another slimmer volume, this time a P.E.N. book, published under the auspices of the Pen Club, *Critical Thoughts in Critical Days*. The awkward play of ideas manifested in this title (strange that so dry a name should have so rancid a flavour), is typical of the donnish jokes and prim, but tittering flights of fancy, in evidence throughout its pages. The author, Mr F. L. Lucas, a god to his readers and himself, sits in his motor, while the ghost of wretched Macaulay is made to materialize beside him, and obliged to listen to the unrolling of an insufferable priggishness. . . . 'Here', writes Mr Lucas, '. . . stands the first of European writers, to me in many ways the finest still.' . . . Thus Homer obtains his school certificate. Nevertheless, he does, it will be seen, distribute praise as well as blame, but the praise, with the single exception of a greasy compliment to poor Mr Desmond MacCarthy, is reserved for the dead. Only Homer Shakespeare, Milton, Thomas Hardy and the Shropshire Lad, running saucily along to catch them up, are good enough for Mr Lucas, so superb a fellow is he, with his tic-tac style, like that of a curate learning to use the typewriter. He is no tomb-breaker; reverently he scratches and clucks among the graves, like a hen strayed into a churchyard. He even has a word of commendation for those who one would have imagined would have most disliked it, Roger Fry and Lytton Strachey. An air of poisonous superiority inhabits his every cliché. 'Reopening Thucydides at odd moments since the war, I have been shocked.

[301]

He had shrunk. Was the fault mine, or the war's or his? . . .' All three of them, you will notice, Thucydides, the war and tiny little Mr Lucas, are on the same scale. . . . At any rate, you may object, he does praise a few writers, even if they *are* dead. Yes, but for what virtues? Because they help *him* in time of trouble. So may the sparrow, twittering upon the broken golden frieze of the Parthenon, give thanks to the makers of Ancient Athens for having built so fine and sunny a perch for him. . . . No, Mr Lucas, that is *not* why they wrote.

'True,' says our paragon elsewhere, 'true that I have read again with wonder passages of Ovid, Seneca and Lucan. One forgets how brilliant they can be. . . . Brains they possessed, as Meredith and Shaw and Wilde possessed them. And brains are never common. . . .' (Oh yes, they are common sometimes, Mr Lucas.) 'The Sagas,' he remarks two pages later, 'live for me because they tell of men rammed with life, though dryly scant of words. . . .' *Rammed*, one hopes, being one of the words of which these Vikings were 'dryly scant', though a *ram* is a male sheep, or tup, and, as such, doubtless dear to Mr Lucas— or must we blame the printer for snatching still another cliché from Mr Lucas's grasp?

. . . Elsewhere in this odious little volume we are told that 'the years seem to make Coleridge only shabbier and flabbier', while Keats is reproved for not writing 'more things like *The Belle Dame Sans Merci*!' (I can hear the conversation:

' 'Morning, Keats.'

'Good morning, sir. . . . How clever of you to recognize me.'

'That was rather a nice thing of yours, Keats, in *The Cambridge Non-Pareil*, the other day: I hope to see more things like that. . . . Come to me if you have any trouble with your iambics. Always glad to give you a hand, you know.'

'Thank you, sir, oh, thank you kindly.')

Now, this mimic Hercules, clad in his mouse-skin, this tit-titan, heroicks it, draws his toy wooden sword and charges upon the moderns, calls Mr Eliot a sewer—in an exquisite pun 'to the sewer, all things are sewer'—trounces D. H. Lawrence for not foreseeing the advent of the Nazis—whereas he was precisely the one writer who as early as 1920 or 1921 foretold it[1]—and denounces me for having written that 'the multitudinous seas . . . learned to "yap like a Pekinese" . . .': a thing, of course, I never said. The waves that lap the Monte Carlo beach are not 'multitudinous seas'. The younger poets are also insulted, but more in general than individually as with the older writers. . . . Yet how—to be frank—such a poet as this Mr Lucas dares to criticize other poets of any age or sort, I do not know. Listen!

> 'To think I shall not see you for a week,' he said,
>   'For a week—eternity!
> But you'll ring me up before you go to bed
>   Each night and talk to me?'

That is the first verse of a poem by Mr Lucas entitled 'Ringing False': the last—and those between are neither better nor worse—runs:

> 'For the spell was broken. A little while,
>   And we parted, bitterly.
> And that is why,' with a sudden smile,
>   'I always wire,' said she.

What a comfort such broken-toothed lyrics will be to the sparrows of the future!

You asked me why men like Lord Elton—and I add Mr

---

[1] In his published correspondence. He says that the heart of Germany has altered, that she is no longer a Western country, and has thrown aside Christian civilization.

Lucas—attack the authors of the last twenty-five years with such peculiar venom. I think it is a quite natural dislike; because the interbellum in England possessed a record in the arts of which any country and any epoch might be proud; but neither Lord Elton nor Mr Lucas was its most conspicuous ornament. It gave birth to some of the most vital and inspired writing, painting, music and literature—which fact must remain of the most interest to you and me—that England had produced for centuries. Politics were the whole undermining of us: that is true. But they were not the artist's dominion; and, if they were, no one in this country would pay attention to what he said: (For though Mr Gladstone was able to make the fortune of Marie Corelli, and Mr Baldwin of Mary Webb, yet, by an unfair paradox, no English writer has ever been able to discover and present a politician—unless it was Disraeli, who lavished his successful efforts upon himself.) No, the period was damned by its politicians, by the cruel and gigantic unemployment they allowed. That, and the not-caring which permitted it to exist, were its most tragic and lamentable features. . . . But the danger, and indeed the horror, you will have to face will be of a different order; *over-employment*. You may see the whole world tied to a machine that will not let go of it. The price of bread will be a life sentence. Only once or twice a week, perhaps, 'time off' will be allowed for machine pleasures, such as the cinema. . . . But I would fight—and I know you would—for the right to be idle. We would always oppose the ants in their awful paradise.

The last war—the First War to End Wars—broke out when I was twenty-one; the present war—The Sequel—when you were twenty. Formerly there were only the ordeals of the private and public school to be endured, concentration camps that were certainly vile enough (there I have seen bullying—and in one instance upon a Jew—which would have taxed the ingenuity of German storm-troopers). But the men of your generation have never for a moment been free: and, unless you conquer in the battle for the hours, there will be no liberty left. The embryonic writer of after-the-war will have, not only the schoolmaster and the captain of the games, as you say, for his two enemies, but the drill-sergeant, the gym-instructor, the leader of the fire squad, the Civil Defence Expert, the Inspirer of the Youth Movement, and afterwards, when he grows up, the official of the Labour Exchange and the shop-steward, as well as the politician and the critic. Such an existence is death to the artist; because, to be able to work at his best, it is necessary for him to have an endless vista of hours and days, within the space of which he can write or paint without any interruption except those which are casual or that he makes for himself. But the modern development of 'healthy citizenship', as it is called, under which every man is obliged to take a hand to repel the attacks from land, sea and air brought upon him by his incompetence as a voter, sterilizes all talent. To be able to exist, you will have to give up twenty-two hours out of every twenty-four. Men are no longer wanted, but only numbers; a man today—and if you are not careful, tomorrow as well—is only valuable to the extent that he can supply man-hours—or ant-hours—of labour to the politicians, and at the end a death with which to crown their policy.

As an inducement to this kind of life and a reward for leading it, the voter, the Little Man, is flattered morning and evening by the Press, and fawned upon by his slave-masters. He is told he is World Champion No. 1, that no one can compare with him. In each country he believed himself to be absolute lord. Moreover the mental food fed to him renders him unduly excitable in the realm of gross ideas, while, too, the people of every nation are profoundly xenophobic. These last facts, unless they can be modified through education (of which development there is no sign), make popular government in the present sense of that term impossible; but they also enable any government, however bad and incompetent, in every country, to achieve an easy and invariable popularity by abuse of foreign countries, or, in more rational cases, by a governessy upbraiding of them. Hitler, for example, may not have truly represented his people in everything: but he does—and did— truly represent them when he denounced foreign nations. Alas, the feeling of innate racial superiority which inhabits the mind of the Common Man in every country, and is to be examined in its most blatant form in Nazi doctrines, equally must in every country be encouraged, in order to persuade him to consent willingly to the eventual loss of life and fortune. Yet 'Love Thy Neighbour as Thyself' remains the only foundation stone of sound, peaceful relations with foreign countries. A policy founded on a collection of Jenkins's Ears, and atrocity stories generally, cannot endure, however violent it may be, and however attractive it may appear while it lasts.

Thus are men persuaded to yield money, career, freedom, health, life itself, to the boundless folly or iniquitous ambition of the demagogues, autocrats and politicians: men who in England, during the last twenty years, have scarcely produced a leader. Churchill was the last, but by origin, as by ability, he was out of the ordinary run, half aristocrat, half American, and in no way derived from the middle classes who govern both here and in France, and who, by their lack of intuition and energy, except in the realm of finance, have proved so great a blight upon their countries. . . . It is only fair, however, to admit that where, as in Italy and Germany, the middle classes *have* yielded and the lower classes have taken over, the leaders who have arisen are, if less purely incompetent, far madder, more unbridled, violent with the violence of the turbulent mob from which they spring. Yet they are merely a reflection of those whose energies they sap and whose lives they ruin.

What can *our* politicians say in their own and our defence? They can say that here, as opposed to the enemy countries, all that has been done to render war probable was done by mistake, and not on purpose—but to an unprejudiced mind, does not this make their responsibility worse? The strangulation of your life, the chief calamity that involves every man and woman, befalls you because war is total. But remember, it is only total because the politicians allowed it to be so. The governments of the last two decades have lied and deceived— no doubt often not of intention—so consistently, they have been so free of unfulfilled and specious promises, that the point has now been reached where the people feel they can only trust a statesman who comes to them with the terrible words 'I can promise you nothing but blood and tears and sweat': the enunciation of a policy, which though in a way noble, could hardly be surpassed in menace by the threats of foreign autocrats, bellowing across the water what they will do to us when they get us. . . . (So might the Jews have welcomed the words of King Rehoboam, who promised them scorpions for whips.) . . . And, indeed, whereas in former ages of barbarism the whole populations of whole countries were uprooted and enslaved *after* a war by a victorious foe, now every government uproots and enslaves its own people *during* a war. Only thus can a country survive in total war. This is total war. It is therefore the chief job of your generation to see that the kind of men who deceived themselves and us, and led us into total war, shall never again be returned to Parliament.

If, in states vowed to death and to fights without a finish, the lot of Everyman is, of course, hard, that of the artist is especially abominable. Here, unless some special status is allowed him, as elsewhere, it will mean, in fact, that he becomes a helot. Had Mozart been a modern Englishman—or, for that, a modern Austrian—he would have spent the last four years training to fight, fighting or engaged in forced labour, and since he died at thirty-six, this would have constituted a large slice of his art-life. Conceive the loss to the world had conscription been in force! Imagine, too, how greatly a modern government would relish wasting several years of Shelley's brief span by making him a fireman, or enjoy sending Keats, with his weak lungs, upon a gas course. Yet our governors are humane; they prefer muzzling an artist to his downright destruction. 'Give the creature a safe job; make him write what *we* like.' . . . Can you imagine Shelley or Blake at a desk in the M.O.I., or Byron flitting in and out of the studios of the B.B.C. You are, alas, destined to live in an age in which no painter will be supplied with paints without a permit from the Director of the National Gallery, no writer with paper save by grace of the Paper Controller. For, in a democracy, the artist, first smeared with his own honey, is then staked down upon the ant heap. . . . In the end, however, the artist and the thinker win. Even starvation cannot prevail against them: it has been tried before. . . . Nevertheless, for your own sake, think the matter out, sum up your position.

It is wise not to underrate the difficulties, the cruel difficulties before you. It will be harder for you than ever it was for your father. The true artist has always had to fight, but it is, and will be, a more ferocious struggle for you, and the artists of your generation, than ever before. The working man, this time, will be better looked after, he will be flattered by the Press and bribed with Beveridge schemes, because he possesses a plurality of votes. But who will care for you or your fate, who will trouble to defend the cause of the young writer, painter, sculptor, musician? And what inspiration will you be offered when theatre, ballet, concert-hall lie in ruins, and, owing to the break in training, there are no great executant artists for several decades? Above all, do not underestimate the amount and intensity of the genuine ill-will that people will feel for you; not the working man, for though not highly educated he has a mild respect for the arts and no preconceived notions, not the few remaining patricians, but the vast army between them, the fat middle classes and the little men. And here I must first make special mention of the civil servant as enemy. Throughout your career your liveliness will provoke his particular attention, and so you will suffer the continued passive obstruction that his resistant softness opposes to the will of the artist, towards whom he bears an inborn loathing. He envies the artist's liberty of disposition and path of enjoyment, although officially he rates the gummy persistence of the limpet above all other virtues, above the wind-swift speeding of the greyhound or any species of conscious thought. At the best, you will be ground down between the small but powerful authoritarian minority of art directors, museum racketeers, the chic, giggling modistes who write on art and literature, publishers, journalists and dons (who will, to do them justice, try to help you, if you will write as they tell you)— and the enormous remainder, who would not mind, who would, indeed, be pleased, if they saw you starve. For we English are unique in that, albeit an art-producing nation, we are not an art-loving one. In the past the arts depended on a small number of very rich patrons. The enclave they formed has never been re-established. The very name 'art-lover' stinks. The small army of art-lovers that still exists, trailing round the smashed and empty galleries, belongs to the Victorian Age. When it moves, the rattle of camphor balls sounds like a rain of bullets in the echoing scagliola halls of houses thrown open to members of the art-loving congregations.

Decrepit it may be, but it still retains its power to injure. It only cares for old masters, and you will be surprised at the vigour and satisfaction with which it will always trample on the new.

The privileges you hold today, then, as an artist, are those of Ishmael, the hand of every man is against you. Remember, therefore, that outcasts must never be afraid, and that to a writer, courage should, before physical courage, signify moral courage—during wars a quality often at a discount, whatever the packs of journalists may bleat to the contrary. As an artist, the only crime you can commit is to fail to support and uphold your peers, to agree in your heart with the herd, and, above all, to be *afraid* of ideas, *afraid* of beauty. You must never take heed for the morrow, never be afraid of the morning, for you have no more to lose than you brought with you.

Yet cultivate guile; be not, as I have been, too outspoken. Invent several manners and try them on those who like them. Consider everything upon its merits, for you need not give your own conclusions until tempers are cooler—and heads, I may add, clearer. When I was a boy of your age, in the Brigade of Guards before the war, one of the things we young officers were taught was never to argue with a drunken man. See him the next day, and interrogate him then. Similarly I counsel *you* never to argue; join in, and after the hysteria has vanished, after Lord Elton has changed to some other and more pacific tune, after Mr F. L. Lucas has a little descended from the heights, remember to administer splashes of cold water over a long period against a recurrence. (For there will be a morning-after.) But, in whatever fashion you may act, do not appear 'cynical'; Swift and Pope and Shaw were 'cynical', and it lessened their just authority.

On the contrary, join in, as I say, accept the situation and

[310]

rejoice. We live in an age of world-wide hysteria—and not without reason—when not to believe as many atrocity-stories as your neighbour believes puts you not only in danger of hell fire, but, if he has his way, exposes you to the rigours of persecution. You would rank as a heretic, as one who refuses to place credence in the Thirty-Nine Articles, or who, by declining to take part in a witch hunt, numbers himself openly among the witches. You were even denounced the other day— for I heard it—for saying that you did not believe that in a stadium in Poland Jewish babies had been seized from their mothers' arms and used as footballs by storm-troopers. It was most injudicious of you. Do you want a martyr's crown of that kind? It can always be obtained. . . . No, adopt the homeopathic system, but prescribe large doses. Be inventive. Use your creative gift. Pretend to believe and then go one better. Enjoy yourself. Sicken the enemy with the blatant non-sense you pour out. Tell them you know their stories are true, and repeat everything you have ever heard in the same line, however improbable. Pile it on, until *they* begin to argue against *you*. *Insist* on believing everything with a firmer belief than they do; go a hundred times better. Whenever the crowd mentions Italians, shout 'wops!', 'dagos!', 'ice-creamers!' It may prove difficult for you, since you lived in Italy as a child, but you must persist. Tell them that Raphael, Michelangelo and Leonardo, Titian and Veronese, were all really English-men with American mothers; and declare that Noël Coward is worth all Dante. (Point out that Dante never wrote the music for his 'lyrics.') . . . But, notwithstanding, at the end of all this, when a reaction has set in, you must let them know this much of the truth; that you abhor brutality, from wherever it comes, and whether shown to Jew or Christian, and that you know, and have long known, the Germans to be a brutal race; that you had been brought up to believe it, even at the time the

[311]

crowd were praising them, saying they preferred them to the French, and that 'they are just like us!' (What a curious, recurrent, dangerous hallucination is that!) Otherwise, unless you emphasize this point, you will leave them in the right to the point that their hysteria may at least have arisen from a hatred of oppression.

When you have satiated and disgusted them with your atrocity stories, agree with them that *perhaps* they *are* right not to believe everything they are told. And add, quickly, before leaving them, that perhaps the ability *not* to be taken in by superstitions, not to bow the knee to Mumbo-Jumbo, whether in West Africa or South Kensington, whether outside a kraal or a town hall, decorated with flags, may be, after all, the test of a civilized man. Remember, for your own comfort, that you are only exaggerating for the sake of moderation; because you must ever pursue the golden mean, the most difficult of all ideals for the artist, with the clashes inherent in his temperament and his need for expression, to follow. And after the war—for it will end one day (when a silly woman once asked Chekhov, apropos of some contemporary fracas: 'How do *you* think the war will end?', he replied, after some thought: 'In peace, I should say'): after the war, then, when we may relapse to easy ways, it will become your duty once more to remind people of the brutality of the German race.... No doubt, we shall revert to type. The hysteria will pass, for we are not, like the Germans, a feminine, emotional race, but a tolerant, masculine-minded people, who can be worked up only by outrageous events and the wickedness of the Press.

You must do more, however, than recall the nature of the Germans, in case we forget it: for that would be a purely negative contribution. You must harness your vivid sense of fantasy to the cause of reality. Be practical; practical in the way the Chinese were when they used to recruit their prostitutes from among the blind. You realize, I know, that a certain proportion of Germans are born into the world with an especial love of fighting, and you must see that they get it, before they can inflict their will, first upon the stupid but crafty and slavish majority of their own countrymen, and then upon the world. . . . Ask yourself what can be done to obtain the correct solution; *viz.*, to kill off this ruffianly minority at regular intervals, and before it attains power, and if possible to satisfy its deep urge to kill and be killed in such a manner as to enable it gradually to feel a certain self-respect. Thus, though you cannot cure snakes of their bite, you can at stated intervals deprive them of their venom and, by manufacturing a serum from it, use it for the good of humanity, as a cure for certain diseases.

Now the solution that I propose, and recommend to you most seriously, is derived from the instinctive and traditional treatment of the same problem in other epochs, and I believe it would prove successful and at the same time solve another and even more acute difficulty. During the eighteenth century, the British people had little trouble from the Germans, because they hired German troops to fight their battles, and so procured the death of the most naturally ferocious of the German race. (Indeed, because these were slaughtered in this fashion, the left-over German, with his beer and pipe and dirty moustache, became the very emblem of peace.) Unfortunately in the nineteenth century the idea spread that it was immoral to obtain the death in battle on your behalf of any but your own people—and soon, in consequence, Germany was unleashing her hordes of trained killers upon France. . . . The League of Nations failed because it possessed no armed force to back up its authority. Well then, restore the League, and recruit the army necessary for the enforcement of its laws from among the German people. Those who love fighting will volunteer, and, by being made to serve an ideal, and, at the same time, a useful purpose, their tone will gradually be raised; they will feel that the future of civilization depends on them, and will respond. The fact of being dressed in a uniform will quiet many of them. And, of course, we must see to it that they are, in the interests of the whole world, decimated every few years in border clashes and in fracas in Thibet and Central Africa. This is the sole solution that will de-totalize war: for within a generation all the Germans who would most *like* war will have been given a taste of it, have become its victims without involving the rest of their race and the rest of the five continents.

The worst of conscription is that, unlike the system adumbrated above, it involves and kills off those who hate war as much as those who love it. For this reason, and also because I think that, in spite of the efforts of envenomed fanatics who find in these tragic years their happy hour, we shall return to the purely English methods of life that we have through the centuries evolved, I find it difficult to believe that we shall continue to enforce conscription for ever after the war. Directly a war—for which we are always unprepared—descends upon us, the nation demands compulsion as a measure of sacrifice, equivalent to lethal dust and ashes: we do not examine whether it is judicious. Yet conscription should never be more than a matter of convenience or its reverse; it should never be a question of religious principle or a measure of self-immolation. And it is doubtful whether military conscription has ever suited this country, with its tremendous naval tradition and its industrial power: it is doubtful, indeed, how far it has helped any country, for it only enables the old, pre-the-last-war militarism to continue until the next outbreak. In France it was in force up till 1870; after that Germany adopted it for the whole Reich, and was defeated in 1914. Then France and

England forbad Germany to have a conscripted army, and the French was the largest, and, by old standards, 'the best in the world'—as *all* our politicians reiterated: the result was, that, after the German Army had been reconstituted by Hitler, the French were defeated. The two greatest and most successful military organizations of modern times, Russian and German, have been built up *since* the last war, and after a clean sweep. A triumphant nation should always celebrate peace by the destruction of the War Office—then, at the right time, and if our politicians *must* continue to make us these presents of wars, a suitable organization and army could take shape. . . . The Englishman, when of sound mind, recognizes the truth of these facts by instinct, more fully than would a continental; he recognizes the wickedness, and, above all, the folly of mega-lomaniac conceptions. He wants no youth movements, no *ballilas* and black-handed gangs of tub-thumping tots and thugs in miniature, no great organizations to cripple and pervert the minds of the young. And if, during real peace, an English government proposes to continue conscription, then the English people, unless they have altered their character, will tell it to go. . . . But of what you are to do, if it *does* continue, I will speak later, at the end of my letter.

You asked me, when I last saw you, what were my politics, and I find it a question difficult, even now, to answer. I belong to the balance of the body politic, and have at one moment felt, and acted, in one mood, at another, in another. I believe in trying to achieve the fullest liberty for the individual within the bounds of human and political conscience. With the late D. H. Lawrence, it is my opinion that, where finance and economics are concerned, it is man's chief misfortune that at present those who are most active and eager in these fields, i.e. in the pursuit of money or in planning to take it away—and whose ideas are therefore the most likely to prevail, unless we can marshal the disinterested—are the most unpleasant, the most material-minded, of all men, either the most greedy, the most anxious to exploit their fellows, or the most dry, kill-joy doctrinaires. In any case, money is a convenience we have ourselves created for our own use, not a god or a religion. And it should remain so—that is to say, money is made to be spent. But so long as the money-world is ruled by the beaked and bloated tribes of the great capitalists, whose fortunes must be considered as a kind of elephantiasis, or threatened by the dour, sour looks of our old enemies, the Puritans, what can you expect?

I would not like to see—though no doubt I shall—hereditary wealth abolished. Today men seem afraid to defend it. American ideas of ant-labour prevail. But, in all truth, the only kind of wealth worth having is the kind you do not earn; it is unassociated with the mean and slavish virtue of thrift. You have time to learn how to spend your money, and time in which to spend it. Obversely, I would like to see the possession and privileges of inherited wealth extended universally. To abolish hereditary possessions today, instead of insisting on them for everyone, would be equivalent to the action of the Elizabethans who decreed the abolition of glass in all windows, because it was only to be found in the houses of the rich, and thereby prevented its use from becoming general. Samuel Butler maintained, in *The Way of All Flesh* and in his *Notebooks*, that one day it would be as anomalous to be born without an annual income attached to you of three or four hundred, to come to you when you had reached the age of twenty-five or so years, as it is today to be born without arms or legs. Evolution should provide each of us with a fortune, as with a face. I think he was right.

I was told lately, by an American who had been in Paris at the time of the Germans entering that city, that German officers could be seen sitting in the fashionable tea-shops, gnawing huge lumps of butter, or sometimes with twenty or thirty cakes piled on the plate in front of them: this was, of course, the ugly result of underfeeding. A gross fortune is, similarly, the result—and as indecent a result—of poverty, the most degrading of human afflictions. But the stupidity and financial fecklessness of successive governments in Britain has at least accomplished this much, that we can say that any man who today sets out to make a great fortune, must be either a great fool or a great philanthropist, and—if he succeeds, a great knave; for he pays 19s. 6d. in the pound as income tax and at least two-thirds of his possessions must go to the State when he dies. For though governments in the past feared to overtax the people they ruled, or pretended to represent, they have now made what must be to them a most joyful discovery; that, so long as the situation arises from sheer muddle, lack of foresight and incompetence, and not of intention, they can squander the national income up to any limit (and this is of benefit to them—at least indirectly—by increasing their importance). If, that is to say, they take your money, not because they believe in doing so, not because they are advocates of socialism, but because, on the contrary, having continually opposed it, they yet have floundered, of their own accord, into a position so tragic and untenable that it becomes their sole chance of rescue; nothing else remains to be done except to cling to an expedient in which they have no faith; then to reproach them becomes unpatriotic. But you and I would surely, even though we are not Socialists, prefer to live in a State that was Socialist by principle rather than by virtue of the amazing ineptitude of its politicians.

Yet it is not, perhaps, for a writer to complain. If an artist, it is scarcely probable that he will make a great fortune in a capitalist State, though it is true that he occupies, at any rate financially, a special place in it. For one thing, the proceeds of a book, which may have taken him five years to write, are liable to income tax and super-tax—though a great portion of the money should surely be regarded as capital; for another, it has long been recognized that a writer's particular form of property, the copyright of the books he has created, is on a different footing from all other property, is not inalienable, and should, in fact, be snatched from his family or heirs as soon as this can be accomplished without an appearance of indecent haste. On the other hand, such an attitude is by no means confined to the old-fashioned democracies. The more modern and democratic is the State concerned, the less it allows to authors—at any rate, foreign authors. Thus, in the United States of America, piracy in books is no crime; while in Soviet Russia it is a duty.

So much for the writer's financial status. What the artist should do, then, for his own sake, I think, is not to advocate that money be taken away from its present owners, but to support a policy which will undermine its attraction for the material-minded by diminishing the value they can set upon it. Rationing, for example, already accomplishes this. It soon becomes plain that there is little object in making too much money, if there is little or nothing to buy with it. Confine the rich to the pastures of a restricted Fortnum & Mason's. Advocate heavy permanent taxes on jewellery and old masters and decorative objects, and then you will be able to say to the rich, in the continual effort you make to educate those of them who need it: 'Look! modern pictures and books remain; their value *may* increase, while that of investments is bound to sink.' Plug that over, every time.

Money, though, is not so important to you as liberty: I recur to that. You must carry out a continual campaign against civil servants, dons, masters-of-hounds, schoolmasters,

professional football players and all friends to national
sclerosis everywhere. Use once again your sense of fantasy and
of fun. Hit them where they least expect it. If, for example, it
should prove—which I do not believe—that the character of
the English people has changed, should it transpire that the
young are to be enslaved, and the artists subjected to continual
domination by pin-heads, then charge the foe. If you find that
it has been planned for the intelligent, the intellectual, above all,
the creative, and those who live for things of the spirit to
spend a large portion of their lives after the war in undergoing,
one after another, courses in gas and bomb-throwing, then
loudly, and on every occasion, you must demand in the name
of Sacred English Fair Play, that the philistines who hate art
and literature and love to handle and throw bombs and to fire
guns and, generally, to be as noisy and destructive as possible
and to live with a continual B.B.C. programme from opening
to close, should, as compensation, be obliged to suffer six-
weeks-long compulsory courses in Dutch Painting or Persian
textiles, and to pass endurance-tests in the Art Element in
Chinese Calligraphy and in English Romantic Poetry. Torn
from their peace-time occupations of golf, darts and reading the
papers, they must be made, during these courses, to live under,
for them, the most uncomfortable circumstances possible;
they must be forced to sleep on planks, eighty in a hut (unless
they show a liking for dormitory life, when they should be
placed in the solitary confinement of a comfortable bedroom).
No radio should be allowed in any hut or mess. At meal-times,
they must listen in silence to Beethoven quartets, and after
dinner attend orchestral concerts of Mahler and Stravinsky.
The examinations in Byzantine jewellery and Turkish tiles
should be conducted to the appropriate music of the countries
concerned. During the Netherlands School of Painting Course,
they should be taken by train, starting from London at

midnight, to that flat part of East Anglia which somewhat resembles Holland in configuration, and there be made to lie for hours in a damp ditch, so as to observe the sun rise over the river from the correct angle. During the daytime they should be made to adopt the proper physical attitudes of Teniers boors, one foot in the air, an arm extended, and later to dance in the same jolly and abandoned style. They should be forced to carry with them always a Field Art Notebook, in which to make entries. . . . The unsuccessful candidates for promotion, the recalcitrant and stubborn, could be ordered to take further courses in French Symbolist Poetry, as well as English Romantic, and be examined minutely on the works of Baudelaire, Verlaine and Rimbaud. Those who showed any symptom of being refractory could, even, be commanded to attend a lecture on the latest art movement by Group-Dupe Herbert Read. But you should be humane as well as stern, and first-aid should be ready on all occasions for the mind as well as the body.

I implore you to take what I say seriously, even when I put it in a form to amuse you. You are a cavalier by type, and not a roundhead, and you will need all the fun you can make for yourself and others, as well as all the fighting spirit you can muster, if you are, as I hope, to carry on a long one-man campaign against stupidity and priggishness wherever you see it. Never allow yourself to be discouraged, however hopeless at any one moment the struggle may appear. . . . I must end now, for my letter is long, and at present you have not much time for reading: but there still remain several subjects on which I must talk to you in my next letter. . . . Take care of yourself.

Your affectionate father,

OSBERT SITWELL